Between Breaths

Between Breaths

A TEACHER IN THE ALASKAN BUSH

Sandra K. Mathews

University of New Mexico Press | Albuquerque

Library of Congress Cataloging-in-Publication Data

Mathews, Sandra K., 1963–
  Between breaths : a teacher in the Alaskan bush /
Sandra K. Mathews.
      p. cm.
  Includes bibliographical references and index.
  ISBN-13: 978-0-8263-3877-8 (pbk. : alk. paper)
  ISBN-10: 0-8263-3877-1 (pbk. : alk. paper)
  1. McGladrey, Donna Joy, 1935–1959.
  2. Teachers—Alaska—Biography.
  3. Education, Rural—Alaska.
  I. Title.
  LA2317.M365M38 2006
  371.10092—dc22
  [B]

                        2006012480

Design and composition: Melissa Tandysh

To Donna Joy McGladrey

whose life and letters made this story possible

⁓

Aubrey Anne (1987–2003)

Charlie Russell (1990–2004)

Contents

List of Illustrations

Acknowledgments

Numerous people provided invaluable knowledge and resources during the course of this research project. Primarily, I need to thank Donna herself for writing such meticulous and thoughtful letters, and so beautifully recording so many aspects of her life and of those around her. Her parents, Leslie and Verna McGladrey, made this book possible by their willingness to hold on to the past with such delicate care. At every stage of the way, Donna's sisters Dorothy Mathews and Joan (Engelsen) Eik have encouraged me, provided me with innumerable irreplaceable sources, and have shared their stories with me. Their husbands, Jack Mathews and Alf Eik, deserve credit for allowing me to visit their homes or for their travel to visit me, so that I could then interview their wives at length. Hours of taped interviews are the result.

Without the assistance of Andy Tooley, Sara McCroden, Trisha Randolph, and Chanté Bauer—all promising young scholars—this project would have taken me many more years. I will always be grateful for their enthusiasm and interest in this project. I credit former Provost Norval Kneten and department chairs Ronald C. Naugle and Elaine Kruse for allowing me to hire these research assistants. Student and office assistant Jessica Furst also provided many important services for me instead of working for Mary Hoylman, our gracious department administrative assistant. I also have to thank my Spring 2000 Women of the American West History class. As willing (or unwilling) students, they read all of Donna's transcribed letters. They read with fascination, getting to know Donna during her year at Dillingham. I withheld the final section, however, so they would not read ahead. Their comments and questions helped guide me when I began my research and I thank them for their candid responses. Although she graduated in 2000, Amy Ziems continues to encourage me with her questions about my progress. Others in the class I must also thank by name include P. J. Book, Ariella Zinn, Heather Olson, Ashley Gummere, Crystal Buhrmann, Heather Houghton, Stephanie Owen, Jennifer Safarik, Libby Steiner, and Jasmine Wagaman. Additionally, I thank my Fall 2002 Women of the American West course for being the guinea pigs for the earliest version of this manuscript, giving me encouragement, constructive criticism, and direction. As a promise to them, I thank them by name: Jeff Bernadt, Amanda DeBrie, Amy Engle, Angela Goebel, Caramae Jordison, Abby Keeler, Stephanie Keeler, Kristin Maricle, Trisha Randolph, and Timothy Rasmussen.

NWU colleagues, including Professors Dale Benham and Maxine Fawcett-Yeske, and staff members Cindy Sindel and Alana Little, encouraged me after either reading portions of this manuscript or hearing presentations on campus. Furthermore, Norval Kneten found value in the project and provided me with a course release for the Spring 2002 semester to begin work on the manuscript. A special thank you to Rachel Pokora and former colleague Carol Langer who listened to me babble on endlessly about this project. Never-ending pats on the back and encouragement came from Loretta Fairchild and Janet Lu. And to the many faculty, staff, and students who attended those talks, I am grateful for your comments, questions, and enthusiastic encouragement.

But I must cast my net much farther geographically. My dear friend and fellow author Catherine Lavender read a short version of this work and offered me very helpful suggestions. Colleague Susan Richards helped me by forcing me to tell the story and asked me questions as I described Donna's experience. This exercise helped me enormously in understanding the story I planned to write. Susan's suggestion that Donna wrote with the "eye of an anthropologist" helped me refocus my research and ask new questions. Evelyn Schlatter was my energizer and motivator when my progress slowed. Most recently, my new friend Christine Starr, an aspiring novelist, has given me critical and most beneficial feedback on the final manuscript. I can never thank her enough for the gift of a most fitting and beautiful title.

In Anchorage, Archivist Diane Brenner, formerly of the Anchorage Museum of History and Art, directed me to photograph collections of Dillingham and Chugiak from the 1950s, just prior to the time in which Donna lived in those communities. She put me in touch with a very special person, Tim Troll, then the CEO of Choggiung, Ltd., in Dillingham. Also a local historian, he lent me piles and piles of books, took me on tours of Dillingham, and introduced me to key individuals in town. He even arranged two flights on a bush plane with John Paul Bouker, owner of Bristol Bay Air, so that I would have a better sense of Bristol Bay and the Nushagak region, as well as of the dangers of flying in Alaska. It was the adventure of a lifetime. Tim also introduced me to Verna Lee Heyano, one of Donna's sixth-grade students, who happened to be the hotel manager of Dillingham's Bristol Inn. From these two contacts came many others, including JoAnn and Richard Armstrong, formerly of Armstrong Air Services. I must thank JoAnn for sharing her memories of Dillingham in the 1950s, of Donna, and of Donna's roommate Ann Carr. I thank Wendy Hladick, formerly of the Dillingham Chamber of Commerce, for her assistance, as well as for sending me copies of newspaper articles from the *Bristol Bay News* in Dillingham.

In Chugiak, Hermann and Hilda Kroener provided invaluable information about Donna, Richard, and living in Dillingham during the 1950s. I can never repay them for their assistance and friendship. Shirley Mauldin, an active member of the Chugiak Methodist Church who corresponded with Donna's mother Verna McGladrey, introduced me to other members of the community who also provided a valuable perspective of Chugiak and Donna: Les and Dorothy Fetrow, Zona Dahlmann, and Margaret Swanson. I am in debt to Donna's close friend Tressie Vander Hoek, who answered some very important questions about Donna's life in Dillingham, the type of questions that no one else could answer. As Donna's friend and the one who accompanied Donna and Richard on their first "blind date," Tressie knew much about Donna during her time in Alaska, as well as about Donna's on-again-off-again relationship with Richard Newton. Tressie and Donna's enduring friendship meant a great deal to Donna, and to Donna's surviving family too. I can certainly see what Donna saw in Tressie! She connected me with Don Wagner, who used to work with Richard and Charles Newton at Matanuska Plumbing and Heating Company. I cannot thank them both enough, as well as Tressie's daughter Carol.

I would also like to thank Juanita Pelagio and the Bristol Bay Native

Corporation, Bruce Merrell (Archivist at Alaska Collection, Loussac Public Library), Bruce Parham at the National Archives Pacific Coast Branch in Anchorage, Pam Khiani at the United States Bureau of Land Management, Emily Roberts, Natalie Brooks, Don Warton, Bill and Marie Andrews, many people who work for the Federal Aviation Administration both in Alaska and in Washington, DC, and a nice gentleman who gave me a tour of Merrill Field (pointing out a Cessna 175 for me on the tarmac).

In Nebraska, I am indebted to Paul Eisloffel for helping me turn old reel-to-reel and wire recordings into manageable cassettes, which Sara or Trisha could then transcribe. As an objective historian, I sat down to listen to the first reel-to-reel tape that Donna's family found. The first voice I heard was the booming voice of the Reverend Leslie David McGladrey. I instantly broke out into tears when I realized that it was the grandfather I so dearly loved, but whose voice I had not heard since he came to baptize my little sister Janet in the fall of 1973, when I was not yet ten years old.

Without the Ameritas Faculty Fellowship, I could not have completed this research on any decent time schedule. Ameritas's generous support of faculty research and development projects provides a much needed source of assistance for faculty who pursue creative goals. I would like to thank the generous foundation and encourage them to continue their support of this type of project at NWU. It enhances the quality of our teaching—therefore our students as well. Without the financial assistance of the Faculty Development Committee at Nebraska Wesleyan University, I would not have completed this project. In particular, I would like to thank the former vice president for Faculty Development, and NWU director of the Masters in Forensic Science, Jody Meerdink. I wish also to thank Maya Allen-Gallegos, most gracious and patient managing editor at the University of New Mexico Press, for her support for this project and encouragement. Linda Kay Quintana's assistance cannot be overstated, for she helped take this manuscript to its final stages with her excellent suggestions and critical eye.

I am indebted to other family members who have assisted me with this project: my sister Janet Mathews-Flynn and her husband Mike Flynn, my sister Diane Mathews, and my cousin Karen Engelsen. I thank my "kids" Aubrey Anne and Charlie Russell (both of whom I miss greatly) and now Dulcinea. They sat uncomplainingly by as I typed away on my computer, waited impatiently for me to return when

I left the house for many days to do research, and happily greeted me at the door, furry tails flying. And special thanks go to Joan Eik and Dorothy Mathews again for their assistance with the final preparation of this, our manuscript.

Most important, however, is Donna herself. In one of her first letters she wrote, "I want to write a book about my experiences someday." With this in mind, she wrote with the eye of an anthropologist and historian, one who carefully recorded even the most mundane experiences. Without this incredible collection of letters, and the willingness of her family to share them and talk with me, this book would never have happened. Donna, you finally got your book.

Sandra K. Mathews, Ph.D.
Lincoln, Nebraska

Introduction

> We were met in my new home town by the incessant rain and swarms of hungry flies. Dillingham is a growing town, but is unlike Anchorage in many ways. Anchorage is lucky enough to have plumbing, modern looking buildings, streets, stores, and so on which are similar to what a small town in Illinois might have. But Dillingham has no plumbing in most of its shacks, no streets, stores that don't resemble stores I've ever seen, and the general outlook of an unorganized primitive village.
>
> —Donna Joy McGladrey,
> October 1958 (form letter to family and friends)

The story of surviving hardship on the frontier has mesmerized readers and moviegoers for generations. Life in a far-off and exotic land, surrounded by cultures unknown and difficult conditions, seemed like a great adventure, one worth recording for family and friends. While men traveling the overland trails to the West recorded simple details about the journey, women's diaries and letters immortalized the ever-present unremarkable chores and daily occurrences along the trail. They recorded the number of graves, the injuries and illnesses, the collection of buffalo chips for fires, and the social milieu. Upon arriving at their final destination, they wrote about the hardships they endured, of hauling water, watching out for snakes and spiders coming through sod-house walls, and caring for children who needed to understand a new set of boundaries for living in the wilderness. They wrote about everyday things that informed future Western historians about actual life on the frontier.

But when Frederick Jackson Turner wrote in the 1890s about the closing of the frontier, he missed the point.[1] The frontier was not a place for "savagery" to meet civilization but instead approximated a social and cultural construction grounded in group or individual experiences and their cultural programming as well as their coming into contact with a different place and set of values, lifestyles, and tools. In this sense, the frontier continued long after Turner proclaimed it was over. While Frederick Jackson Turner was correct in seeing the frontier as both place and process, he could not dig deep enough into the long-term effects of the frontier to expand upon the idea that place and process were not static and would therefore continue to evolve long after the geographic definition of frontier no longer proved viable. The place may no longer have existed in the Trans-Mississippi West, but it still existed into the twentieth century in a very different sense.

Alaska, then, allows historians to retest the theory of westward migration (or northward as well, as this case might have it) and its impact on the psyche of the migrants and, when possible, on the original inhabitants. What caused the explorers and pioneers to move outside the boundaries of a comfortable lifestyle, friends, and family, as well as the security of towns and cities filled with others like them? Oftentimes, the answer seems to be similar to other "frontier" experiences—even between centuries. Alaska in the mid-twentieth century typified a more recent and perhaps more of a personal frontier, one based on cultural designations and social distinctions of modernity. The fewer pleasantries available (like flush toilets and running water, shopping centers and music stores, railcars and highways), the more the interloper perceived him or herself as having stepped into the past and a different set of circumstances—as Donna McGladrey termed it, a frontier. Alaskans native to the region, however, would not have deemed Dillingham, a bush village in Bristol Bay in southwest Alaska, a frontier. To them, Dillingham had grown significantly in the years before Donna's arrival, and in fact had grown into a regional headquarters for the salmon industry. And, as Donna would learn, many outlying communities were far more "primitive" than Dillingham.

Donna Joy McGladrey, the daughter of a Methodist minister, entered her own frontier in 1958, one that challenged her perception of herself, the wilderness, Alaska natives, and other "pioneers" (as relatively recent Alaskan arrivals called themselves). She learned about adaptation and doing without, deprivation and resulting illness, cultural (the Inuit and Aleut) and family differences, the pain of separation from loved ones and the joy of creating new friendships, and perhaps most important, how to make do. In 1958, when Alaska was still a territory, she left the relative comfort of the modern city of Chicago and moved to Dillingham, a remote fishing village in southwestern Alaska. Here she would reinvent herself, find a new sense of purpose, develop self-worth and confidence, as well as maintain a firm connection to home through letters, photographs, and moving pictures. Donna's story exemplifies the story of a single woman moving to the frontier, whether in the nineteenth or twentieth century. While the technology and opportunities for women differed, the personal and psychological adaptation to being separated from family and friends and home did not. Donna pined for her family and begged them to move to the frontier with her. She thrived on the adventure, yet the deprivation and remoteness of her new home caused her to feel great sadness and loneliness, especially around the Christmas season.

The stories of the privation and hardship she endured, as well as her numerous advances and successes, fill the letters she wrote from Alaska between September 1958 and December 1959. Interestingly, like many overland migrants and merchants who labored along the Oregon and California Trails, she understood the importance and relative uniqueness of her experience. She was aware that by moving to Alaska on her own, she was going against societal expectations, particularly that a young woman's priority should be finding a husband and starting a family. Nevertheless, her parents had encouraged her to get an education, so she graduated from college. Even though she grew excited about her developing sense of independence as she completed her education and struck out on her own, she yearned for a husband so she could "settle down." Until she found that man, she struck out on her own and learned how to depend upon herself. And during this reinvention process, she wrote more than one hundred letters to her parents in Chicago, her older sister in Minnesota, her twin sister in Evanston, Illinois, as well as to her many friends. She worked long hours, scrimping and saving in order to buy a camera with which she recorded Dillingham's daily scenes, as well as aerial shots around the Bristol Bay region. Almost all of these letters, photographs, and other memorabilia remain in family archives today. After all, Donna had hoped to write a book someday. While she never had that opportunity, her family's diligence in saving her recorded history makes a book possible. Donna's story is an intriguing one, a story that pulls a reader into her life.

The Story

I grew up knowing in the recesses of my mind that my mother Dorothy was a twin, but she never really talked about Donna. And since I had never met my Aunt Donna, I never understood what it meant to be a twin. I never witnessed that tight bond that purportedly develops between siblings who shared the womb, grew up together, shared birthdays and clothing, and learned about life's experiences together. I have since heard stories that twins can feel the pain that the other endures, whether physical or emotional. My mother said she did not share that psychic closeness with Donna, but her sister Joan did. When Donna died, Dorothy did not sense it, but Joan felt some unease.

I never remember seeing my mother cry—except during those particularly sad episodes of *Little House on the Prairie* where we sobbed together while my older, more stoic sister Diane watched us in bewilderment. I do remember Mother crying when her father died—I was ten. My grandfather, a Methodist minister, had the most amazing voice and the most wonderful and biggest hands. He and Grandma (Verna) had just visited to baptize my baby sister, Janet. While there, he sang songs about a robber who hid under an old maid's bed—but the robber was nearly frightened to death as she took off her hair and took out her teeth.[2] He read to us our favorite books, *Winnie the Pooh* and stories about Raggedy Ann and Andy. He imitated their voices and heartily laughed when the Camel with the Wrinkled Knees tripped and fell down. He held my little sister so tightly to his heart that I thought she would burst. He loved his daughters and treasured his grandchildren.

Within days of his death, we traveled to Sycamore, Illinois, to be with Grandma at their mobile home, and to attend my grandpa's funeral—my first. I do not remember much, other than playing a whodunit board game called Clue. My Aunt Joan was there, as was her husband Uncle Alf Eik, a Norwegian immigrant who married Joan after her first husband Malvin Engelsen, also a Norwegian immigrant, died several years before. One of the most entertaining couples that I know, Joan and Alf helped us all through those difficult days.

When I attended high school, Grandma Mac, as we called her, lived with us for four months while she awaited Oak Crest Retirement home's completion in DeKalb, Illinois. I was a typical high school student: self-centered, impolite, and, well, a teenager. I did not take much time to be with Grandma. She liked to make up her own rules for games, and she hated to lose. After she left us for DeKalb, I remember the emptiness and sensation of guilt, for not having taken advantage of her friendship and camaraderie. Now I realize I should also have learned from her about her past.

I visited Grandma Mac during Spring Break of my junior year in college. When most kids my age were going to South Padre or Mexico, I went to see Grandma Mac. Something just made me want to go see her. She invited me to watch one of her numerous and carefully scripted slide shows, of which she was so proud. She and Grandpa used to love to travel, and she was a master photographer, taking beautiful photographs of each national park or monument they visited. She brought them home, chose only the best, and scripted well-written narratives of their trips, which were interspersed with religious messages and that left her church audiences spellbound. She had been trained as an English teacher, after all, so her narrative was flawless and engaging. She showed me slides of Alaska. They were amazing.

She then mentioned something I had completely forgotten: my mother's twin sister. Then Grandma showed me something that I would always remember. She pulled out an 8.5 by 11 inch book of typed paper, bound together with spiral binding. She began to tell me about Donna, the aunt that I had never met.

The Letters

Verna's pain became evident, but it was tempered by her love of teaching. She told me a little about Donna and asked if I would like to read Donna's letters. As a history major, I was excited about the possibility and responded with an enthusiastic yes! A few weeks later, I received in the mail a bound collection of Donna's letters, typed lovingly by her mother's hands. I quickly read through it, nearly emotionless, and set it aside. I never remember asking my mother about the letters, or what it felt like to lose a sister. Apparently I was still too self-absorbed. The letters would have to wait.

Years later, while taking Women of the American West with Elizabeth Jameson during my doctoral program at the University of New Mexico in the 1990s, I learned about the forgotten or ignored people in Western history—women.[3] I remember distinctly that she wanted us to "nudge the boundaries" of Western history to include women and minorities. We read about Spanish colonial New Mexico, African Exodusters, and Hispanas in twentieth-century California. She told the class that *every* family, *every woman*, has a story to tell. Then I remembered Donna's letters. I reread them and they broke my heart.

I shared the letters with Dr. Jameson, whose excitement over the story inspired me. She said I should write a book. Drat. I was just starting to write my dissertation. Once again, the story would have to wait. And it did—until after I defended my dissertation in early 1998. Sadly, as I defended in New Mexico, my family buried Grandma Mac in Illinois next to Donna. They had not told me she died until after I arrived in New Mexico. She had lived to ninety-five years of age, but death always has a way of ambushing you—even when you think you are prepared. How could I find out more about Donna now that her parents had died? How could I write Donna's book without them?

I reread the letters again, so touched by the tragedy that tears streamed down my face. But my training in history forced me to ask questions that I had never asked before. Why did Grandma omit portions of Donna's letters when she transcribed them? Did more letters exist? Did Donna send letters to her sisters as well? If she did, did they keep those letters? How could I learn more about her experiences in Alaska as a young pioneer woman, one whose emotional journey typified those pioneers from the nineteenth century? Later that summer, as my mother and her sister began sorting through Grandma's things in our basement, I asked them casually if they had come across Donna's letters. Not yet, they said, but they would look.

The Research

By summer, my mother and my Aunt Joan had begun the arduous task of dividing up Grandma's things. Aunt Joan brought with her the letters Donna had written to her, and so I gently asked my mother about Donna's letters to her parents again, reminding her that I would love to see Donna's handwritten letters, and she again promised to look for them. Weeks and then months passed, no letters. I kept pressing, "Certainly Grandma wouldn't have thrown them out." Eventually Aunt Joan and my mother both found letters, but not letters that Donna sent her parents—rather letters Donna had sent to them. I begged them to share the letters with me, which they did. I dutifully copied them, then I read them, page by page.

But the letters were confusing, out of order. In the spring of 1999, Joan and my mother put the letters into chronological order. I then transcribed the letters, with the help of student assistants. My mother found and shared Donna's childhood memory album with me. In it, I learned more about Donna's childhood, adolescence, and college years. I learned about a happy child who participated in choirs, plays, synchronized swimming, musicals, and who grew into a strikingly beautiful young woman. Her love of cats was apparent in a two-page layout of Donna with her cat's kittens. I was excited to see the photograph of Donna and her Alaskan boyfriend Richard on a boat together near Susitna, Alaska, next to which Verna had scrawled "Photographed by Herman[n] Kroener on a trip on the Susitna River, fall of 1959, near Mrs. Newton's homestead." Who was Hermann Kroener? I pondered. We turned the page and clippings of newspaper headlines announcing the disappearance of the Newton plane, with Donna inside, overwhelmed Mother and me. The articles, clipped, saved, and glued into Donna's album, overlapped each other—and went on for pages. Mother and I cried together—she reliving the pain of forty years ago, and I, experiencing the loss of an aunt for the first time. Grandma had saved everything! Then I remembered that in one letter, Donna begged her mother, "Please save my letters in your chest or dresser, I want to write a book someday about my experiences in Alaska." Donna could not write the book, but I was infused that day with a sincere obligation to write it for her*.

I knew that other women in Alaska had written their stories, like the well-read book by Robert Specht, *Tisha: The Story of a Young Teacher in the Alaska Wilderness*, but they seemed to highlight either the nineteenth century or earliest years of the twentieth.[4] I had found no other book

---

*The transcriptions of personal correspondence in the text are true to the original material, preserving errors and variant spellings.

that highlighted the mid-twentieth century as a comparison. After conducting preliminary research on Alaska, I realized that nobody yet had published such a book about a woman's experience after the 1930s or 1940s. Donna's book could illuminate the views of a recently arrived, urban white woman in a remote bush village in the 1950s.

Shortly thereafter, Mother finally found the original letters that Donna sent to her parents. Sara McCroden and I transcribed them and soon an amazing story emerged. I began to interview Dorothy and Joan about their early childhood, about their parents Verna and Leslie, and about Donna. During the summer of 2000, I realized I needed to go to Alaska to follow Donna's footsteps, for I believe one truly cannot understand a person or a place without being there and experiencing it firsthand.

Since then, I have been to Alaska four times. I have met Donna's best friend Tressie Vander Hoek, Richard's sister MaryAnne Mateson, his sisters-in-law Ruby and Mary Newton, Donna's landlord, coworkers, students, colleagues, and more—all of whom provided immeasurable assistance with this book. I have met so many generous people in Alaska. Most important, I felt divine assistance—Donna must have been watching over me. At the Chinese restaurant by the boat harbor in Dillingham on my first research trip, my fortune cookie read, "You Are On the Right Course—Follow Through." My newfound friends, Tim Troll and his wife, and I were stunned. I have since followed the course and have pieced together her life through research, interviews, and diligent reading of her letters from college and from Alaska.

As an historian, however, it pains me to write her story without including detailed and numerous footnotes. I have chosen to eliminate the abundance of notes and references that I had originally created for this manuscript, including only the most necessary. The bibliographical essay, however, will guide the reader to the key documents held at public and accessible locations. But this manuscript is based mostly on meticulous research; Donna's letters; numerous interviews with Donna's and Richard's families, friends, colleagues, and Donna's former students; as well as my own travels to follow Donna's path. Without Donna's letters and the help of Dorothy and Joan, Donna's sisters, I could not have written her book.

I hope that you will find her story as wonderful and enjoyable as she would have wanted it to be.

CHAPTER ONE

Growing Up A "PK"

"It seems like so many years ago," lamented Donna's sisters, Joan and Dorothy, as they sat to talk about Donna's life, then tragic disappearance and death in Alaska over forty years ago. Even though the life they discussed had ended so abruptly, leaving her family in utter disbelief and grief, Donna's sisters have a marvelous sense of humor. Riddled with laughter, our discussions of Donna's life went on for hours. They eagerly shared stories of their childhood, as daughters of a Methodist minister in Minnesota and Illinois, their adolescent years, and growing up. Most important, from their stories I learned about Donna. And I wanted to know everything, so we started at the beginning.

On April 19, 1935, Verna and Leslie McGladrey joyfully welcomed their new twins into the world at the Methodist parsonage in Mora, Minnesota.[1] Leslie served the Mora community as the Methodist Minister. Then just over three years old, Joan remembers the day the twins were born at home: "I was quite small . . . I recall very vividly one day being sent out to play with Beverly Engstrom and I had to stay out and play and play and play and play and I was getting really tired of being outside and playing. Nobody would let me come back in the house. But eventually, before the day was done, I came back in and I found I had two sisters, which changed a lot of things." The birth

of the twins meant many things to Joan: new playmates, but also sharing resources in an already strapped family. She remembered clearly
that life was difficult economically with just one child in the family.
Then again, she recalled years later, everybody suffered during the
"Dirty Thirties."

Before 1939, the small family moved often. As many families did,
they also experienced economic frustration due to the Depression itself.
Leslie did his best to provide a comfortable life for his little family. As
a Methodist minister during the Depression, however, he did not bring
home enough money to provide daily necessities. Verna, therefore,
watched every penny—as her parents, Wilson and Lillie Belle Higbie,
had taught her. Wilson Higbie had been a successful businessman until
the Depression and therefore understood the importance of tracking
expenditures, something Verna practiced religiously until her death in
February 1998.

Verna's fiscal talents proved useful in Minnesota, for Reverend
McGladrey's very minimal salary sometimes did not come at all. But
at least the Methodist Church always provided them with housing.
Nonetheless, they still had to cut corners to acquire basic necessities.
They scrimped, saving energy and money wherever they could. Joan
recalls how Verna closed off the entire house, except for the kitchen, in
order to conserve heat in the wintertime.[2] While never luxurious, the
Methodist parsonages sufficed. Joan remembers that the walls always
had old wallpaper, almost always beige in hue. They never had any
"homey" decorations, because whatever they owned, they would have
to pack up and transport to the next parsonage when the Methodist
Church reassigned their father, which occurred every couple of years
or so. Joan and Dorothy remembered the few items that they took from
parsonage to parsonage to make their house more special: lace cur-
tains and pull-down shades, and a rug or two they could roll up and
move. Nothing they owned showed extravagance, or even a modicum
of luxury.

The young girls had many obligations associated with the home and
their father's vocation as a minister. For the household, they did the
sweeping, mopping, dusting, washing and ironing, and even took out
the trash. On Sunday mornings, they had to fold the church bulletins
before they could read the Sunday paper. Everybody worked hard in
order to support the family. But it never seemed to be enough, and
while Leslie tried to hide the stress of his job, the tension always seemed

to filter down to Verna. Unfortunately, as a minister's wife, she also had to deal with other, more externally oriented pressures. For perhaps no one was under such scrutiny as Verna, who only by association had to follow a certain lifestyle—that of a minister's wife.

Verna always carefully monitored her own behavior, actions, and appearance. She, as well as the girls, conscientiously noted attitudes of the parishioners toward the family—there was a distinct and fairly unyielding set of expectations for religious folks and their families. Verna told Joan that one day she was behind the house working in her garden and a parishioner approached her and chastised her. "'You're a minister's wife, what are you doing back here?' As if she should be above that." Dorothy recalled that her mother "had to be careful about what she wore and [that] she didn't wear any makeup." Verna's active role in the church—as organist, pianist, Methodist Youth Fellowship (MYF) director, and secretary—meant she was constantly under the social microscope.

But more important to Donna, Dorothy, and Joan, the community also carefully monitored the children of ministers, or "PKs" (Preacher's Kids). Joan remembered how she had to be careful about her actions and words. "We couldn't play [card] games . . . we couldn't wear lipstick . . . when I was introduced I was very often not 'Joan McGladrey,' but I was 'Joan, whose father is a minister,' as if that were my last name." The girls both remember that they had to behave better than anybody else, but not be "snooty." Besides behaving at church, teachers and fellow students expected them to perform better in school and during stage productions (in which they participated). The McGladrey girls learned that this public scrutiny did not, however, preclude them having a good time. While the girls regularly enjoyed playing games, such as softball, in their backyard, they did share responsibilities at home and with their father's work. The girls learned how to save resources (whether financial or otherwise) and thereby the value of money and of family, yet the family always seemed to maintain a balance between their responsibilities and having fun.

One of the few luxuries they did enjoy was music lessons. Music had an important role in their family.[3] Verna played the organ at church, and their father had an amazing, beautiful, deep, and penetrating singing voice. In the McGladrey household, it was therefore natural that music lessons quickly became an important priority. And the girls enjoyed these lessons tremendously. Music lessons provided an important diversion, but also formed the basis for Donna's future education and employment.

The money for lessons did not come easily to the McGladrey family, however. Leslie and Verna made great sacrifices to pay the seventy-five cents per week for the lessons for the three girls. Joan recalled her mother saying that before the twins were born, sometimes they had no food in the house. "No money, no food. But somebody would come to the door with a piece of deer meat or a loaf of bread and it was okay. I don't think we were aware of that because we had a garden and we lived in small towns during those years until 1939." In that year, they moved to Pullman on the south side of Chicago and Rev. McGladrey began working a side job for Railway Express, procuring a little extra money with which they purchased necessities. After working for Railway Express

Left to right: Donna, Joan, and Dorothy McGladrey at Greenstone Church, Pullman in Chicago, Illinois, 1939, photograph courtesy of author.

between 1939 and 1940, he began supplemental summer work as a hail adjustor for America Fore Insurance Company in 1940. He held that job for many more years. Joan maintained that had it not been for her father's extra jobs, the family would have struggled far more.

While in Pullman, which had already deteriorated somewhat by the 1940s, the children began to experience a little bit of freedom.[4] Not that far away from their row house sat a park. Because of the traffic and other urban dangers, however, Verna warned Joan not to let the twins cross any streets without holding someone's hand. Once, the twins desperately wanted to play at the park, so they grabbed each other's hands and took off for the park—carefully stopping for the light at the corner. Joan did not think much of the incident, but when Verna came out and wondered where the twins were, Joan reported that "well, they went to the park or something." Later Dorothy replied innocently, "Well, we were told not to cross the street without holding on to somebody's hand so we held on to each other's." Their mother was fit to be tied!

After the difficult year at Pullman (1939–40), the Rock River Conference of the Illinois Methodist Church assigned Leslie to Plainfield, Illinois, for three years. While preaching at Plainfield, Leslie's work with the America Fore Insurance Company took him to Illinois, Indiana, and Ohio during the summers. He worked five days a week investigating farmers' hail damage claims from April until early fall, spending a week at a time away from home. He really enjoyed this work because "he liked to drive, and he liked to talk with people, and he liked to be out on the farm." When he went on these many business trips, he slept in the car to save money. Joan remembered that by 1946, the family had an old Nash Rambler that had a folding seat upon which Leslie slept while on his hail adjusting trips. Joan recalled that "when he turned in his expense account he had meals on the expense account but he didn't have anything for hotels and the bosses called him in and said 'you're making the others look bad because the others had motel bills and you don't' so he started staying in hotels sometimes." He used to keep his accounts on a sheet of paper that he wryly referred to as his "swindle sheet." He was so used to thrift that he had a difficult time charging the company for such extravagances as a restaurant meal or a hotel room when sandwiches and the car seat had suited him so well in the past.

In Plainfield, the girls continued to grow and learn about life, relationships, and more. Because Joan was a little ahead of other schoolchildren her age, the school let her skip a grade. Dorothy and Donna started their school career in a day care in 1940, then attended the first and second grades there in Plainfield. During these years, there were other memorable events as well. In August 1941, their uncle Merlin, Leslie's brother, got married and Dorothy and Donna wore matching dresses at the wedding. And then U.S. involvement in World War II began that same year with the bombing of Pearl Harbor on December 7, 1941. Merlin W. McGladrey was an Air Force chaplain who would eventually be stationed in Great Britain and correspond with the girls from there during the war.[5]

When the twins turned nine, they began to attend church camps, and it soon became the highlight of their summers. They got away from their parents and the hot city, enjoyed making new friends, swam, and just plain had a great time. Spending time away from home allowed the girls an opportunity not to be PKs, out from under the watchful eyes of their parents, parishioners, teachers, and classmates.

As an older sister, however, Joan often had different experiences playing with her classmates. While she also attended summer camp, she distinctly remembered that her mother allowed her more freedoms than her younger siblings. For example, her best friend's father worked at the Joliet State Penitentiary. Occasionally on Friday nights, Joan accompanied her friend's family to the prison, to a darkened room, where she enjoyed watching movies with the inmates. During one of the movies, she recalled distinctly, she needed to use the restroom. Since it was men's prison, however, the bathrooms had simple row toilets without walls. She found a seat and perched herself upon it. An inmate came in, saw the little girl perched upon the toilet, said, "Oh, 'scuse me," and walked out. Joan described not being afraid, but knew that the men had committed serious crimes (she later learned one man had killed his wife). She recalls most of her experiences were quite positive, but a young girl going to the Joliet State Pen on a Friday night to watch a movie with convicts would not be every mother's idea of a safe evening! Neither Dorothy nor Joan can figure out why Verna would have let her go to a prison to watch movies with murderers. Joan remembered it many years later as "weird, especially since we weren't allowed to go to the movies otherwise until after about 1947."

Their home provided security and a constant reminder of the importance of family, sharing, and of course, frugality. Therefore, living arrangements were not the best. The parsonages provided by the church were usually not spacious. Normally, their Grandma and

Grandpa Higbie, who lived with them, stayed in the front bedroom, or the master bedroom, while their parents occupied another bedroom. Since there were two, the twins usually commanded a third bedroom. When Leslie moved his family to Christ Church in 1945, the house had only two and a half bedrooms. The grandparents slept in a bedroom, Leslie and his wife slept downstairs on a hide-a-bed, and the twins had a bedroom. Joan remembers sleeping on a single bed in what was supposed to be a closet. The girls certainly had adjusted well to doing without—something that would serve Donna well in Alaska many years later.

While their Grandma Higbie did all of the cooking at the house, she still found time to play with her grandchildren. She was extremely quiet, but a very warm person. She did not interfere in her daughter's child-rearing, but constantly served as a presence in the household. In those days, she had long flowing white hair that she used to tie back into a bun with bone hairpins. Joan used to call her "Pinky" because of her little round nose that was always pink.

Grandma Higbie understood how to teach a child a lesson. Joan illustrated her deep love and respect for her grandmother's lessons of life with a story:

One of the warmest feelings I ever had in my life was [when] I had gone to a friend when I was fifteen. Mom and Dad were gone, and [Grandma] was in charge of us. And I was out a little bit later than I was supposed to, not a lot late because I didn't do that, but maybe half an hour to an hour and when I came home she was sitting on the steps to go upstairs and she was crying, and I asked why she was crying and she said, "Because I didn't know where you were." And I sat down on the step and we both cried. But I think of that as being one of the sweetest reprimands anybody could ever have. And I behaved very well after that. For her, and for my dad.

Unfortunately, in 1953 Grandma Higbie fell and broke her arm. Joan and Dorothy think she might have had some sort of blood clot that went to her heart, or a stroke, causing her to black out and fall down. She passed away on February 4, 1953. She died just short of her eighty-second birthday. Lillie Belle Higbie had earned the deep respect of her granddaughters who still miss her, even some fifty years later.

As even-handed and humane as Grandma Higbie's interactions remained with her grandchildren, Verna's tactics at child-rearing seemed far more harsh. Dorothy recalled one time in particular that Joan confronted her mother about something. Within moments, they began yelling. Shortly thereafter, Dorothy remembered, "Mother had Joan in a corner, with a broom, she was attacking Jo and . . . going after her with the broom." Joan remembered that one time her mother got her under a table, but could not reach her. As Joan tried to get away, Verna began kicking at her. Years later, Joan laughed, offering her mother an excuse, "Maybe this was menopausal time . . . she had terrible temper flares, just terrible temper flares." Besides her temper, Verna also had some difficulty with other communication issues with her daughters.

Verna loved her daughters and tried to protect them from harm, but she did have a way of issuing warnings about such things as marijuana and other dangers that made the girls squirm. "Our stomach would churn sometimes," Dorothy said, shuddering slightly as she recounted the feeling. Joan remembered her mother describing boys as "smarmy, real smarmy . . . whatever it means." Verna had very high standards for her daughters' boyfriends. If one of them did not live up to her standards, she let the girls know. She described relationships with boys in such a way that made the girls feel "crawly, creepy crawly." It is no great wonder that Donna did not date boys while she lived at home. Perhaps these warnings impacted her decision to attend all-women's MacMurray College in Jacksonville, Illinois.

Even though Verna warned the girls about boys, her own marriage provided the girls with a good example of a successful relationship. The couple enjoyed each other's company and it showed. For example, they liked to go on car rides together, a common diversion for people after the war and wartime gas rationing. Besides Leslie's regular business trips, the family sometimes piled into the car for a leisurely drive around town or the surrounding countryside. Leslie drove with Verna at his side, while the three girls sat in the backseat. The girls often took off their shoes and stuck their feet out the window, or wrapped them around their dad's head. The longer the ride, however, the more the elbows began to fly. Dorothy and Joan even figured out how to poke Donna so that she got into trouble, instead of the instigators. Soon Verna would lose her temper and demand that Donna sit up front between her and Leslie. It confounded the backseat occupants, however, when

Donna McGladrey
on horse, Chicago,
1939, photograph
courtesy of author.

Donna seemed to enjoy sitting in the front seat! Either way, it left more room for Joan and Dorothy in the backseat.

Leslie and Verna enjoyed Donna's company in the front seat as well. Donna's sisters, after all, believed that their parents doted more on Donna than themselves. Dorothy recalled, "There was always something separate and special about her. Now, I don't know if that's because of the way she was treated, I mean, she was cute." Both Dorothy and Joan remembered the time that the family lived in Pullman and they came upon a man taking photographs of kids dressed up in western garb on his beautiful palomino-colored Shetland pony. Perhaps it was Verna that decided to let Donna on the pony and to have her picture taken. The parents could only afford a photograph of one child; therefore, they did not offer to do the same for the other daughters. Both sisters agreed in interviews much later that this was yet another example of their mother's favoritism for Donna. In fact, years later that photograph showed up in both Dorothy's and Joan's childhood memory albums—a frustrating reminder of their parent's preference for Donna. Such jealously did not last, however, and in their unstable and very mobile existence, the girls found themselves without friends again and again, and they learned to cling more tightly to each other. Closeness with the family helped them adapt to their constant moves throughout their childhood years.

Whether they had favorites or not, Leslie and Verna loved all three daughters without question, taking them on trips as often as money and time would allow. One early car trip memory was in the winter of 1941, the same year Uncle Merlin was married and the December that Pearl Harbor was attacked. Immediately after their father conducted the Christmas Eve service, they packed into their car and headed south to Alabama to visit their grandparents Higbie who wintered there every year. They drove through the night, hanging their Christmas socks in the car. They celebrated Christmas morning in the car, arriving later that day across the bay from Mobile at Fair Hope. Dorothy received a dolly for Christmas that year, and remembers being amazed that Santa could find her in the moving car!

A particularly memorable camping vacation by car occurred in 1946, the same year that the McGladreys moved to Chicago. The family took a five-week camping trip through Illinois, Minnesota, the Black Hills in South Dakota, Yellowstone in Montana and Wyoming, Salt Lake in Utah, Rocky Mountain National Park in Colorado, across Kansas to Hannibal in Missouri, and finally back home again to Illinois. As a safety measure, Verna safely kept the family's money in her girdle. Years later Dorothy remembered that girdle, which Verna wore during "all waking hours"—even though in Kansas the temperatures soared to 110 degrees! They took the trip in the Nash Rambler that their father drove during insurance adjusting trips. Joan recalled that "it lacked bumpers because metal was still scarce," adding that she thought they utilized wood boards for their bumpers. On that trip, she reminisced, their parents slept in the car while the kids stayed in an "ancient tent, me on the cot without a bottom." She also remembered that on that trip a bear approached the car and "Dad rolled down the window and growled 'get outa here' and the bear went." Their dad's calmness and quick response taught the girls never to fear wildlife, but instead to appreciate it in its own environment.

Joan and Dorothy remembered that the most wonderful experience of all of their family trips was the songs that the family sang together in the car, playing "Cow Poker," the Alphabet Game, and other car games. Joan remembered that her dad always won the Alphabet Game because he was farsighted and could take off his glasses, seeing signs long before anyone else. For this musical family, the car songs provided hours of entertainment on long trips. They sang folk songs, children's songs, and church songs, including one of their dad's favorites, Earl Marlott's "Are Ye Able." At one point in this favorite tune, he slipped, accidentally changing the words from "Yea the sturdy dreamers answer" to "Yea the dirty streamers answer," and a cacophony of laughter would break out in the car and they would laugh all the way to the next state. (Sometimes, Dorothy remembered, he would even sing the erroneous phrase by accident in church!) Harmony provided by the parents would be balanced by the girls' beautiful voices as they grew older. Even the car occasionally accompanied them, providing the beat by which they sang the songs. Dorothy remembers well how the "old time cars" and their electrical equipment were not as good as cars today. The windshield wipers, plopping from side to side, would speed up or slow down, depending upon whether they traveled up or down a hill. So, the family used the wipers as a metronome, "We'd be singing really slow and the windshield wipers were going slow 'cause we're going uphill then we'd go real fast 'cause we were going downhill. And we'd just laugh and laugh, laugh so we could hardly sing." The sisters remember these times together as a family with fondness. Family vacations provided a key time for bonding, as well as an important role in their development.

The girls enjoyed family trips and spending time with their sisters. About Donna, Dorothy commented, "No matter where we went, we had each other." Feeling comforted and safe became more important to Donna, for as the years went by, she had recurring health problems. She developed a case of cat scratch fever—a particularly devastating event for someone who loved cats so much. Donna also seemed to develop a nervous condition that caused her to break down into uncontrollable tremors as an adolescent. Joan recalled that it took all the strength she, her father, and Dorothy could muster to hold Donna down during one of these episodes.

The oldest of the three, Joan did not have a "built in best friend," like the twins did. But as the years progressed, Dorothy began to grow closer to Joan. Joan had an adventurous edge that intrigued Dorothy. But even as Dorothy and Joan became closer, Joan graduated from high school at sixteen in 1948 and headed off to college. Joan matriculated at Kendall College in Evanston, one hour from the McGladrey home by elevated train.[6] Two years later, she transferred to Hamline University in Saint Paul, Minnesota, where she finished her degree. With her older sister in Minnesota, Dorothy no longer had her closest confidant at her side. She and Donna would spend the next few years together making their own friendship and sister bond even closer.

Remembering their years together under Verna's tutelage, Joan and Dorothy often broke out into fits of laughter. The sisters summed up their experience in two words: "The shoes." Verna always wore the same style and brand of shoes. The girls knew the wrath of their mother by the clump, clump, clump of her Dr. Scholl's heavy soled, lace-up, high-heeled shoes. They clicked loudly as she crossed the floor, and Joan remembered that they "scared the heck out of me when I heard them coming!" After Verna's death in 1998 when Joan and Dorothy found themselves cleaning out their mother's room, closets, and storage, they found several boxes of those shoes—never opened. In her later years, Verna apparently had ordered them, not realizing she had many spare pairs—in many different shades of neutral. The daughters gave most of them away, but saved one pair that appeared well worn. That summer, both of their families vacationed as they had since 1948 at Camp Nawakwa, the YMCA camp in the north woods. One day, the two women solemnly carried Verna's shoes down to the rowboat and headed to Verna's favorite fishing spot out on the lake, called "Verna's Cove" by her family. With all of the dignity they could muster, they remembered their mother with love and honor, then plopped the shoes overboard as a lasting memorial to their mother's love of fishing, the outdoors, and Big Crooked Lake. They watched them sink, tied together, floating end over end until they lightly touched the lake bottom, kicking up a pouf of sand and debris. It was as if they were ceremonially burying all of the pain that they associated with the shoes, but also letting go of the mother they so dearly loved.

CHAPTER TWO

Defining Moments:
Camp Nawakwa

The water glistened, rippling in the south winds that snaked around Big Island, whistling through the pine and birch trees that hung precariously out over the small coves, sometimes large enough for only a fishing boat or two. The small peninsulas provided homes for raccoons, birds, otter, and other wild creatures, which dotted Big Crooked Lake in Northern Wisconsin. Splash! The silence was broken for the sunbathing twins who woke up from their lazy slumber on the raft when the Wicker boys tossed their friends in the lake, only to engage them in a fierce game of "King of the Raft!"

Without a doubt, Camp Nawakwa was the McGladrey family's favorite summer destination. After planning for the trip for weeks, the girls packed in anticipation, eagerly awaiting the nearly day-long drive north. On the road, they played games and sang songs as they traveled, watching the view change from concrete, buildings, and street corners, to beautiful stands of birch and pine, interspersed with lakes and streams. It even seemed to get cooler. Anticipation built as they reached Lac du Flambeau, then the train station at the corner by the water tower, then the winding road that led to Camp Nawakwa Road. Along the way, they passed by a long driveway that disappeared into the thick forest, they giggled, having heard that it led to Al Capone's old haunt. They became excited as they took the last left turn, and leaning into the front seat, begged their daddy not to miss the right turn onto the unassuming road to camp that beckoned them. Once on that road, they drove past the little office on the right and headed toward the sand parking lot and lodge ahead. The excitement became almost unbearable! They could hardly wait to unpack the car, throw on their swimming suits, and head for the floating raft. They ran through the woods, located their cabin, unpacked, and raced each other to the cool, clear water. During their first few years at camp, they found new friends, some of whom would join them year after year, the same weeks of the summer.

Camp Nawakwa became a fixture in the McGladreys' lives while Leslie traveled for America Fore in 1948.[1] Leslie drove his family to northern Wisconsin with him, dropping them off at the YMCA-run family camp near the town of Lac du Flambeau (part of the Lake Superior Band of Ojibwe Indian Reservation) for weeks at a time. This beautiful and serene location provided them a welcome respite from the intense heat of Chicago's summers. In addition, Chicago's many factories belched pollutants into the air, and with the humid and hot summers on the South Side, the stench was at times overwhelming. The Windy City also had the largest slaughterhouse in the world, which periodically dumped untreated refuse, such as the unusable portions of hogs and cattle, into the waterways. The rivers stunk and sometimes one could see animal parts floating down river.[2]

They stayed in a cabin called Lakeview that first year in 1948. At the Lakeview cabin, they considered themselves lucky to be one of the closest to the brand new outhouse! Before the early 1950s, campers "bathed" in the lake or took sponge baths and emptied their "ugh" buckets (porta-potties) in the outhouses—if they chose to have a bucket in the cabin. By the late 1960s, Nawakwa had running water in the cabins, and some would even have indoor bathrooms. For those without, Nawakwa installed community bathrooms (which had toilets and showers with cold concrete floors). These new facilities, complete with spiders and mosquitoes, were located up the hill from the beach just minutes from their cabin, or seconds if it was raining.

The girls felt the exhilaration of being in the wilderness and enjoying the pristine conditions of nature that surrounded them. They reveled in their weeks spent in cabins with nothing but bunk beds, kerosene stove, lanterns, army surplus dressers, a small icebox, a few chairs, a wooden picnic table, and a sink in which to wash the dishes. They had electricity, but only with the assistance of a generator that was on only

Left to right: Joan, Donna, and Dorothy McGladrey on steps
of Lakeview cabin at Camp Nawakwa, Wisconsin, in 1948,
photograph by Verna McGladrey, courtesy of author.

from 6:00–10:00 P.M., then it was "lights out!" They did not mind hauling water from the camp's well. The pump, located by the bathrooms,
sat at the top of the hill above the beach and behind the North Camp
Lodge, Dorothy remembered, "so you got good muscles for doing that!"
And depending upon where their cabin sat in a given year, they might
have to walk perhaps as far as 250 yards. None of the McGladrey girls
were wimps!

They spent their time at camp canoeing, fishing, swimming, and
square dancing, as well as playing all sorts of games with camp residents such as sand volleyball, softball, capture the flag, king of the
raft, and gunneling canoes.[3] Touched forever by the beauty of the
north woods, the clear environment, and good friends, many years
later Donna referred to Nawakwa in her letters to help explain why
she would take a teaching job in Alaska.

Donna and her sisters and friends took out canoes and rowboats to
find good fishing spots where they would sit quietly for hours. They
hiked the one-mile sand and dirt road from North Camp to South Camp
to play softball. Returning to North Camp under the moonlight was
always a favorite time to walk arm in arm with friends. They listened

for bears in the woods, or mischievous boys hoping to scare young girls into a screaming dead run, guided only by the evening moon shining through the trees parted by the narrow sandy road. And Donna enjoyed the wilderness with her friends that returned each year, whether middle class or poor, for at Camp Nawakwa social and economic class did not matter. Everyone lived in similar cabins without "luxuries." If someone had a sailboat or a motorboat, they shared. The McGladrey family, especially Verna, could finally let their guard down, not having to live up to the standards of being a minister's family. Both Joan and Dorothy remembered that their mother seemed more at ease and gave them a comparatively generous amount of freedom at Nawakwa. They theorized that because the Reverend's congregation would not appear at inopportune moments, Verna could be herself.

While Verna relaxed her control over her daughters at camp, one rule stuck firmly: No Fishing on Sundays. Fishing was work to the McGladrey family who lived partially on what they caught during summers at Nawakwa. On one particular Sunday, temptation overtook the three girls and they snuck out during their mother's nap time, got their fishing poles, and ran down to the rowboat—giggling all the way—and went fishing where their mother could not see them. "We were just really bad." Joan continued, "Yeah, that's the kind of bad thing that we would do. That was a big piece of rebellion, wasn't it?"

Donna, Dorothy, and Joan built solid and lasting relationships with the friends they met at camp, such as the Wicker family—a fun-loving bunch from Milwaukee that Dorothy and Joan remember as if they had seen them yesterday. Joan and Dorothy recalled that "there were always ten to twenty teenagers with the ringleaders being the Wicker boys who knew every fish and tree and rock and trail." Dorothy explained that Lou Wicker, the wife of Ken Wicker and mother of four boys and one girl, knew "where all the berries grew, where the fish hid, where the fungus could be found, and shared her knowledge with all." In retrospect, Dorothy commented that maybe Mrs. Wicker had not shared all of the secrets about the best fishing spots. Lou Wicker was an incredibly athletic woman as well. On one occasion, her sons had climbed up into the rafters of the old lodge and jumped from rafter to rafter to catch bats. When they refused to come down, she climbed up into the rafters herself and dragged them down, one by one. The Wicker boys were exceptionally handsome "and vital" young men who provided a great deal of entertainment. As "real good-looking" men, they were "willing to hang out with us and show off their macho-ness . . . and how they could [survive in] the woods and paddle the canoe" and "throw knives." These young men, and their animated mother, enjoyed spending time with the McGladrey daughters and the other campers. The Wicker boys gave the girls an opportunity to interact with the opposite sex in a safe place, an important lesson for the girls.

Mrs. Wicker's handsome sons, particularly Gordon (Googie) and Chuck, caught Dorothy and Donna's notice. Dorothy talked about how these handsome boys made them feel comfortable around young men, regardless of their mother's attempts to intimidate them. They enjoyed each other's company tremendously, not as couples or as someone engaged romantically, but rather as a bunch of friends. Sometimes they paired off, but it was only for a more quiet time, not for ulterior romantic motives. Donna seemed to prefer Googie, who was muscular, tan, and knowledgeable about the "wilderness," but as far as her sisters can remember, Donna never dated.

The Wickers, the McGladreys, and their friends especially enjoyed spending endless hours on the raft in the swimming area. Visitors to camp used the big army surplus rubber raft for wrestling during the numerous and exciting King of the Raft contests. They also used the raft for transportation to "The Pines," a hidden cove on the far side of the lake where the campers met for weekly picnics. The rubber raft was as long as a car, Joan recalled, perhaps twelve to fifteen feet long. "The sausage part was long enough for six to seven footsteps before we fell off." Because of its rather large oblong size, they usually matched two people together and wrestled each other until one of them flipped off into the water. On one occasion, Donna and Mrs. Wicker, paired together, spiritedly defended their inflated post. As the situation became more tense, Mrs. Wicker's teeth came out and sank to the bottom of the lake. Her sons, as mischievous as they normally were, quickly leapt to her assistance and began diving the eight to ten feet to the bottom to search for the teeth. Dorothy and Joan both recall laughing so hard that they could barely breathe. After numerous dives, "Mrs. Wicker's choppers finally came up."

While Dorothy thoroughly enjoyed the outdoor activities, she admits that Donna was more athletic than she. But together they enjoyed hiking, canoeing, swimming, walking, softball, ping-pong, and even chopping wood with an axe for the family. Joan and Dorothy recalled one time when Donna had the duty of chopping wood—but she missed the wood and hit her foot instead. Joan and Dorothy recalled that Donna had to soak her foot in Epson salts, but neither sister remembers if she actually went to a doctor. Dorothy remembered with a scowl, "She should've had a tetanus shot." Chuck Wicker fashioned a crutch out of branches for her to hobble around on, but as a result of having an open wound, she could not go swimming or participate in any water sports.

While that year might not have been Donna's favorite, at the end of every trip to the family camp, a sense of longing and sadness overwhelmed the girls as their father packed them up and drove them down the drive that seemed so much longer than when they arrived just a few weeks before. They passed by the water tower and train station, Lac du Flambeau, and then turned south to Illinois. Soon their lives would be back to "normal" and school would begin and consume their energies.

CHAPTER THREE

Becoming Donna

In 1946 the McGladrey family moved to Englewood, a neighborhood on Chicago's South Side, where the twins spent their final seven years at home. Joan had already left home for college when the twins entered the University of Chicago Laboratory School (high school). Some students who attended were known as the "Whiz Kids"—exceptionally smart and therefore needing additional stimulus and training to reach their full academic potential.[1] By sending their twins to the Laboratory School, they hoped to give their children greater opportunities than the public schools could provide. While attending a new school and studying fascinating subjects seemed practically painless for Dorothy, Donna struggled a little more. After one year, however, Leslie and Verna realized that they could not afford tuition at both the Lab School and Joan's college, so the twins transferred to Parker Public High School.

During their senior year, Donna participated in the Carnival—a variety show put on by the students, faculty, alumni, and the Parent Teachers Association (PTA)—in hopes of raising enough money to buy a large-screen television for the school's auditorium, apparently a big enough accomplishment to merit an article in the *Chicago Daily Tribune*. Both girls participated in water ballet, volleyball, and many extracurricular activities. The twins also did well academically, becoming members of the Honor Society and the Senior Honor Society. Donna had perfect attendance and earned a Certificate of Merit. To ensure Donna would receive a college scholarship, teacher Henry Jarvis wrote a letter on her behalf (likely including her perfect attendance record for her year at the lab school):

> I find that Donna Joy McGladrey has unusual ability in studies at Parker High School. Her attendance has been perfect, for the entire 4 years. Her integrity is above reproach and her personality though not seemingly adjusted, because of many talents and interests is focusing toward a sweet and talented attractiveness. Donna is a beautiful girl that has inherited and acquired a fine mental and physical fitness. The family background is certainly superb although their financial means are quite limited. D. J. McGladrey will be a credit to any organization. I wholeheartedly recommend a chance for a scholarship.

Donna made a positive impression upon her teachers, for she focused so diligently on her talents and interests.

In a special Glee Club autograph album for her senior year, Donna's friends and colleagues wrote messages of encouragement, friendship, and gratitude during her final few weeks in high school:

> "Dear Donna—You were a swell president. We'll all miss you. Love Doloris Poitle"
>
> "Donna—All I can say is loads of luck. It's been swell wonderful and anything else! Myrina"
>
> "Dear Donna I never thought I'd ever get to this front table, but I did. We both did. It's been swell knowing you and I know we'll bawl together on the 24th. You were really a swell president. Love always, Lynne '53'"
>
> "To the prettiest girl in Glee Club—Judith"
>
> "Best luck to a wonderful gal. I enjoyed all the years I've been with you in school. Here's my best for wonderful years to come. —Margie Zacharias"
>
> "Dear Donna—it has been my pleasure since my stay at Parker to meet such lovely friends as you. Good luck, Love Freda."
>
> "The Glee Club will be lost without you. We will be thinking of you always.—Nancy Helps"

"Dear Donna—I wish you all the Luck and Happiness in World.—Barbara Langston"

On June 24, 1953, Donna, Dorothy, and their friends donned their graduation robes and headed to the Chicago Teachers College Auditorium. During the ceremony, Dorothy was honored for having the fourth highest scholastic average, and Donna the seventeenth. Donna directed and performed with the Girls' Glee Club and they graduated in a class of 187 students. Donna and Dorothy both received a National Honor Society Award (gold tassels), a Minor Service Award, and a Major Service Award. Donna asked Jimmy Swatosh to her senior prom, one of the only dates her sisters ever remember Donna having in high school. But the friendship never developed into anything serious, and after graduating from high school in 1953, the twins headed to Camp Cutter to work for the summer. They had little choice, for they had no place to live. Their father was transferred from Christ Church to Mount Greenwood and the parsonage was not yet ready. Of her month at Camp Cutter as a counselor, Dorothy recalled, "I think I didn't enjoy it at all. Icky." At the end of the summer, the girls went off to college: Dorothy to Northwestern University (graduating with a Math major in June 1957) and Donna to MacMurray College, then an all-women's college, in Jacksonville, Illinois.

At MacMurray College, Donna had even fewer opportunities to meet men, but she truly enjoyed her time there. She participated in freshman initiation and enjoyed being with her friends, even taking a trip with them to New Salem, Illinois. Together they participated in outings at parks where they grilled hot dogs and marshmallows and played softball. She joined numerous groups on campus and, with an old camera, took snapshots of musical rehearsals and just being silly in the dormitory hallways. But she missed her family and home, so in her room on her dresser below her big mirror, she had a photograph of her beloved sisters Dorothy and Joan, as well as white stuffed cats and kittens sitting on a lace runner.

During her first year, Donna enrolled in general courses required for graduation, as well as Music Theory, Organ, Piano, Music Orientation, Swim Life Saving, and Madrigal. She took a total of twenty-seven hours during her first year, and she enjoyed French, Music, and Life Saving, but had a tougher time in English, receiving a D and then a C. During her second year, she enrolled in Music Theory II, and kept a straight A average the entire year. She took yearlong courses including Organ, Piano, Voice, Archery, Badminton, Tennis, Bowling, Choir, and Methods of Teaching Music. She maintained a B average, but excelled in Music Theory and the History of the Early Christian Church. During her junior year, she took mostly yearlong courses including Teaching in Music, Choral and Orchestra Conducting, Organ, Voice, Piano, and Choir, as well as Archery, Badminton, and Social Recreation. She also took Woodwind Instrumentation, Percussion, and Brass Instrument classes. During her senior year, she took mostly music classes, but had to complete other requirements for graduation. Her courses included the History of Music, Teaching in Music, a String Instrument class, Orchestration, Church Service Playing, Organ, Voice, Piano, and American Public Education (for which she received her first D since her English class). Except for her first year, she always took eighteen credit hours—a heavy load certainly for students of music who demanded several hours daily to practice both organ and piano, as well as vocals and instrumentation. She obviously enjoyed music, as well as recreation classes that always seemed to find a way into her schedule.

Donna's classmates included Senior Class Vice President Phyllis Wong, an already accomplished pianist from Hong Kong. With her

Donna McGladrey, MacMurray College, 1956, photograph courtesy of author.

friends, Donna participated in the MacMurray College Choir where she performed across the United States. With the Wabash College Glee Club, they performed a program that was broadcast over the Mutual Network on April 4, 1955. She was also a member of the Organ Guild and Music Educators National Conference. Like other music majors, Donna presented many recitals, performing as a soprano, mezzo-soprano, and on piano and organ at Ann Marshall Orr Auditorium in MacMurray Hall.[2] On Senior Recognition Day, November 27, 1956, Donna sang in a quartet with Barbara Moor, Nanci Weeks, and Phyllis Wong.

Donna had taken the message of MacMurray College President Norris's speech to heart during her college career, "The world will know you by your values." Donna set very high standards for herself, so high in fact, that she complained to Joan that she could not seem to keep her performances and abilities in line with them. She blamed those same high standards on the fact that she had no self-esteem and even told Joan that as a result of her lack of confidence, she was just "a stupid-dumb 'old-maid-to-be.'" In a heartfelt letter to Joan, Donna explained her frustration and predicament that she could not seem to change. "I was so terribly tired. . . . Everything I do eventually winds up with the same deficiency—that of my self-consciousness, lack of self-confidence and all as a cause of my inferiority complex. I'm making myself miserable by being the way I am. I need someone to watch me—a psychologist or a psychiatrist—who'll analysis me and eventually pull me out of my shell." She knew that her own psychological issues made her question her abilities and frustrated her intensely, but she could not seem to change. She then explained the root cause of her inferiority complex, "I have such high standards in everything. Not only for myself but in everything I do or hope to do. I always look to the bad side of everything whether it be the way my hair is parted, or a piece I sing or a fellow I date. Anything!"

To make matters worse, she reported that she and her father had their first big "blowout" over music, "the first argument I've ever had with him." Leslie realized he could not convince Donna that she had a beautiful voice and had incredible musical talent. He loved his daughter dearly, but he simply could not discuss the argument logically with her, so he left the room. Verna, however, would not let it drop until Donna finally "burst into tears exploding at her—screaming for her to stop." Verna encouraged her to not expect so much from herself, that nobody could achieve perfection. Donna wrote, "It was all over my high standards. She just couldn't realize that I can't change my whole thoughts etc personality etc by snapping my fingers. I realize I am as I am but how can I change—? I want to terribly, but I can't overnight." Donna found herself in a desperate and perpetual cycle of disappointment and self-loathing.[3]

Dorothy later postulated that since Donna seemed to be the favorite, it "may have set up unrealistic expectations for her." She never received "from the outside world the recognition that she had [received] from home." But deep inside her heart, Donna understood that her parents were right, she did have talent. Yet Donna continued torturing herself by having unattainable expectations for herself, both personally and musically.

Donna had clearly encountered the same things that most young women did: lack of self-confidence, worrying about success, wondering if she would ever find a man that would love her and marry her, and worrying about her appearance. Donna understood that these concerns would pass, but not quickly enough in her estimation, "There are so many things to life that are so difficult. The biggest problem is in growing up." She knew she would mature with time, but the wait proved excruciating. She wanted to "enjoy life like most everybody else," but she lamented that her "dog-gumed hi-standards won't let me." At least she recognized her problem, "If I could just acquire a ton of self-confidence I'd just about win the whole battle in one sweep. My music would improve 100% and I'd begin to live. But—again them there Hi Standards chase away my confidence. What am I to do?"

Truly mystified, Donna drew a blank. She seemed to understand that the process of finding a solution was part of growing up as well. She then apologized to her sister and began writing about more mundane topics, dismissing her tirade by simply stating, "Anyway, you know I'm a mixed up kid." She hoped to move to the Twin Cities (Minneapolis-St. Paul) where Joan lived to find a job in the summer. She had to repay her mother, whom she nicknamed "the greedy old lady," for school costs. By the time Donna graduated, she figured she would owe fourteen hundred dollars, mostly to her mother, but also to her twin sister Dorothy. "Isn't that a neat sum to owe when starting one's career. At that rate I won't get to Europe until I'm 85. The folks are going to Europe when they're rid of me—guess on who's money!?! Bah Humbug." She then asked Joan to bake and send her cookies for final exam week, and asked that they come to her graduation in "138 days."

Donna worried about finding a job after her graduation, knowing that she had to come up with a plan for the upcoming fall. She considered teaching in Illinois, near Urbana. She wanted to be near a university where she could work on her master's degree—and the University of Minnesota, she told Joan, was "lousy for grad study in Music." But she thought she could use it as a "safety" school.

While her future seemed uncertain, Donna learned something important about her prospective career during the Spring 1957 semester: she did not want to teach beyond elementary school. As part of her course work, she began working with second graders twice a week, and fourth and fifth graders two other days during the week. She really enjoyed the second graders. "They are so responsive and love to sing and learn anything. It's such a great difference from those stubborn independent 6th graders." She told Joan that she had never worked with children before. She enjoyed it, but when the music teacher invited her to jump in and teach, she declined. She explained to Joan that she did not know how to "treat them." She learned that she had fun, and "that's why I should teach in elem[entary] not Hi. S[chool] or Jr. Hi." She also realized

Donna McGladrey practicing for graduation ceremonies at MacMurray College, Jacksonville, Illinois, May 1957, photograph courtesy of author.

something else important that would guide her future decision about where to teach and live: "I really feel that I should go someplace where I know no one and get a clean fresh start in a new world of my own, but the whole thing frightens me." She wanted to redefine herself, yet the fear of striking out alone troubled her.

Before setting out on her own, though, she had to graduate. Festivities began and on June 1, 1957, the Music Department at MacMurray College put together a program entitled, "Hour of Music" at the Ann Marshall Orr Auditorium. Phyllis Wong started the program with a song, and after Nanci Weeks performed on the piano, Donna came on stage to play "All Saints' Day Meditation: 'Gaudeamus'" by Everett Titcomb on the organ. Later, Donna's beautiful mezzo-soprano voice sang "Voi che sapete" from the *Marriage of Figaro* by Mozart. The next day, MacMurray College Commencement was held at the Annie Merner Chapel at four in the afternoon. Donna graduated with a Bachelor of Music, along with five other music majors.

Just before graduation, she received an award at Honors Chapel for "most outstanding achievement in the field of music." Donna wrote to her parents:

Hurrah for ME! In Honor's Chapel today I was awarded $5.00 for the most outstanding achievement in the field of music. Now ain't I sumin? $5.00. Hurrah—Cheers.

The music prize I won was really something. The faculty voted on who should get it. And Mrs. Gerson said it was unanimous. Everyone was in my favor. That's what makes me feel so good that the whole faculty thought I had made the most improvement over 4 years. I rode on clouds for days! Also Mr. Glasgow, who is as stuffed and nasty as possible, even complimented me and said many nice things about me in the faculty meeting.

Donna had earned her accolades and by the time she graduated, had signed her first teacher's contract for the 1957–58 academic year. She agreed to teach for the Board of Education's School District No. 28, Cook County, Illinois, for a salary of $3,900 a year. She signed her contract on April 4, 1957, which specified payment of $325 per month. She would specialize in "special education teacher in vocal music," according to a small local newspaper article.

Before she began teaching, however, she had to survive the summer.

Donna moved to Evanston where she landed a job at General Motors Acceptance Corporation (GMAC) in the lending department. She roomed with her sister Dorothy (Do), Lynn, Barb, and Julie. "Julie is a very poor roommate. She's very hard to get along with—betwix her and me I don't see how Do can stand it. If I had to live with me I'd move out. I can't stand people like me." Donna again disparaged herself. Donna rationalized, however, that soon Dorothy would marry "that dumb Dr. friend of hers." Donna obviously hurt inside because of her twin's engagement to Jack Mathews, a tall, stocky, handsome former football player from a small farming community in northwest Missouri. Donna described Jack as nice, "but I don't like him too much. . . . Of course my main complaint is he's taking my only faithful friend away from me." When she reported that Jack was not very considerate, she obviously meant that he was changing Donna's life forever and did not seem to realize it. She explained to Joan why losing Dorothy as a roommate would be particularly difficult. "Being as I am I've never had a real personal friend so Do's had to be that and is not really." Already she had started to distance herself psychologically from her sister so that eventually Dorothy's departure would not affect her as much. As a result, Donna began to spend more time with Joan than she did with Dorothy. And recently graduated Dorothy had a lot on her mind that summer. She had begun working as a technician in a laboratory owned by a woman and preparing for her wedding the following May. Dorothy's nuptials were another reminder to Donna of the unspoken requirements for women during the 1950s, to marry and raise a family.

Even though she worked eight-hour days at GMAC, Donna appreciated the newfound freedom that came with earning her own paycheck and having a car. No doubt after she began teaching, she would look back with fondness on the "good old days" at GMAC where she never had to bring work home with her at night. At the end of the summer, she took her first teaching job in Northbrook, but it did not work out as she planned. She did not enjoy her experience, moaning and complaining about school politics to her roommates and Joan. Some of Donna's frustrations included "a problem with funding. She wanted to get some instruments and she was up against the Board of Education. She thought kids learning music should have something to do music with," Joan recalled. Imagine teaching music without instruments, Donna must have thought. After getting permission from the principal, she sent a letter home with the children for the parents asking them to buy recorders (under two dollars at the time). She had all of the parents' permission and the parents purchased the instruments, but the Board admonished her for sending the letter. Dorothy remembered that the kids came from an affluent suburb and Donna felt that the kids were coddled and spoiled.[4] Joan recalled that Donna did not play the "political game," instead she was vocal when she disagreed with the Board. So by the second semester, she had decided not to return to Meadowbrook School for the 1958–59 school year.

Her dad congratulated her on her first year of teaching and encouraged her to renew her contract late in the spring of 1958, but Donna had had a difficult year. Leslie nevertheless urged Donna to secure a position there for the upcoming year. He told her that after graduating from college, she would find herself enrolled in "a post graduate course in the 'University of Hard Knocks.' I know for I have been in that school for a long time!" He continued to encourage her, telling her that everyone makes mistakes, that one must face adversity, and that "mistakes and failures are the stepping stones to success." He then reassured her that she actually had not failed, but rather had "met some difficult situations" and had not "pleased everybody. That's all it amounts to. Let it go at that." He then used his own life as an example, telling her that he made a lot of mistakes, but chose to go back for more training in summer school. He suggested to her that "summer school would be worth all the sacrifice it would take." He obviously loved his daughter and wanted her to succeed, without just giving up when the times got tough. He ended his letter by saying, "Mother and I are betting on you. We know you have got what it takes." It is no surprise that Donna kept that letter, for in it she was reassured by the man she loved and respected the most.[5]

On May 3, 1958, Dorothy married Jack Mathews at the Methodist church in Waterman, Illinois. When she did, Donna felt as if she had lost her closest confidant. Shortly after Dorothy's marriage, school ended and Donna decided to forego her father's advice of enrolling in graduate school and instead returned to her job at GMAC. She moved into an apartment on West Juneway Terrace in Chicago, but this time without Dorothy. It took her days to clean up the apartment before her new roommate Mary would arrive, which frustrated her because she needed the help. To make matters worse, she tripped and fell down some stairs at work and "nearly broke" her ankle. After having to walk home in a driving downpour, she laid upon her bed with her foot up on a pillow feeling helpless. "If I had somebody to wait on me it would be fine. I could die and no one would know the difference." Feeling sorry for herself, she lamented not having a spouse to dote on her. Donna's independent spirit dampened when her life became lonely and challenging, and she longed for companionship and assistance.

She continued working, enjoyed the company of her roommates when they finally joined her, and watched her newly purchased TV (she loved the show *Maverick* with handsome young James Garner). She enjoyed inviting friends for dinner. In early July, she cooked up a "genuine Chinese dinner" for MacMurray college friends, including Laura Hsu. She was exited to show off her cooking abilities to her Korean and Chinese college friends. Even as she enjoyed her friends, she no longer enjoyed working at GMAC; although she did like the pay, some $273.39 per month. ("That ain't bad.") But she worried about not having a job for September—nor even having any leads. Her job at Meadowbrook had been a frustrating experience and she refused to talk about it in letters, but she did discuss alternatives. Her parents had always talked about a camping trip to Alaska, but could not afford the gas. The more they talked, the more she began to think about teaching in Alaska. "I've been thinking since I hate hot weather so violently I should go up to Alaska to teach. Doesn't that sound exciting?" Thus appeared Donna's first mention of a potential and major move to Alaska, and she related the potential decision to escaping the heat of Chicago in the summertime—something their family had done for years in the northern woods of Wisconsin.

Her parents began preparing for the trip of a lifetime to Alaska that resulted from a chance dialogue between Verna and Leslie, and Donna's Great Aunt Florence Langley (just a few years older than Leslie) at a celebratory party honoring Jack's graduation in June 1958 from Northwestern University Medical School. Shortly after the ceremony, Dorothy and Jack hosted a small party at their apartment on Foster Avenue for family and friends. Jack's parents drove up from their family farm in Missouri to attend the celebration. Dorothy's parents, Verna and Leslie, also attended the gala, as did Leslie's Aunt Florence. Florence, Verna, and Leslie began talking about trips, places they had visited and would love to see, and the Territory of Alaska popped into the conversation. At that very moment, Florence, Verna, and Leslie decided they would take a camping trip to Alaska. They left a few months later in July. Leslie and Verna never could have afforded the trip, but since Aunt Florence did not have a car and could not drive, she promised to pay for the gas for the trip if they would take her with them. Donna even gave her parents $150 for use on their Alaska trip.

The trio drove from Chicago to Seattle, to Dawson Creek, then up the Alaska Highway through Alberta and along the Canadian Rockies. Verna and Leslie took dozens and dozens of photographs of their trip, later putting them together in a carefully scripted slide show that they shared with friends and church groups. From the moment she was able, until August 1984, Verna had shown her slide show to over sixty groups of people including various Methodist Women's groups. The script described details about their trip, with Biblical verses scattered throughout the narrative. They particularly enjoyed retelling how the Canadian Mounted Patrol stopped them for broken headlights—smashed by the cars that had passed them on the dirt and gravel highway. By the end of the trip, they had broken many more headlights, had a huge crack in the windshield, six big dents on the hood, and a broken rim (due to a large rock). But it was worth it, for along the way they passed beautiful lakes, rugged mountains, cemeteries, log churches, rivers, abandoned gold mines, and they even encountered a forest fire that licked precariously at the road they traveled. As they passed Whitehorse (Yukon, Canada), they began following the Yukon River, where they encountered the forest fire's wrath. It had jumped the road and they were forced back to Whitehorse to wait out the blaze. As they settled down to a nice meal at a local café, an earthquake struck. They learned later that over a half million acres were ablaze, and when they returned, nearly 1.5 million acres of forest had burned, the largest fire in western Canada until the summer of 2003.

After traveling 3,450 miles, they had finally reached Alaska Territory. Roads improved as they entered the territory—they were paved! As they reached the end of the highway at milepost 1523, they arrived at Fairbanks at last. They visited Leslie's cousin Marion "Red" Langley, who lived in a home he built himself on the permafrost. But the heat of the home was causing the permafrost to melt and the house was sinking! Verna snapped photographs of the many taverns and bars, referring to them in her slide shows as the "innumerable dives" and "hovels." While camping throughout Alaska, Verna remembered waking up one night around 1:30 A.M. and seeing her watch as plain as daytime, for as she wrote, "the sun never went down." They continued on to Valdez, Devil's Elbow in the Tsaina River Gorge, Worthington Glacier, and

Nelchina Glacier on the way to Alaska Methodist University—which they were excited to see. They then traveled down the Kenai Peninsula to Seward, Kachemak Bay at Homer, Ninilchik, Grewink Glacier, Portage Glacier, snapping photographs of the churches—especially the Methodist churches—that they saw along the way. They returned to Anchorage, where Verna took a photograph of the airport. "With very few roads, Alaska would still be in the dog sledge era if it were not for the bush pilots who pilot these planes," Verna wrote. Their trip nearly over, Verna wrote, "Now we hurry back to the Alaska (AlCan) Highway, leave it to fly down to Juneau from Haines and Chilkoot. We returned by boat up the Inner Passage." Upon the end of the "show," Leslie used to read a poem about a traveler finding his way back home.

During the McGladrey's trip, they wrote home telling Donna and the others about the beauty that surrounded them: the trees, the lakes, the mountains, the rivers, and nature in general. Before the end of their trip, Donna had contacted her parents and asked them to see about teaching jobs in Alaska. She expressed her desire to get away from the Chicago area. Her parent's description of Alaska, after all, reminded her of summers at Camp Nawakwa. Leslie and Verna found the necessary information and Donna then wrote to apply for a job, to Alaska Territory Commissioner of Education Don M. Dafoe.

Dorothy remembered that during the 1950s, Alaska desperately needed teachers as they began to open more and more schools. Alaska had become an important strategic post during WWII, and Anchorage had gone from a quiet town to a bustling community due to the resettlement of hundreds of people from the Pacific Northwest coast to places like Elmendorf Air Force Base on the outskirts of Anchorage. These newly arrived "pioneers," as they termed themselves, then had children who by the late 1950s needed more schools and teachers. Therefore schools popped up all over the territory, in particular near the military bases and outlying areas. When Commissioner Dafoe informed Donna that jobs were available, Dorothy remembers that "telegrams went back thick and fast . . . it was cheaper than telephones." Donna took a job as the first band instructor in Dillingham, a remote fishing village 350 miles west of Anchorage. Donna's father "attributed her decision in part, to the 'adventurous nature of her parents and two older sisters.'"

Donna's excitement for the adventure outweighed her family's trepidation about the impending journey. Donna's sisters had great pride in Donna for "going away on an adventure like that, and we were happy for her that she was doing something she really wanted to do." Yet, they lamented her leaving; it was terribly far from the rest of the family. In the days before e-mail, the family simply could not keep in close touch with Donna due to the expense of telephone calls. Dillingham had only one outgoing line, a party line onto which the entire town could eavesdrop. Donna would learn that sometimes people listened in on telephone conversations coming in and out of Dillingham. Still, she was excited to go. While Joan felt hesitation about Donna moving to the Territory of Alaska so far away, Verna enjoyed bragging about Donna moving to Alaska. Leslie was much more demure, he would simply grin. Leslie was "proud of all of his kids, no matter what they did. At least that's the impression I got," Dorothy recalled.

CHAPTER FOUR

An Introduction to Dillingham

Donna's decision to move to Alaska created a sense of excitement, for she could finally move far away to reinvent herself, prove her worth to herself and others, and become independent. She had chosen to leave her comfortable life in the city, with trains and cars, music stores and concerts, not to mention her family and friends. Like the many women who chose to move west during the nineteenth century, she saw the experience as unique, special, and important, and she intended to keep a good record of her experiences. She knew nothing of Alaska Territory, except its unrivaled beauty that her parents had described during their camping trip in the summer of 1958.

As Alaskans began planning statehood, the Lower 48 began to show a greater interest in its land and people. Donna dutifully reported her experiences in Alaska, for she knew that friends and family back home had developed a great interest in Alaska and she intended to record her experiences, as well as to share what she learned or witnessed in Dillingham and the surrounding communities. Donna would eventually write, "It seems people in the 'lesser' states are becoming aware of Alaska more and more and are all hungry for news about it. I find life among these people a very interesting experience. I wish I could describe in detail all the things I have observed about these people. Alaska is indeed the 'last frontier' and I'm thankful for the opportunity to be here and see things first hand." She knew that her "Alaskan adventure" was unique to her family and friends back home, so she begged her mother to save all of her letters in her trunk.

The territory had become front-page news during World War II with the Japanese invasion of the Aleutian Islands. Response to the Japanese invasion included an increased U.S. military presence in Alaska and, therefore, a rapid growth in population. As more non-Natives arrived throughout the 1940s, through military or civilian service, pressure increased on local Alaska Native populations. The United States also desired to know of the resources and capabilities of the land and people. As a result, the Alaska Indian Service (AIS) became more involved in trying to understand Alaska and its people, under the auspices of the Department of the Interior. Immediately following the war, the AIS completed a study of Alaska, "Post War Planning Survey," to research the resources of native communities in Alaska. Researchers studied Alaskan communities, resources, people, and economies and recorded the information for the AIS in Juneau. Muriel Speers was in charge of investigating Snag Point, which later became known as Dillingham.[1] In the thirty-page report on Snag Point, Speers described what Donna would only hint at later in her letters. In her report, Speers believed that 90 percent of the homes needed rebuilding, and all of them needed major repairs. Yet of the Alaska Natives that needed new homes or repairs, only approximately 50 percent of the population could actually afford to make the necessary changes. Shipping in building materials proved cost prohibitive for the majority of Bristol Bay inhabitants.

According to Speers, the Alaska Natives in Snag Point had long since abandoned the majority of their traditional ways. They had torn down their *maqi* (community steam bath) and they no longer depended upon native foods for their survival. Only 10 percent depended upon native fuel (wood) for cooking and heating their homes, or upon skins and furs for clothing. She did report that the Alaska Natives in the area performed an annual dance, "similar to the old Potlash or Potlatch."[2]

While Snag Point residents did not have electricity, they did have oil to heat their homes. A few residents utilized windmill-generated electric systems. For light, the majority of residents had gaslights, kerosene lamps, and candles. Speers reported that most of them fished and trapped as their chief occupation. Only one Alaska Native individual owned a local business: J. Pelagio and Company, which operated the Hotel Dillingham ($15,000 net worth). The Hotel Dillingham had six to eight rooms that served the community, a very important service as few other hotels even existed. But the hotel had no potable running water. Even a decade or so later, the hotel had no potable running water, and still boasted only seven rooms.

Sanitation and lack of acceptably clean water concerned Speers. Spring-fed wells provided water for the town, and she reported that "everyone dips his buckets in on the average of twice daily." The wells provided sufficient water in both winter and summer, but they were subject to contamination. The community had no water filtration or chlorination systems; therefore, according to Speers, their water was "Polluted!" Lack of proper sewage disposal exacerbated the problem. "The white families do have cess-pools. (Natives have the front and back yards!)"[3] In regard to garbage and refuse disposal, "sometimes trucks haul a winter's accumulation away during the summer. Some people have drums, which had previously held heating oil, which they utilized as incinerators." Locals improvised with their discarded items and refuse. They even converted the oil drums into doghouses for their sled dogs, which provided transportation due to the lack of road systems and the high cost of shipping motorized vehicles to the bush. Because of the contaminated water and the refuse in the yards, diseases permeated the community and resulted in many residents' demands for a public health facility and a nurse.

Recent diseases common among Dillingham residents, Speers reported, included more than a half dozen cases of measles, innumerable colds, and nearly a dozen schoolchildren had impetigo. A handful of children contracted tuberculosis. She reported that recent causes of death included paralysis, jaundice, tuberculosis, ruptured appendix, old age, drowning, killed by truck, and suicide (a twenty-five-year-old). The only hospital in the area, Kanakanak Hospital, provided service for Alaska Natives, but non-Natives could use it for emergencies. Even sixty years later, this remains the case. In the two years prior to Speers's report, over 75 percent of the dogs in the community were killed due to an epidemic of distemper; only fifty dogs survived. The loss was devastating, but even today a veterinarian does not live in Dillingham. Speers reported that in the 1940s, a dentist never came to Snag Point, and a doctor arrived only once every month—and that depended upon weather conditions. As a result, poor tooth and gum conditions permeated the community, and would continue until fluoride was added to the water much later.

For entertainment, Speers reported that the community enjoyed

"Moving pictures—public dances—skiing, sled[d]ing, dogteaming, etc." Apparently, the activities provided adequate diversion for the population, for even though the town had a U.S. Commissioner (Eric D. Femne) and a U.S. Deputy Marshal (John Bradshaw), practically no crimes were committed in the small community. Consequently, the jail often sat empty. Occasional crimes included "Supplying liquor to minors; petty larceny; con't [contributing] to the delinquency of a minor." Even though minors in possession at times became problematic, as a whole the village supported the locally licensed liquor establishment. Finally, Speers added that no local Alaska Native governing body existed at the time, an important point for her superiors at the Indian Bureau.

During the 1940s, Speers reported that only two churches had any active programs directed at the Alaska Natives, the Church of Christ and the Seventh Day Adventist Church, neither of which boasted regular members from among the Alaska Native community. Unemployment seemed an even worse and more immediate problem. In 1950, Snag Point had a population of around 570 people, yet the labor figures Speers included in her report illustrate the lack of positions available:

TYPE OF EMPLOYMENT	# EMPLOYED	PERMANENT OR TEMPORARY	PREVAILING WAGE
Clerks—Lowe Company	about 6	P.	about $250
Clerks—Felder & Gale Co.	4	P.	[$] 200
Clerks—Fisherman's Coop	3	P.	[$] 225
Waitress—Hotel Dillingham	4	P.	$30–50, Room & Board
Help—P.A.F. Cannery	300	P.	$1300 season
(none) Danielsen's store		P.	
Scandinavian Cannery	1	T.	$125
Road Commission	3	T.	[$] 260

Speers suggested that reindeer could be introduced as an important economic asset to the Alaska Natives, "under proper supervision and *some* planning." After all, only fifteen people in Snag Point had permanent, year-round employment. While an additional 304 had summer employment, many of those individuals were Alaska Natives from small surrounding communities that moved into the wood frame tent community near the cannery along the beach.

Cannery tent village, located just west of the PAF cannery,
"Dillingham, Eskimo tent town—they worked in cannery, 3 June 1955,"
McCutcheon collection #19034, printed with permission of
Anchorage Museum of History and Art, Anchorage, Alaska.

Finally, Speers had some suggestions for Dillingham, which she put together in conjunction with unnamed village planners. At the top of her list, she stressed the community's desperate need for the "introduction of sewers maintained by outside funds." Speers argued that the community did not have a budget large enough to construct, much less maintain a city sewer system, at the very least, "a housed community pump." She urged that a city medical clinic be built and a regular doctor be hired (something that would not occur until the late 1950s). Concerning educational, cultural, and social developmental needs, she urged the community to build a gymnasium for diversion and public programming. Self-government was "good as is," but a "town hall, gym, with stage facilities" would be beneficial to the community. Economically, Speers suggested that with fertilizers, perhaps the ground would yield results. Too many had given up growing gardens; only 1 percent of community members even bothered. Gardens would reduce the community's dependence upon produce flown in to Snag Point year round at often exorbitant rates. She suggested that the landing strip located on the north end of town be extended (it was forty feet wide by 886 feet long, not nearly long enough to service passenger or larger cargo aircraft), or that an entirely new one be built. A major and expensive improvement should be considered: a dock like that at Valdez, which "would allow boats a mooring." More accessibility would lower prices and lessen the economic burden on the community of acquiring daily necessities. Speer's report argued that various other industries simply would not work: "forest[ry] and logging, grazing, arts and crafts, Native Cooperate stores/tanning/canneries/etc." She saw economic potential for Snag Point, but misunderstood the environmental constraints on possible industry for the area. The region was indeed a major canning center, and arts and crafts would help feed the economy in later years when tourism brought wealthy travelers to see the walrus at Round Island and fish on the Mulchatna River and at Wood-Tikchik State Park.

Snag Point's school was relatively small in the 1940s. The children attending the grade school consisted of only twenty-four Alaska Natives, some having less than one-half Alaska Native blood. She reported that no three-quarter or full Alaska Natives attended the school, however six natives attended the Territorial High School. In other words, less than 10 percent of the students were Alaska Native, but a total of more than 30 percent were at least part Alaska Native. Already by the 1940s, Snag Point had become an integrated community of migrants from all over the world. She reported that ninety-four students attended all schools. Every adult had at one time attended school, and less than 0.5 percent could not read or write. All spoke English. Education obviously played a key role in the community.

Former schoolchildren from those early days recall that the first territorial school began servicing students from Snag Point and Olsonville in 1939, and additional students from Kanakanak when their old BIA school closed. The original territorial school was replaced by a much larger school with rooms upstairs for the teachers. Snag Point residents like Lyle Smith and other young boys used to haul water upstairs to the teachers every day for a nickel a bucket since the school had no running water. Historic photographs reveal that outside the school next to the outhouses, a very large metal tower—a former windmill—stood. Longtime resident Lyle Smith explained the story of that windmill.

Native cabin, Dillingham, Fall 1958. Residents were running to the right to watch a grass fire. Photograph by Donna McGladrey, courtesy of author.

In the "old days" the school was powered by a large windmill that sat just to the northeast of the school, providing electricity that was stored in huge glass cell batteries that occupied approximately half of the school's basement. On Bristol Bay, sustained winds blow with great force, and Dillingham has clocked sustained winds of over sixty miles per hour. One day the whole town could hear the windmill screaming in the stiff, howling winds. Lyle, who lived across the street at the first ice cream shop in town (they also had a few rooms to rent), saw sparks flying as the blades spun around, pulling the windmill farther and farther off-center. Like other townspeople, he feared that the windmill would tip over. According to his recollection, no one else seemed to be brave enough, so he decided to climb up the large structure and pull the brake to stop the blades from spinning. He was just a small, gangly kid though, and while dodging the sparks, he could not budge the brake, even while using his entire body weight to attempt to maneuver the brake lever. He shimmied back down the windmill tower and watched as, one by one, the wind tore the huge blades from their mooring and out across the tundra. The town searched for months, but no one ever found the twenty-foot blades.

When the windmill broke, a dilemma arose: how would they power the school? Luckily, Lyle's father had a generator in his basement that had more than enough capacity to provide electricity for his home and for the school, so he strung a line from his ice cream shop and house to the school. Like all frontier towns on the edge of dependable energy technology and sources, the inhabitants made do by sharing their resources. Every night at 10:00 P.M., Lyle's job was to shut off the power to the school. Sometimes Lyle got in trouble at school and, in retaliation, he would shut off the power a little earlier. The teachers scrambled for their candles as he watched giggling from across the street. In order to alleviate the power issues in town, local resident Carl Nunn had pushed for public power in Dillingham and the Rural Electric Association began

The Dillingham school where Donna taught, with the new addition immediately attached on right, with Church of Christ on its right (building with steeple). To the left of school is outhouse, windmill, and in background, Nushagak River. "Dillingham, School Houses, 3 June 1955," McCutcheon collection #8879, printed with permission of Anchorage Museum of History and Art, Anchorage, Alaska.

to operate in 1947. Nunn served on the organizing board and championed the importance of public power. By mid-March 1956, the Public Utility District officially organized to distribute electric power. By the time Donna arrived, Nushagak Power and Electric Company provided electricity, even lit a few streetlights, in Dillingham.

Carl Nunn, like many other Dillingham residents such as Eldon Gallear, David Carlson, and David Harrison, was instrumental to community building in Dillingham. Nunn built Dillingham's first youth center. He recognized the need of Dillingham's children for a place of recreation and to gather. Eventually, however, the community's need for a fire rescue station seemed more immediate and outweighed the children's need for indoor play, so the village converted the youth center into a fire station. Heating-oil drums attached to the side of the homes, as well as fires for heating, caused fire dangers to escalate in the winter months. Before the first fire vehicle arrived, residents lined up from the town's wells and hand carried buckets to dowse house and grass fires. After building the youth center, Carl Nunn had another vision—to build a library for the community. The log cabin structure he built so many years ago continues to serve as Dillingham's library. Additions to the original structure now house the Chamber of Commerce and the amazing Samuel K. Fox Museum, formerly operated by the Dillingham Historical Society. Nearly all of the old buildings that Donna would frequent, however, have since burned down due to insufficient firefighting facilities and staff.

The fishing industry also developed in Dillingham, making it the regional center for Bristol Bay. By 1951, powerboats could be utilized in the fishing industry in Bristol Bay for the first time. Previously, only double-ender sailboats were legal, a much less efficient method of fishing. Since Pacific American Foods (PAF) owned the boats that the fishers utilized, it would have been expensive to purchase enough new motorboats for all the fishers during the salmon harvest.[4] Bristol Bay canneries exerted pressure to disallow motorboats in Bristol Bay in order to keep their monopoly on the fishing industry.[5]

Besides the fishing industry, other major changes occurred in Dillingham during the 1950s. In 1952, the community formed the first Public Health Council at Dillingham with Edna Crawford serving as the first public health nurse. The health center did not have a building, however, and so it acquired a room in the basement of the territorial school as its first office. Finally, by 1954, local town leader David

Carlson, acting as president on behalf of the Nushagak Area Public Health Council, wrote a letter to C. Earl Albrecht, M.D., Commissioner of Health in Juneau, urging him to press the Territorial Legislature to finance a health center and living quarters for the public health nurse in Dillingham. It was four years in the making, but by the beginning of the school year in 1958, the new health clinic was operational. By this time as well, physician John Libby had established a permanent residence and medical practice in Dillingham. He worked with the Public Health Council to attempt to bring hospital facilities to Dillingham. During the fall of 1958, a new public health nurse, Diana Fearby, began to agitate for a sanitarian to come to Dillingham, citing the community's desperate need for a water and sewer system to alleviate health problems—something Muriel Speers had asked for in the 1940s. The committee determined that since Dillingham would be expected to pay half the cost of the system, and that the service would not be a revenue-making venture like the new electric energy system, Dillingham would forgo the sewer and water system. It would take almost another ten years to have a system in place. JoAnn Armstrong, as a member of the Public Utility District (PUD), became instrumental in convincing the city council to acquire a water and sewer system in the 1960s.

The second territorial school, for whose teachers young Lyle hauled water, consisted of a large frame structure with a high pitched roof (to keep snow from sticking and collapsing the roof), as well as gabled windows emanating from the teacher's quarters originally located upstairs. The student cafeteria and glass cell batteries were in the basement, with the classrooms on the main floor.[6] But the community continued to grow as Dillingham became the canning "capital" of Bristol Bay, so the town had to add to the school to accommodate more students. An enclosed hallway addition connected the old school with the newer addition added in 1952, which sat on a north-south axis and bordered the curve on Main Street. Just west across from the school sat the Alaska Mission, later known as the Church of Christ, on the corner of Main Street, Second Avenue, and Alaska Street. The church periodically provided overflow classroom space. While the enclosed hallway that connected the two school buildings has since been torn down, both the original school and the addition from 1952 still stand.

In 1948, students began to publish *The Blizzard*, an irregularly published school newspaper that reported news and events at the territorial school and around town as well. In *The Blizzard*, one could find advertisements for air service, cargo shipping, hotels, restaurants, and local resident Oscar Larsen's bakery. While published by the typing class at school, the children diligently collected stories from around town and provided an important service to the relatively new community. The newspaper continued through the years that Donna lived in Dillingham as well. They reported on the new addition to the school, as well as the construction of a new high school up the hill. In the late 1950s, workers were finishing construction on a new high school on Seward Street, north and west of the original school with an expected completion date of January 1960. The new high school had a gymnasium and library, which served the community as well as the students—just what Speers had envisioned more than a dozen years before. The building had indoor plumbing and a heating system as well. But until it was completed, the students would continue to learn in the old territorial school, with its outhouses, crowded hallways, and outdoor well.

As Donna planned her trip to Alaska, she knew nothing about the changes that this bush community had experienced. Even though she might have wanted to learn more, she had little time to investigate the region or its inhabitants. Besides, few resources existed on the town at the time. Donna had only belatedly contacted Alaska Territory's Commissioner of Education, Don M. Dafoe, about a job. He quickly responded with a telegram on September 3, 1958, "Re: Letter Stop Offer You Music Position Dillingham Stop If You Accept Wire Night Letter Collect And Further Instructions Will Follow=Don M DaFoe Commissioner Of Education." On September 9, she received another

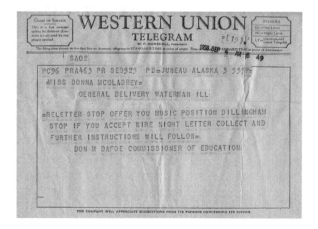

Telegram sent by
Don M. DaFoe to
Donna McGladrey,
September 4, 1958,
Juneau, Alaska.
Courtesy of author.

telegram sent from Juneau at 6:49 A.M. (underscoring the urgency of the message itself), "This confirms your acceptance Dillingham Music position. Contract and information being forwarded to Supervisor Arnold Granville our field office Anchorage K-326-I Street Telephone 5-5075. Recommend you proceed there first available air transportation. School has started. Notify us travel schedule. Don M. Dafoe, Commissioner of Education." Donna's great adventure had begun.

Donna's plane left Chicago at 1:00 A.M. on September 12, just a few months before Alaska Territory became a state. Donna packed forty-four pounds of belongings, not a lot for a year away from home, but all that the airline allowed at the time. The plane took her to Seattle where she exchanged planes for Alaska. (She lamented that she had no time to see her Uncle Merlin McGladrey, who was by then stationed at McChord Air Force Base.) When she finally arrived in Anchorage, the bus from the airport dropped her off in front of what she described as the main hotel. No rooms were available. She lugged her suitcases over to the Anchorage Hotel. No rooms. Hoping for assistance, Donna called Commissioner Dafoe who put her in contact with the supervisor, Mr. Hatcher. Hatcher helped her find a room and brought over the teacher's contract to sign, which she did on September 12, 1958. Her base salary would be $5,500, plus a $300 housing allowance, giving her a total of $5,800 per year. She would be paid in "monthly installments with one tenth ($1/10$th) of each check withheld, said amount to be paid as final installment less any adjustments upon termination and release from the school." Obviously Alaska had difficulty keeping teachers in remote bush villages, and this clause would theoretically protect the schools from teacher flight during mid-semester. The contract had an interesting list of requirements to which she must agree, one in particular indicative of the McCarthy era in which she lived:

1. Perform the duties of teacher in the Territorial Schools during the 1958–59 school year . . . for a total of not to exceed 180 school days
2. Affirm and swear that she is a United States Citizen
3. Affirm and swear to a non-communist oath in the same form as set forth in 11-1-8 ACLA 1949.
4. Abide by and be bound by the rules and regulations of the Board
5. Authorize deductions for the Teachers' Retirement System or F.I.C.A. withholding if eligible.

Donna took the oaths and looked forward to finding her new home, settling in, and getting to know her students and colleagues.

Since she had not made arrangements to get to Dillingham, Donna spent her first night in Anchorage. In a mimeographed letter to all of her family and friends, she wrote, "By this time I was lonely, scared and homesick and ready to give it all up and go home. I was mighty close to tears that afternoon." Donna hated flying: "I'm sick of planes. I was so scared. I sat next to an old timer who put my mind at ease." The next day, Supervisor Hatcher and Donna would leave for Dillingham. Donna told her family what she had heard of Dillingham, a small village 379 air miles west of Anchorage, and described it to her family

Aerial shot of Dillingham. At the top of the image is Ball Air Strip, the road meandering through the middle of the image is Main Street, and the canneries are located along the bottom left-hand side. On the far right in the middle is the school and the new addition with the darker roof. "Dillingham — Air, 3 June 1955," McCutcheon collection #26738, printed with permission of Anchorage Museum of History and Art, Anchorage, Alaska.

from a photograph someone showed her: "It's terribly primitive." In 1950, the population of Dillingham itself was only 577, dropping more than 150 by 1960, even though Donna reported the population at nearly 900. The population drop directly correlated with the poor salmon harvests that decade. Therefore as Donna moved to Dillingham, it had suffered from a temporary downturn in population and industry, yet the town was far from dying. Instead, the decline was merely cyclical. The community had already organized and built their first Public Health Center and hired Diana Fearby to be their nurse. Nearby communities, however, did not see the growth that Dillingham experienced in the 1960s. The only nearby village that grew was Aleknagik, located north and west of Dillingham. In the entire Bristol Bay region, the census reported a mere 1,636 inhabitants for 1950.[7] After 1960, however, the population of red salmon began to grow and when Dillingham became incorporated in 1963, it had become a regional center for nearby communities and canneries. The geographic location and local community leaders and their efforts made this possible.

Those who lived in Dillingham in 1958 had strong roots in the community, local Alaska Native affiliation, successful businesses, or simply could not afford to move. The small homes and tin houses in which much of Dillingham's population lived were sometimes built from materials recycled from torn-down canneries or other abandoned structures, adapting what they could find into their own home. Few people could afford to have new building materials shipped via boat from Anchorage or Seattle, so they made do. Even their sweat lodges (smaller non-ceremonial versions of the maqis behind many Dillingham homes) were made of leftover materials, serving a very useful and important role. While Donna never took a sweat, she could see these small buildings dotting the hill from her hotel, which looked southwest toward the broad Nushagak. At one point, she even referred to her Dillingham Hotel kitchen as becoming as hot as one of the "Russian steam baths."

The sweat lodges, along with the pieced-together homes, appeared to Donna as an unsightly community that, at first glance, looked worse than anything she had ever witnessed in her travels or growing up in South Chicago. She described her first impressions of the town: "This town is a typical Eskimo fishing village. It is by far the largest fishing village in this area, but as barbarian, primitive, uncultured, remote, dirty, shacky, miserable, etc., as anything anywhere. The slums in Chgo [Chicago] are far better than the houses here. For me + those like me It's

Spent oil barrels, small homes, and outhouses in foreground, with
Dillingham school and windmill tower in background. "Dillingham, School
House, 3 June 1955," McCutcheon collection #8880, printed with permission
of Anchorage Museum of History and Art, Anchorage, Alaska.

bad, but the people don't know any better."[8] Yet with time, she truly
grew to appreciate the community and the people who seemed to survive on the edge.

Despite her appreciation of the beauty of the region in general, which
she would write about at length, her introduction to Dillingham itself
impressed her not in the slightest. She wrote that a "cloud of insects"
(likely mosquitos, no-see-ums, and biting flies) and rain greeted her
when she arrived. In the rain, she trudged around Dillingham trying
to find a place to stay. The small community had only two hotels, the
Opland Hotel and the Dillingham Hotel, and neither had vacancies.
"The apartment situation is far worse in Dill[ingham] than N.Y. or Chgo
could even imagine." A young engineer that Donna met expressed his
frustration about housing. He had searched for weeks before he found

anything for his family. Two days into Donna's search, Opland Hotel manager Jean O'Connor decided that she would move to a downstairs room in order to secure the hotel's entrance.[9] When she moved downstairs, Donna and another teacher who flew in late on Donna's flight, took over her "penthouse" apartment, consisting of two bedrooms and a kitchen, upstairs toward the back of the hotel for $150 per month (which included her meals, electricity, kitchen, and cleaning). Not bad for Dillingham, Donna wrote, even though she did have to share the space with a roommate.

But Donna had difficulty adjusting to being alone so far away from home. Donna wrote, "I'm still so insecure." She expressed her certainty that when winter hit, she would no longer like Alaska. Even though enamored by the environment and the people, she wrote, "some of this town nauseates me." No doubt she found some of the refuse pits in yards and observed the run-off or sewage running down the street in the rain. She witnessed men wandering around "Hardliquor Square," just across the street from the hotel where she would live during her first month in Dillingham. Her early letters clearly expressed her emotions as they vacillated between the awesome beauty of her surroundings, to the "backwards" nature of the remote village, to her excitement of adventure, to the persistence of drunks in the streets at any time of day.[10]

While she might have periodically disparaged the community of Dillingham when she first arrived, she learned that teachers in other communities—such as Ekwok, where only one man and his wife taught the twenty-five local children—were far worse off. Recognizing the telltale signs of a new teacher's depression, Supervisor Hatcher invited Donna to go check on schools in nearby villages. Together they traveled, and later she described her impressions of various communities:

[Ekwok] with its racks and racks of drying and decaying salmon (the stench was nauseating), its mean-looking, much abused dogs chained everywhere, its bear skins in process of tanning, its caches built high above the ground to keep animals away, its moose meat hung here and there in the open where mold and flies feasted on it, its old Russian steam bath houses, its fish nets hung to dry and the dwellings that weren't fit for human habitation all seemed to make Dillingham the best and most modern town in this area. The people in this region are mainly Aleuts and especially in Ekw[o]k not too far up the ladder from the stone age people.

Donna McGladrey in Dillingham with pilot on way to Ekwok
and Aleknagik, September 1958, photograph [likely with
Donna's camera but taken by Mr. Hatcher] courtesy of author.

Dillingham certainly did not seem as isolated as Ekwok either, which
was accessible only by small plane or a very long boat ride up the
Nushagak River from Dillingham in the summer. The next town
they visited, Aleknagik, was a bit more inviting and certainly more
"civilized." In fact, "Aleknagik Road" was the only other road out of
Dillingham besides the road to Kanakanak. Although only seven miles
long, the road would eventually be expanded to twenty-three miles,
finally reaching Aleknagik several years later.[11]

At the outset, Donna described Dillingham as only slightly more
"civilized" than Aleknagik and Ekwok. She ascertained that Dillingham
was comprised of "mostly Aleuts, Phillipinos, Jap[anese], Norwegian,
and mixtures. It's a very strange combination." Donna enjoyed interacting with the ethnically diverse children whom she described as quite
musical, but unfortunately with little musical training. (She lamented
that the only music they heard was on the radio, and the only radio station played rock and roll.) The longer she remained in Dillingham and
visited nearby communities, the more she learned to appreciate native
culture and standards. She learned that many native communities

still utilized traditional housing, the *barabaras* (Aleut) and what she described as rectangular, partially dugout homes covered by either wood beams and grass and bark, or sod (Yuit). The traditional *kashgees* (or kashims, sometimes called men's houses), had disappeared by the time that Donna arrived.

Donna's appreciation for and desire to understand Dillingham's inhabitants led her to observe and record events that either she witnessed herself, or that she heard about from her new friends. One of her first example "reports" of Dillingham's seedier side occurred during her first night at the Opland Hotel:

> After I had gone to bed, I was startled by noise in the hall. It seems the 7 fellows, who flew in when Mr H[atcher] + I did from King Salmon, had spent the evening in one of the local taverns—became entirely drunk and also got a local gal in the same state. She was dead to the world + several months pregnant with her second illegitimate child. . . . When they were bored they staggered out into the road (street) where he (only two of them) try to undress her. Being as stewed as he was he had a hard time so he slung her over his shoulder half dressed and dragged her up to the hotel where he tryed to take her to his room. Mrs. O'Conner put up a big fight + the fellow was popped into jail + the gal is being sent back to her institution.

Instead of condemning the whole community as backwards, drunkards, and uncivilized, she simply postulated that the episode was related to the negative results of the introduction of alcohol, a depressed economy, and the isolated actions of a few people.

School agent and longtime resident David Carlson, who kept a diary diligently during his fifty years in Dillingham, explained the incident's outcome. He wrote on September 14 that Catherine Nick was held for trial by the U.S. Commissioner, charged with "being more or less unclad in Hardliquor Square." Also held was a young "oil exploration worker who claimed he was trying to help her get her clothes on again." They were both fined; "very good," Carlson asserted in his journal. Donna could have heard the details from hotel manager Mrs. Jean O'Connor, or one of the many friendly conversationalists in town the next morning. She wrote, "You can't walk down the street without seeing at least 1 drunk—anytime of day."

In contrast to these occasionally unpleasant realities, Donna genuinely loved the beauty that surrounded the area's towns, whether Dillingham, Ekwok, or Aleknagik. As an example of her appreciation for the natural environment, she reiterated her enthusiasm for the out-of-doors in the very same letter in which her disparaging words about Dillingham's buildings appeared. In capital letters she wrote, "I SAW A GLACIER! WOW!" As difficult as her first semester was, she recognized and then reveled in the incredible beauty of the land that surrounded her and tried to convey it in letters home. "Fall colors are the most gorgeous I've ever seen. And the mountains—Wow."[12]

When Donna had flown into Dillingham on September 13, she was touched by the incredible beauty of the tundra, scrub forest, and the Nushagak River, which emptied into Bristol Bay. Alaska was a far cry from the sooty, noisy, concrete "wilderness" of Chicago. In nearly every letter, Donna wrote about some aspect of the natural world in which she found herself. "The tundra we flew over was dotted with lakes, rivers, creeks, swamps, etc. and was extremely colorful. The blueberry bushes had turned to red with the aid of Jack Frost and other bushes had turned yellow. These two colors, combined with the green of the spruce and the blue of the lakes, made a breath-taking picture." The colors of fall certainly illuminated the landscape with their brilliance: the blueberries, salmonberries, blackberries, lingonberries (also known as mossberries), cranberries, and nagoon berries. For countless generations, the Yup'iks (and other Alaska Natives) had gathered these berries with their bare hands, walking for two or three days from home to gather the precious, life-sustaining berries for their families. Their thin woven buckets cradled the precious sustenance until they returned home. Then they dug holes, filled them up with water, and placed their woven buckets filled with berries into the hole. Before temperatures dipped, however, they removed the berries from the water to let them freeze in caches high above the ground, to protect them from the marauding bears and other freeloaders. One of the popular locations to collect berries near Dillingham sat to the west, beyond Kanakanak Hospital, out on the open tundra. But all the color would disappear by late October, and by the beginning of November, when the first snows arrived, temperatures would not rise above ten degrees, most of the time hovering around zero.

And the weather did provide its own challenges. "Being so close to the ocean we have lots of precipitation," she wrote. She reported that it had not stopped raining in the two weeks since she arrived. Regardless of the dreary conditions, she wrote about the beauty that surrounded her.

> The colors from the plane were so outstanding. . . . The rivers (creeks) that run all over by the thousands don't go straight—they stagger. It's the oddest thing. You speak of Minn[esota]. being land of 1000 lakes [sic]. Alaska can multiply that by a million and you may come close. There are swan in many of the lakes—and beaver! Wow. The herds of the caribou etc are small and almost vanished from this area. The beauty of the land is enough to hypnotize anybody. The adventure, newness, strangeness, etc., is thoroughly invigorating. When and if I get settled with a roof over my head that is mine till I want to leave—I'm sure I'll have Alaska fever as bad as everyone else.

Dillingham was situated at the Nushagak River's north bank, on the edge of a geological boundary. To the west lay low glacial moraine and drift, to the east lay coastal interlayered alluvial and marine sediments. Vegetation immediately surrounding Dillingham consisted of upland spruce hardwood forest, although the forest might seem rather sparse to someone like Donna who visited the thick forests of Wisconsin every summer. The upland spruce hardwood extended to the north, along the Aleknagik Road to today's Wood-Tikchik State Park, a very popular destination for today's fishers and remote cabin enthusiasts. Immediately north of town was a large expanse of wet tundra that followed the Wood River north and bordered the Nushagak River east and south. It wound northward through moist tundra to Ekwok. Then bottomland spruce poplar forests nestled close to the Nushagak as it snaked its way north to its headwaters at the Nushagak Hills, at the base of the Taylor Mountains nearly 130 miles north as the raven flies. Southwest of town, toward Olsonville and Kanakanak, and even farther to the Igushik River—a traditional fish camp for some Dillingham area residents—the moist tundra faded slowly into wet tundra. As Donna flew over the region, she was struck by the sparseness of settlement, the incredible greenness of the region, the perpetual winding of streams and rivers between low grassy hills, small and shallow ponds and lakes, and the awesome expanse of wilderness that captivated her very soul.

Fireweed near
Dillingham
overlooking
Nushagak River,
photograph by
Donna McGladrey,
courtesy of author.

Even as she appreciated the expansive wilderness and its beauty, she also recognized the austere lifestyle that the environment demanded of its inhabitants. She quickly recognized that her frame of reference could not be the standard by which she judged the local population. She wanted to learn about those in Dillingham whom she thought still lived a traditional lifestyle, or at least a small measure of one. She rarely made condemnatory statements, but rather tried to explain why she saw the town from a different perspective. She also made no reference to trying to force them to change. She accepted their lifestyle, lived within the constraints of the village's culture, recognizing that technological improvements would come and the community would embrace them. After all, this was a dynamic and adaptable community that welcomed positive improvements that arrived—thanks to several dedicated residents, albeit slowly due to the community's remote location. More important, she recognized how unique her experience was to those of her family and friends back home. She described every detail of her experience in letters home.

Even as she learned about the negative aspects of the region, she quickly grew an appreciation for the harsh realities of life in the bush, and how they affected the people who lived there. Residents did the best they could with the resources they had. She had begun to discover Dillingham indeed.

CHAPTER FIVE

Donna Adjusts to Life in the Bush

Donna was lucky to get a room at the Opland Hotel, originally for six dollars per night. She had arrived during a particularly busy time for Dillingham and surrounding homes because the last supply ship of the year, the *Coastal Nomad*, was sitting in the harbor. After school, boys worked as longshoremen offloading all of the goods that locals had ordered for the long winter. By September 18, the *Coastal Nomad* left the harbor for other destinations on the Nushagak River. Donna learned that the supplies strewn across the beaches and boardwalks enticed boys who could not resist mischief. Soon items began to disappear from the pier, particularly cases of beer. Dillingham lived by the barges and ships that delivered goods to the community each fall before freeze, and every spring after "Break-Up" when the ice on the river began to melt, break apart, and flow down the river to Bristol Bay and then out to the Bering Sea. Fresh fruits and vegetables were few and far between after the ice locked in the river. When winter arrived, the only fresh produce arrived by plane, and with a hefty price tag. Shocked, Donna wrote about the high prices and poor food quality. She reported that "sour and rather rotten" grapes cost $.70 per pound, and moldy apples sold for $.20 each. Eggs sold for $1.30 a dozen, bread at $.70 per loaf, orange juice $.30 for a small can, small pork chops at $1.45, and lettuce at $.65 per head. In many cases, these prices were three or four times what she had paid in Illinois. She wrote about the foods that she missed eating: "turkey, roast pork, sirloin steak, ham, liver, milk, <u>fresh</u> eggs, potato chips, cookies, nuts, <u>fresh</u> candy, ice cream, fresh anything."[1]

Eating out at the local restaurant was not much better. At the Green Front Café, considered by most "the best restaurant in town," she complained: "Toast and coffee costs $.40. A roast beef dinner $2.75. A bowl of chicken soup $1.25. You've never seen such prices. The cheapest steak is $4.00. The joint is one that you wouldn't go in in the (smaller) states—even if you were paid to. The stove they cook on is similar to my ancestors—fire built inside—only difference is that it has been converted to oil."

She reported, "We're really ruffing it." She wrote to her sisters, "I guess in comparison—it'll be a lot like Norway this winter—nothing but dead fish and caribou. No milk except powdered." Rent, food, electricity, and heat, were all costing her between two and three hundred dollars per month. She reported to her family that her contract gave

Barges on the beach at PAF cannery, Dillingham,
photograph by Donna McGladrey, courtesy of author.

Dillingham teachers an extra three hundred dollars per year living expenses; "Ha Ha," she cynically added. It helped with expenses that Donna shared the penthouse apartment of the Opland Hotel with fifty-five-year-old English teacher Ann Carr, the other teacher who had arrived on the same plane with Donna. She was a grandmother, vivacious talker, smoker, and drinker; Ann and Donna really had their differences. Donna's two sisters, Joan and Dorothy, recalled feeling so badly for her because she had such a difficult roommate. Donna quickly learned how to adapt to her roommate, however. Donna wryly reported that "the only way I can get along with her is to do exactly as she wants. I have no other choice. . . . At least she's somebody to talk to." Ann was domineering and considered Donna her charge, not a roommate to be treated equally.

JoAnn Armstrong, a fifty-year resident of Dillingham who arrived as a public health nurse at Kanakanak Hospital and later owned an airline transport company with her husband, Richard, remembers Ann Carr as well. JoAnn recalled that Ann liked to involve herself in conversations and steer the discussion her way. She was strong-willed and would interrupt everyone. Ann Carr's personality exuded self-confidence, self-assuredness, and perhaps a bit of hubris as well. JoAnn remembered one occasion when Ann barged into her house and asked JoAnn to dry some new pants that Ann had just washed. JoAnn pleasantly obliged, knowing that she had one of the only automatic clothes dryers in town. Unfortunately for the both of them, the dryer caught on fire. Absolutely unconcerned about JoAnn's dryer, Ann demanded that someone get her new pants out of the dryer before they burned to a crisp.[2] JoAnn remembered Ann as someone whose desires should be met before those of others. Ann was used to getting things her way, and if she did not, she would get agitated. As tough as Ann seemed to be, however, Donna had watched her reduced to tears on at least one occasion by Pat O'Connor, son of the landlord Jean O'Connor.

The mounting conflicts of different lifestyles and mores were compounded by the frustration of having no heat other than that which entered from the hallway. Worse yet was the community "honey bucket" (the chemical bucket that served as a toilet), with its unique smelling blend wafting about the apartment, that needed to be carried outside and dumped periodically. Donna also hauled water—from a nearby spring-fed well, located about three blocks to the east, then southward down the road to the base of the cemetery's hill. When Donna was ill (as she would be often), Ann took over Donna's cooking, cleaning, and hauling duties. Like many of Dillingham's residents, they used the yoke system to haul their water. And nearly all of the Dillingham residents explained that they used "Blazo" cans at the end of the yokes, originally filled with oil to fuel people's lanterns and lights. They cleaned out the cans and hung them on either side of the shoulder yoke. Usually the children packed the water, and on occasion, area residents hired a neighbor's child to haul water for them as well.

Some of the more transitory Dillingham residents, such as the many teachers who seemed to last only a few years in Dillingham, reported that the water in Dillingham was awful. One former resident, Tressie Vander Hoek, remembered a glass measuring cup that had turned

Community well where Donna got her water during her year in Dillingham. Notice the cemetery immediately above the well. "Dillingham, Water pump at cemetery, well-house for about 30 dwellings just below grave yard, 3 June 1955," McCutcheon collection #19035, printed with permission of Anchorage Museum of History and Art, Anchorage, Alaska.

orange forty years before during her one year in Dillingham, and still had a slightly orange tint.[3] Sue Hahn, proprietor of Sourdough Sue's Bed and Breakfast in Anchorage and who taught in Dillingham in the early 1960s, told stories of her clothes turning a strange orangish hue from the high content of iron in the water. Some local experts even suggested that arsenic, which occurs naturally in the area, had permeated some of Dillingham's wells, and is present even today in minute quantities. While the water in Dillingham might not have been the best, Donna learned that some wells, including the well closest to her hotel, had better tasting water. This well sat by the temporary one-room building and windbreak where the priest said mass behind the Opland Hotel. The other good well sat at the base of the cemetery on the hill by the school. Donna hauled water from both of those locations. Such privations were nothing new to Donna, for the many years she visited YMCA Camp Nawakwa in Wisconsin's northern woods, she and her sisters hauled their own water, used outhouses, and emptied their "ugh" buckets in the morning. For Donna, dealing with a roommate who seemed her exact opposite, trying to stay warm in a frigid environment, hauling water daily, battling swarming insects, and having poor sanitation were just part of the "frontier" experience that caused her to record her life more diligently.

All of these challenges unfortunately took a toll on Donna's health. Repeatedly in letters home, she complained of having either a terrible cold, dizziness, the flu, or stomachaches that caused her to lose her appetite, and sometimes her meals. She fainted on numerous occasions, but resolved not to see Dr. Libby. She claimed that she hated doctors. Ann nagged Donna to see Dr. Libby who, more than once, made house calls to check on Donna. The frantic pace of her life, complicated by the lack of proper sewer and water treatment facilities and poor availability of fresh fruits and vegetables, caused Donna to become tired and overstressed and therefore more susceptible to diseases. Regardless of her health challenges, however, she would fulfill her obligations as a teacher and more.

As Donna prepared to teach the younger residents of Dillingham, she recognized that she would have to wrestle with the allure of popular culture, in particular the music. Almost immediately upon arriving, she learned how difficult a challenge that would be. Donna described in letters home how Dillingham's local theater, Lowe's, played a different movie every night. In order to drum up business, one half hour before

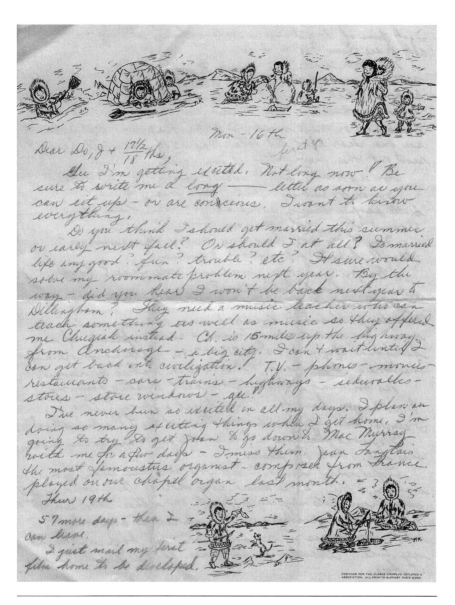

Example of letter from Donna while in Dillingham to Dorothy, Jack,
and their unborn child, March 16, 1959, courtesy of author.

showing the film, Lowe's would broadcast "hill billy+rock+roll" music via a large speaker located on top of the building. The whole town could hear the music blaring. The theater was located only a few yards west of the Opland Hotel on the other side of the street, and unfortunately the speaker faced Donna's hotel room. The music drove her "bonkers." She wrote Dorothy that "We are trying to raise a complaint against that noisy music at the show. It's a disturbance of the piece and I'll go to court to testify. It can be done cuz I talked to the Commissioner (he's a teacher)." She could likely peer outside her window to see the kids standing around, smoking and listening to the music. She reported that at the very least, it kept them out of mischief.

Donna began to recognize the difficulty of living in a community where social and cultural norms were so radically different than her own. The peoples' lives seemed so intricately interwoven with the environment and subsistence fishing, trapping, hauling water, and hunting. And the upcoming summer could be a difficult one indeed, as Donna explained to her family, "You've probably heard the tragic news about only set-netting being allowed this summer [1959]. Very few natives do set-netting. There are going to be a lot of people with out money next year and they'll probably have to declare Dillingham and the Bristol Bay area a disaster area." Dillingham would deal with new challenges as they always had—as a community. Dillingham's residents assisted their neighbors by doing chores, hauling water, and stopping in on the ill. As one of Donna's colleagues from Chugiak explained later, "But that's sort of the way it is as a pioneer. Everyone's on a shoestring, and if . . . something goes wrong you can really be in trouble." Therefore, everyone helped out all who needed help because it might be them in distress the next time.

While community members worried about how they would put that winter's food on their tables, Donna worried about having a permanent home. Donna and Ann's relationship had deteriorated with Opland Hotel manager Mrs. O'Connor and her son, Pat, both of whom seemed terribly unreasonable at times. Donna and Ann were unaware that Mrs. O'Connor had broken the hotel owner's rule by allowing them to stay in the manager's apartment. The infraction did not particularly bother the owner, but by the end of September, the hotel sold to the new proprietors, Bill and Marie Andrews, who were not as understanding. During Donna's first PTA meeting on September 29, Donna and Ann reported that they would be homeless at the end of the month so the new owner's daughter could move into the penthouse. A local family, the Stovalls, generously offered space in their home to the soon-to-be-homeless teachers.

Luckily, however, Donna and Ann negotiated a deal with Mrs. O'Connor to allow them to remain in the penthouse through the end of October. But Mrs. O'Connor changed the terms of their lease. The women would now be responsible for purchasing their own food, cooking, cleaning, and hauling out their "ugh" bucket. Even this agreement lasted less than two weeks, for by mid-October, the Andrewses demanded that Donna and Ann vacate the penthouse. Mrs. O'Connor informed Donna that they would have to move downstairs, even though she had promised Donna that she could stay through the end of the month. Donna located a rental house near Wood River Road on Windmill Hill, a fifteen-minute walk from town. It needed some repairs; they would have to wait until November 1 to move in. Mrs. O'Connor, however, could not allow such a delay due to her agreement with the new owners, the Andrewses. One day after school, Donna and Ann came home to a very unpleasant surprise. Apparently, around 2:30 that afternoon, Jean O'Connor had learned that the new owners were coming into town to check on the hotel. Mrs. O'Connor panicked and became agitated, Donna wrote. Mrs. O'Connor told the teachers they had to move immediately to a downstairs room for $160 per month, $10 more than they were currently paying. To their great shock, Donna and Ann found that half of their things had already been moved out of the penthouse.

Donna explained to her parents that she originally decided to just move and avoid any conflict. But something came over her and she stiffened, becoming resolute, "They can't just throw us out—and trespass with our stuff!" She and Ann marched over to the commissioner's and the marshal's house, located the next street north by the Dillingham Hotel, the only other hotel in town (owned by fellow teacher David Harrison). The commissioner and the marshal agreed that, according to law, the hotel had to give them a ten-day notice before evicting their guests. They returned to their penthouse, followed by Pat O'Connor, Jean's twenty-year-old "hoodlum son," who "cursed us out—raised the roof—threatened us until we were scared to death. His mother was hiding behind his 'skirts.' The two of them said the most insulting things + were so unreasonable + threatening that Ann + I were terribly upset. They hurt her much worse than they did me." Tears streamed down

Ann's cheeks, and Donna headed back over to the Dillingham Hotel, determined to secure a room. On her way, she ran into the commissioner and told him about Mrs. O'Connor's reaction. He immediately went to get the marshal. She returned after an unsuccessful attempt to find lodging at the other hotel to find the law enforcement duo talking with Jean and Pat. In the meantime, Mrs. Andrews arrived at the hotel. She offered Donna and Ann a room at the back of the other establishment they had purchased, the Green Front Café, until that Saturday when the engineers would be vacating the local hotels as they left for Anchorage. Donna believed that the only reason Mrs. Andrews made the offer was to keep Donna from suing her. Donna's frustration intensified. "I'm becoming a sourdough—Sour on Dillingham with no dough to leave!" Donna explained that her tough roommate was ready to get on the next plane for home by October 1. Mrs. Carr did end up leaving the following May.

The house they had planned to move into on Wood River Road was supposed to be fixed up before they moved in November 1. The house still needed a new furnace, tiling, and windows; and Mr. Andrews turned out to be the handyman—a cruel irony. Donna believed that she would never find a place to live. She had already spent most of her money and her next paycheck was late. She had only $30 in her pocket and owed more than $87.50 to the Opland Hotel. The superintendent and others in Dillingham offered her money, but she refused to take it. She wanted to be independent and stand on her own two feet—but inside, she agonized over her situation, becoming more depressed by the day. "I want a shoulder to cry on so bad I could almost die," she wrote. "Ann got all her emotions out yesterday, but mine are knotting me up inside so much that I'll probably have a nervous breakdown." Even as she endured hardships and increasingly frustrating situations, she confronted them head on and found solutions. She needed to be the strong one, she realized, after she watched Ann break down after Pat's tirade. Yet with her growing conviction and self-confidence, she began to hold her emotions inside.

Marie Andrews recalled years later that Donna and Ann stayed at the Green Front Café for a short time until David Harrison had a room open in the Dillingham Hotel. From Donna's letters, it appears the pair spent only one night at the Green Front before moving to the Dillingham Hotel. When they finally did move to the hotel, Donna depended upon a newfound friend to transport all of her belongings. Richard Newton, a plumber from Anchorage, borrowed a Jeep to help her move. She appreciated Richard's assistance in this moment of dire need. She had finally found a permanent home, nearly two months after moving to Dillingham. Even with all of the difficulties Donna experienced, she told her family that she had Alaska Fever: "I love it here!" she wrote, just as she had foreshadowed in one of her first letters to her family.

Donna's new room was located on the top floor of the Dillingham Hotel. She shared a kitchen area with Ann Carr. The situation was slightly better than at the Opland Hotel, with running water for their toilet—no more hauling out their honey bucket like the majority of people who lived in Dillingham. In the 1958 yearbook, *Choggiung*, the Dillingham Hotel boasted of being the only hotel in town with working flush toilets. The hotel utilized a leach pond, since sewers did not yet exist, which emptied the sewage out through underground pipes that released just under the street across the road into the subsoil.[4] Donna did not have to haul water to wash her clothing, hair, or dishes. Unfortunately, she and Ann still had to carry drinking water from the well.

Even though her living conditions might have seemed spartan to many back home in Chicago, Donna recognized that the privations were simply part of living on the "frontier." Donna took on the challenge squarely and expected to make the best of her new austere life. She looked forward to interacting with the children and teaching them about music, instrumentation, and starting a band. The children were not, as Ann Carr had expected, all Scandinavians. Former student and Dillingham resident Hilda (Olson) Kroener remembered that Mrs. Carr commented upon arriving in Dillingham, "All these Olsons and Nelsons and Johnsons and Petersons, I thought I came over here to find a bunch of blondes!" Donna would soon find herself defending the children against other teachers who had less respect for them. More important, she had already begun to redefine herself as a strong and independent woman who proved her mettle admirably in the face of adversity.

CHAPTER SIX

Teaching in Dillingham

Donna's new students' preparation in music was nothing like that of her former Northbrook students, who had come from privilege. The latter had seen musical instruments and heard classical music, and their parents could afford to purchase instruments for them. Dillingham was different. When she arrived, Donna immediately knew it would be a challenge to engage the children with classical music, teach them instrumentation, and get them to abide by her strict discipline. Before even entering the classroom, her presumptions about teaching began to change. Instead of immediately forcing the children to learn classical music, instrumentation, singing in tune, and disciplining without regard to the child's background, she would instead learn about the children and adapt her teaching style to their strengths. She discovered the challenges of their youth and family life and, when she could, tried to correct what she perceived was a lack of direction, discipline, and a will to learn. She asked questions and learned about the environment's impact on the community, primarily that the community depended upon the success of their families during the salmon harvest. Donna understood that the children's success in learning also depended upon their families' ability to survive economically.

Hired to teach fifth through twelfth grade, as well as to start an instrumental program and band, Donna found the lack of instruments and sheet music especially challenging. "Monday morning I met with more disappointments and discouragements," Donna wrote to her friend from Illinois, June Swatosh. She continued, "The school had had no music program previously. Therefore, I have to start with nothing— no music except for a few odd books." Hilda Kroener remembered that "no one played even an instrument at school when she came to town."[1] Even though Donna tried her hardest to be independent so far away from home, conditions at school forced her to depend upon her family to send sheet music. Donna wrote that the only instruments the students had ever heard of were "pianos, ukes [ukeleles], and guitars." They had never heard of clarinets, trumpets, or flutes. "I've had a heck of a time trying to show them the different instruments without the aid of records or pictures or books." While she did have two movies that illustrated instruments and their sounds, they were not very good. Nearly a month later, four of her boxes finally arrived from home and she immediately penned a letter home to sincerely thank her parents for sending the books and pictures of instruments. She displayed the images on her bulletin board for the children. Now that the children had a better idea what the instruments looked like, they chose which instruments they wanted to play. Soon they began to report to Donna that their parents planned to buy them instruments: a cornet, trumpet, clarinet, and three saxophones. Shortly Donna would know whether or not she would have a band. Elated at their excitement, Donna wrote jubilantly that the students showed great enthusiasm for starting a band! But she still had to convince many other parents to help her fill out the band by buying the more expensive instruments for the school: tubas, baritones, and other larger instruments.

Within weeks, she excitedly reported to her family that the children had a great interest in learning music, and that maybe she could have a greater impact on the students than she originally thought. Both Donna and her students gained confidence with each passing day. But until the instruments arrived, the children would only be able to sing in a choir. She thought it rather odd that their excited voices often "soared away from the tune. Others don't try—they shout not sing. Very odd." Instead of chastising them for being off tune, by early October she had already recognized that this difference might be tied to cultural differences and not having access to classical music, not due to lack of ability. Regardless, the students seemed to enjoy her instruction.

Hilda Kroener recalled taking eighth-grade music class from Donna.

"I loved every bit of it [music class]. She . . . seemed like she was just so vivacious, I just loved being in her class because she just . . . made us do the right thing, and when she taught music . . . I guess that's the way a teacher should be." Hilda continued, "I used to wish I was as pretty as she was . . . peaches 'n cream complexion, and the blonde hair . . . there was never a strand out of place. And her figure was gorgeous and just, she was just a nice person. . . . What a nice gal." Juanita Pelagio, who in January 1960 was elected the first president of the Band Club, remembered that Donna "really had control." She was "very quiet, even tempered, was not riled easily. . . . Everyone seemed to learn from her."[2] This had to please Donna, because she focused most of her energy on teaching.

Hilda remembered that "She was just the nicest teacher and easy to get along with. She got upset a few times, never at me." Hilda recalled that she always did as Donna asked and never challenged her, but that several kids in class tended to get a bit rambunctious and "smart alecky." Hilda did not blame Donna for her reactions. Although she never utilized corporal punishment, or at least inferred in letters that she did not believe in its use, she did resort to other methods to make her students pay attention and behave like "little adults."

She encouraged these "little adults" to participate in a festival in order to raise money to purchase instruments for the school. Donna organized the entire festival, complete with music that her family had sent her, which she then orchestrated for the numerous student parts. Hilda Kroener remembered years later how "she had us sing the nicest songs and music . . . the ones where you did rounds and everything. . . . It was so nice." Hilda remembered that she mostly sang, she did not take instrument lessons from Donna, and one song in particular stuck in her memory. They sang it in rounds: "Heigh-ho, anybody home? Food or drink or money have I none. Still I will be very merry." She sighed as she recalled those early years, "I love music, that was my favorite."[3]

Donna held her classes in the basement of the newer addition to the old territorial school that was built in 1952. The space was not large, but neither were her classes, so the students got to know her pretty well. They also got to know Ann Carr who taught eighth-grade English in the same building. Hilda Kroener, remembered Mrs. Carr well. While reluctant to overanalyze a teacher she had known so early in her life, Hilda simply said that Ann Carr was really strict. "She was so strict

Hilda and Hermann Kroener, July 2002, photograph courtesy of author. Hermann passed away the following January.

and so mean we had to abide by her rules and everything and boy, when she came into class you could hear a pin drop." She also remembered that Ann always wore bangle-type bracelets with some sort of charms. When she wrote so beautifully on the blackboard, the bracelets would dangle and make noise. She even recalls Mrs. Carr forcing them to memorize a poem about trees. "I guess she was a good teacher, but she was *strict*." Perhaps it was her age, Hilda thought out loud, but Mrs. Carr did not relate well to the students. Mrs. Carr must have done a good job, though, even Hilda said in retrospect, "She was a good teacher, she knew her subject really well. . . . She was an English teacher, taught me English . . . we all have our favorites."

Donna made such a positive impression on the children that in December 1958, her music students gathered enough money to buy her bronze bookends in the shape of musical notes. And not just the children, but the people of Dillingham showed enthusiasm for Donna's work and readily accepted her into the community. As she walked around town, people stopped her, exclaiming, "Oh yes—you're the new music teacher they've been talking about!" Donna relayed her pride to her family. "It's a thrill to know you're needed, wanted and appreciated," she wrote. After her wretched experience in Northbrook, this had to be a welcome feeling.

But their excitement for her work did not make her job of populating the band any easier. The school still had severely limited music supplies and no sheet music, a staple for music teachers. Donna did what she could, meeting and interacting with the students, and encouraging them to appreciate music lessons, both vocal and instrumental. Donna described the fifth- through eleventh-grade children she taught on that first day:

> My 5th is fine; 6th boys are dreadful; 7th—need help; 8th boys need a whip; 9th—all girls—just fabulous best group; 10th + 11th scared to sing esp[ecially] 3 boys! They have had little or no music + know NOTHING of instruments. They've never had any opportunities to see or hear them. However, they are all enthusiastic about starting a band.

Donna understood that teaching them would be a challenge, in her own words, "IF I live through it."

Unlike her problems at Northbrook, with the school board and spoiled children, her difficulties in Dillingham proved much more basic. In a village based on the annual salmon run, the families depended upon a good harvest in order to purchase instruments, and even then it would take persistence to convince them to use the money for such a purpose. Donna explained to her family that the seasonal nature of the salmon industry made life financially unstable. The only large employer in the fishing village consisted of canneries that operated exclusively during the summer salmon harvest. The villagers and migrants worked for only a few weeks and "went home wealthy or otherwise (depending on the season)." When the students finally had enough instruments, Donna still had a tough time getting them "interested in Bach, Handel, Puccini, or Tchaikovsky . . . when all they have ever heard is Elvis and other rock and roll trash." She obviously referred to the music booming across town over the Lowe's store's loudspeaker. The movies themselves, Donna complained, were of such poor quality that they had no classical music as accompaniment that the children could appreciate. Therefore, Donna expended a great deal of time and energy trying to introduce the children to classical music.

Even as a new and "untested" teacher in Dillingham, with the added peculiarity of appreciating classical music, she still commanded the children's respect. When they did misbehave, she disciplined them accordingly. Even though they wanted to start a band, she still had to fight to keep their attention. She found lack of discipline a major problem among the children, and as a result, assumed that most of the children received no discipline at home. Yet instead of condemning the children or parents, she blamed it on the poor economy and sense of economic despair. Donna did recognize some of the children's misbehavior for what it truly was: mischief—pure and simple.

While Donna oversaw the children's development with firmness, the children remembered her years later quite fondly. Apparently, she did not discipline the children beyond what they could handle. During her first couple of months, Donna described her experience teaching:

> I've had a rough day today. I want to quite! [sic] Grades are due so I gave tests today. From the results I just might as well have been in Siberia these past weeks. It's most discouraging. My 6th grade is composed of "holy terrors." They are ghastly—mean—rude + stubborn. I made them write manners one period and screamed at them the next. They're improving but it'll take all my power + concentration to hold them down. This afternoon the 7th grade was, as usual, noisy, slouchy monsters. I was real mean + screamed. 2 boys decided they wouldn't do as I asked. . . . I did all but hit them. I asked them to sit up (no reaction). I repeated (nothing). Again (still no reaction). Finally I screamed at them. After all that they remained with their noses down + books down + only half descent [sic] posture.

She demanded the same discipline that her parents meted out on her as a child. She hoped to enlist the students' parents in her efforts, or at least find out if they enforced rules at home, but they rarely showed up to Parent-Teacher Association (PTA) meetings.

Donna's teaching responsibilities included attending those PTA meetings that began at the end of September. She thought that the meeting would give her an opportunity to interact with parents, and she looked forward to the occasion. The first PTA meeting took place in the evening, on a cold night in the driving rain. She had to walk directly into the bone-chilling rain to return to school after having supper at home. When she arrived, she discovered that most of the attendees were teachers. She was sorely disappointed. While the perceived lack of interest by parents might seem odd by today's standards, the PTA had only existed in Dillingham since 1953. In more than one interview with Dillingham residents, it became clear that parents really did care about the progress of their students, but they believed that it was the teacher's responsibility to teach their children and could not see the benefit in overseeing that duty.[4] What could they do to help the teacher teach better? "They were the teachers!" a former student declared.

Once she realized that she would have little assistance from parents, Donna determined that she alone would have to motivate the children. With pride, she exclaimed to her parents at the end of October 1958, "I'm beginning to get the brats in line. It's hard but I may have them by May at this rate. Owoo do they drive me insane." Donna's efforts were frustrated by the constant "harassment" of a few young male students who insisted on teasing her about her good looks. Verna Lee Heyano, one of Donna's sixth-grade students, thought back during an interview about how "nice and pretty" Donna was, and how the boys used to tease her, even as early as the sixth grade.[5] They would write things on their papers for her to read, tease her in class, whistle at her on the playground, and generally make teaching her charges difficult. Verna Lee remembers how Donna used to "not take no guff" from anyone, and periodically had to punish the boys. Years later Hilda Kroener and Verna Lee Heyano remember the anguish in the faces of boys as Donna announced she would be leaving over Christmas break. Some of the boys found themselves captivated by Donna's curly blonde locks. They continued to push her harder and harder until she finally had to stop their attempted flirtations by admonishing them publicly in the classroom. While she sometimes commented upon her admirers in letters, the teasing occurred more often than her letters indicated.

Like many other teachers, Donna could not seem to convince students not to slouch, to pay attention, and to behave consistently. She intended to make the children behave properly, sit up straight, and follow instructions, or suffer the consequences. On more than one occasion, Donna had to raise her voice; one time yelling at the children until she was "blue in the face." She made them write "I will not act like an idiot or first grader. I will act like a 7th grader" on the chalkboard, and also kept children after school. The female students recognized that sometimes the teachers had to get really rough on the boys or they simply would not behave. Discipline problems and subsequent punishments took up precious class time.

She must have been frustrated, because even as late as March 1959, Donna described an incident about an eighth-grade boy who "insisted on being a pest." Even after she threatened him with a paddling, he persisted. She asked him to step outside, where she planned to punish the child. She wrote, "He got outside the door and then shot up the stairs, out the door and was half way home before I could blink my eyes. He didn't come back that afternoon either I don't know how he got his coat. Mon[day] morn he brot his excuse for Fri[day] to the Supt. and Mr. Lawvere asked him what was up—giving Wally a thrashing he'll never forget. (Goody)."

And even though the children's behavior sometimes frustrated her, Donna understood that the students had larger social problems that sometimes inhibited their ability to maintain self-control. In response to her mother's queries about Dillingham, Donna described the crimes that pervaded the community, many of them serious and startling. She explained that one twelve-year-old girl was forced to live with her uncle as well as sleep with him. Worse yet, he periodically made her go to other men. She explained how some parents commonly drank to get drunk; no doubt a reflection of the economic conditions, she postulated. Therefore, the kids ran wild and remained undisciplined. Common-wifery, she wrote, was "an accepted thing. Some never bother to marry—some do years later." Promiscuity, especially among teens, was very common she reported. She explained that this often led to early marriages and consequently, they had only one senior and four juniors in the entire school while other class sizes ranged from ten to twenty. She complained that four of their high school freshman got off far too easily when they stole thirty beer cases from a barge in the harbor. Dismayed, she reported that few students actually graduated from high school.

Finally, smoking and drinking started at a very young age, as early as the sixth grade. Verna Lee Heyano remembered that during recess, she and her friends used to escape from the school grounds and run up to the adjacent cemetery and sit down in the tall fireweed, which concealed them. They lit up cigarettes and smoked until a cloud of smoke would appear and a neighbor would chase them back into the schoolyard. Donna argued, perhaps incorrectly in some cases, that their smoking simply represented the lack of discipline that they received from parents at home.

Like Donna, other teachers became frustrated by the students' lack of self-control. But unlike other teachers that held only the student accountable for behaviors, Donna began to defend the students. She and Ann Carr had numerous heated arguments about classroom discipline issues and academic abilities. Donna explained that Ann could not see why "these kids around here have to be so barbarian and unmanageable. She has been used to different kids and is trying to change these kids completely and can't do it. . . . I realize the kids are different but I'm not going to brake my back trying to get them to conform to my ideas. Instead I'm trying to understand why they are as they are and work from there. Ann, I think, has the wrong approach." Donna wrote that Ann disparaged the students, claiming that "a child's background is no excuse for his behavior at school." Donna retorted, "Bah—the heck it isn't (Pardon). When kids have to go home and fend for themselves while their folks go off on a binge, never have clean clothes—proper food, discipline or attention, I don't doubt they are as they are. Their background makes such a big difference on their behavior. But—no—she is been teaching 25 years and knows everything. . . . She's driving me insane!" While Donna did make assumptions about Dillingham's residents, her roommate's callous and seemingly uncaring attitude toward the children and their families upset her. She had witnessed prejudice before in Chicago and chose to identify the root of the problem. She defended the children's behavior, blaming it on their home situations, which in turn she blamed on the economy. Dillingham's salmon industry simply could not support a yearlong economy, and as a result, poverty pervaded the community, and the accompanying social ills resulted.

Donna's teaching, and music in general, consumed her life in Dillingham. Donna must have appreciated the young girls, in particular, who really began to take advantage of band and choir opportunities that she offered. Girls, and even some of the boys, began to practice for hours before and after school. Donna had begun to look at the children differently, respect them, and understand them based on their own cultural norms, traditions, and upbringing. She had finally "arrived" as a teacher and reached them on a level that they understood and appreciated. "I'm gaining a little self confidence," she reported—a major step indeed.

She had begun to feel truly at home in Alaska, and while she continued to report her various flu-like ailments in her frequent letters home, she wrote also of the classroom and teaching experiences. She was proud of her work, of the respect that she had earned, and of her many accomplishments. She knew more challenges would come as the new semester arrived, and they did. She surprised her family with big news: "Today the funniest thing happened. I think it is hysterical. I am now the new Junior-Senior English teacher. The English teacher quit after vacation and his classes were divided up for the rest of us. . . . Wow— me—English! It all came about because I complained about the H.S. student[s] doing such poor work on an essay test that I gave them on opera. Me and my big mouth." Donna's mother had previously been an English teacher and offered her daughter assistance, suggestions, and sent her workbooks and assignment ideas. Even though she already had far more than she could handle trying to teach and raise money for instruments, she relished the challenge and looked forward to teaching English in the spring 1959 semester. "Sounds exciting," she wrote. It would be nice to have a change from music, but she would still have to teach her regular load as well as English. More class preparations, more exams to give, more to grade—yet the increased responsibilities came with no increase in salary.

While the following semester's schedule proved even more challenging, she continued to adjust to the children's learning styles, the additional requirements by administrators on teachers, and her hectic schedule. During the spring 1959 semester, she taught nine classes each day from the second grade through the eleventh. Besides just teaching band and music during school hours, she also taught instrument classes for a half hour before school began and during lunch. Donna also conducted band practice two days a week after school. She often found herself at school from 7:00 A.M. until midnight. Her long hours, however, began to pay off.

In February 1959, the whole town gathered at Lowe's Theater for a concert by the Bristol Bay Mission School from Aleknagik and a week later, Donna conducted the Dillingham school's first band concert. Community support for the band was apparent. Even the Public

Health Committee postponed their monthly meeting in order to attend Donna's concert. On February 11 David Carlson wrote in his journal, "Miss Donna McGladrey did very well considering that she only began to whip it into shape last December. The attendance was fair at 50 cents for children and 75 cents for adults. Mr. Thomas took tickets at the door. We were in the front row but somewhat annoyed by the eldest son of Kenneth Wren bouncing around in his seat." Donna masterminded charging for admittance, which gave her funds to purchase more instruments for the school. They also held an electric blanket raffle, but it failed to raise what she had expected. She learned that the children had sold very few tickets, but they did raise enough money to pay off the baritone and buy some sheet music. Donna acquired the sheet music and then orchestrated it for the entire band and choir.

Donna's programs ranged from traditional classical music to African folks songs and Japanese dancing in costumes.[6] She enjoyed teaching her charges about cultures around the world, something stressed in public schools nationwide only in recent years. And the world had already become a smaller place, at least from the perspective of someone living in Alaska. Donna wrote in March, "I suppose you've heard of our Russian friends in the Bering Sea. They were within 50 miles of Dillingham last weekend so I hear. I don't like them so close." Even in a remote bush village, Donna still found herself confronted by global issues. She also reported that the Japanese fishing industry had an impact on the salmon runs in Bristol Bay, causing Alaska to limit fishing to set-netting during the upcoming summer. All the more reason to understand global issues, she no doubt argued.

Besides teaching in the classroom, she continued taking on more assignments (individual piano lessons, musicals, fund-raising, teaching English, leading teacher's band, and organizing concerts). Of course, she also spent a great deal of time grading papers. Overall, the biggest constraint on her time was copying music. She described her life as constantly busy, and it seemed to her family that she was constantly rushing from one obligation to the next. Her health continued to concern them and as the snow began to thaw that spring, her physical health seemed to worsen. In April, she pulled together as much energy as she could muster and, with the children's help, made her big Spring Festival a great success. The day after the festival, she reported to her parents on the outcome. "I'm glad, but there's still no let up in the work. First thing this morning I had to begin work on graduation music.

I have only 4 weeks to get 5 numbers ready with the chorus. And the band has 3 numbers to get ready. I don't see how they can make it." Even though she worried about the program, it went very well. She thought the program would last an hour and a half, but it took almost three. Donna told her parents that her kids did well, most of them anyway. "The brats carried on with courage. I've had lots of compliments so I guess it was a success." While records do not elucidate whether she demonstrated her pride to her students, Donna was guarded in her praise of the students in letters home, but inside she was bursting with pride. She sent her parents a copy of the program, but sadly reported that she had forgotten to tape-record it for her family. She told them, "I was so proud of the Band. They didn't goof or get off beat nor nuttin'! I nearly died I was so pleased." The chorus had even learned how to sing in three parts. "Two was their limit up until a month ago. They love to do it, too," she wrote. They had the raffle drawing after the performances to raise money to purchase more musical instruments and sheet music. Donna was disappointed with the children's efforts again, for they had only brought in forty-nine dollars in sales. The money did allow her to complete payment on a trombone for the school, as well as some money to buy more music.

While the raffle sales disappointed her, the concert made her realize that she had succeeded in reaching the children with music and instrumentation. As she prepared for the graduation festivities that would follow in May, she became more nervous about the students' abilities and in particular, their attention spans. She had enjoyed her year teaching in Dillingham, but she had much more work to do. With the increased stress of the end of semester rush, she began to have serious stomach pains and nausea. Dr. Libby could not determine the cause of her ailments, which frustrated her. Over the semester, she had reported some form of malady in almost every letter home. Unlike the early letters, however, her last letters from Dillingham that described her teaching experiences there were positive: "As much as I've complained about this fishing village deep in the wilds of Alaska, I sure am going to miss it. It's been a good year and I'll never regret the experience. I've done a lot of growing up and feel I'm more prepared to face life than I was last fall."

CHAPTER SEVEN

The Social Scene, and Richard Newton

On the surface, Donna did not seem to fit in to the culture of Dillingham. Hermann Kroener, a German immigrant and plumber who worked in Dillingham during the 1950s, wondered "what is a . . . nice pretty girl like Donna coming to Dillingham to teach for anyway?" Hermann's wife and former student of Donna's, Hilda, remembered that she looked "like she came straight out of Scandinavia." His comparison included many of the young unmarried teachers that moved to Dillingham and quickly became bored, spending their spare time at bars. Instead, Hermann and other residents saw Donna spending her sparse free time doing schoolwork or volunteering at one of the local churches. Donna also frequented the Green Front Café. Located less than a block away from the school to the west on Main Street, the Green Front Café was an unassuming place on the outside, but inside it had a warm and friendly atmosphere. It was the only local restaurant that served lunch and dinner in more formal dining areas, as well as coffee and ice cream in the parlor, complete with a jukebox and booths for enjoying conversation and a cup of coffee. Since hotel rooms were terribly small, the Green Front Café offered patrons a place to meet and enjoy friends, as well as to escape roommates, cold apartments, and the stress of work. It also gave Donna a safe opportunity to be part of the larger community of Dillingham.

The economic situation of Dillingham had improved slightly with the recuperating fishing industry of the 1940s. Unfortunately, few year-round jobs were available in Dillingham. Some of the businesses that operated in Dillingham during Donna's year teaching included Jessie's Pool Hall, located just around the corner from the Opland Hotel, and the Willow Tree Inn and Bar, about a fifteen-minute walk west of town on Windmill Hill. Together with the liquor store next to the post office and the Sea Inn owned by Carl Nunn, many opportunities existed for acquisition of alcohol for the unemployed, bored workers, minors, and even off-the-clock teachers. Donna, however, did not partake in these sorts of activities. Her benign leisure time activities are still remembered by the longtime residents, such as attending and performing musically in the numerous churches around town, and working late into the night on hand-copying and orchestrating sheet music for the entire choir and band.

Her students saw her eating and gabbing with friends at the Green Front, and years later they wondered why she chose Dillingham and why she behaved so properly and "morally," an aberration compared to many of her colleagues. When Hilda learned about Donna's strict upbringing, it did not surprise her. "I gathered that," she responded, remembering that Donna was not wild. "I've seen a lot of teachers come to town and they just dated and drank and danced and went out partying and Donna didn't do that. Donna was a church-going girl. And she had good morals. I didn't see anything wild or she didn't use bad language. I mean, she was very prim and proper. . . . She really was." Dillingham residents remembered seeing Donna at various churches, participating either as a member of the congregation, singing, or playing the piano or pump organ. She made such an impression that even local businessman David Carlson recorded in his journal that Donna had come forward as one of the "harvest" at the Moravian Church during a week-long Revival in March. She truly lived a spiritual life, far from the debauchery that she described as surrounding her. She dedicated her spare energy mostly to church-related activities, but also to community meetings such as Chamber of Commerce and a Health Center Committee meeting. One day with her new friends Roberta (Bobbie) Tew and Martha (Marty) Jay, lay missionaries with the Church of Christ and only a few years younger, Donna attended a Public Health Council meeting. The meeting consisted of a slide show and was held at the Willow Tree Inn, a local dance hall, restaurant, and bar—likely the only time Donna would ever enter the building. Local resident Mr. Connery presented a program of slides he had taken of Alaska and Guam.

With relatively little to do in Dillingham and traveling so cost prohibitive (especially for teachers and missionaries), the slides provided local residents with a wonderful "escape" from their daily lives. Whether watching a slide presentation, attending meetings or church, or just having coffee at the Green Front Café, Donna enjoyed spending time with Bobbie and Marty and meeting new friends.

Donna's busy agenda did not keep her from adding more to her schedule. She endured illness after illness that year in Dillingham brought on by stress, poor sanitary conditions, overcommitment, lack of proper nutrition and sleep, and her nervous disposition. The addition of her first long-term relationship with a man, and all of the implications that would bring to her life, added yet another level of stress. She met Richard Newton through her new friendship with Guy and Tressie Vander Hoek in the fall of 1958.

On one afternoon in September while enjoying coffee at the Green Front Café, Donna met an electrician who was working on the new high

Roberta Tew and Martha Jay at Homer, Alaska, while on trip with Donna in Fall 1959, photograph by Donna McGladrey, courtesy of author.

school on Seward Street, Guy Vander Hoek. An avid conversationalist, according to his wife, Guy enjoyed talking with Donna. He told her about the community and his wife Tressie who would be arriving in Dillingham soon. Tressie and Donna were about the same age and both new to town; therefore, Guy insisted that they meet. While many years later Tressie cannot remember exactly how or when she met Donna, they became close friends very quickly after Tressie arrived later that September. Tressie had come to Dillingham with her son Richie while Guy worked on the school. Like Donna, they also had a difficult time finding a place to stay. Eventually Tressie and Guy found a nice rental home on Windmill Hill, across the street from The Willow Tree. It was a rather large home, one of the most spacious rentals in the community. As a result, Tressie invited many people out to enjoy the space that her home afforded. She had also planned well for her move to Dillingham, like the many others who moved to the bush, so she always had something prepared for her visitors to eat or drink. Before she left Anchorage, she purchased nonperishable groceries in bulk: many cans of pie filling and soda pop, bags of flour, and much more. Although Tressie lived a mile west of town, Donna trekked out to visit her often. Tressie recalled that visits seemed to become even more frequent after Donna met Richard Newton.

Richard was a plumber who, with his brother Charles, owned Matanuska Plumbing and Heating Company. Richard had met Guy at the construction site, and Guy mentioned to him that he had only recently met a young woman named Donna. Shortly after the two men became friends, Richard found out that Donna, Tressie, and Guy planned to see a movie and Richard invited himself along. After that "blind date," Donna described Richard to her family. "He's 27, been married before—it ended in divorce—she was untrue and it hurt him deeply. That was 3 years ago. He's a Baptist but basically has no allegiance to any one Church. He is a very fine, kind, thoughtful Christian young man. You'd approve of him, I'm sure. He's good looking and has a beautifully built muscular form. Just the perfect specimen I guess . . . I like him far better than I've ever liked anybody else but I don't know if I'll ever love him."

Richard's previous wife, Dorothy Clayton, was from Haines, Alaska. Richard had met Dorothy while he was working there. After the two married in December 1952, according to Richard's two sisters-in-law Ruby and Mary Newton, Dorothy left Richard. When Dorothy returned, she was pregnant with another man's child, yet she wanted Richard to help her take care of the baby. Dorothy began attending Richard's Baptist church where his embarrassment and anguish became public. The outcome of the relationship had devastated him, leaving him nervous about future relationships. According to his younger sister MaryAnne Mateson, "Richard had always held tightly to his girlfriends," and this incident seemed to intensify his grasp. During Donna and Richard's first blind date, he must have told Donna about his past, for she immediately expressed sympathy for him in her letters home.

Donna respected his painful past and feared hurting him again. Therefore, she approached the relationship slowly and cautiously. His past caught Donna, as well as her family, a bit off guard. Yet she allowed Richard to pursue her, even when his constant attentions later would cause her to write that he "bothered" her "every evening." By the end of October, Donna described Richard to her twin sister as being

Donna McGladrey and Richard Newton, date unknown [likely at Anchorage Newton family home at Christmas 1958], photograph courtesy of author.

"tall enuf, handsome enuf, muscular enuf—gentlemanly—just great." But as Donna learned, Richard was not the only eligible bachelor in Dillingham. In fact, Donna wrote that "a goodly number" of bachelors existed in Dillingham, and she had met several of them. One of them, Mr. Hatcher (the supervisor), impressed her so little that she described him as "an effeminate weak livered goon." Another bachelor, Steven Ahl, took Donna out on several dates. He was a "smoothie," however, according to some women of Dillingham who remembered him in later years. Richard showed his obvious and intense jealousy when he found out she planned to go out with Steve. The evening after her date with Steve, she wrote Dorothy:

> Anyway—I'm mad at Richard, too. He is very possessive and jealous and selfish—won't doesn't want me to go out with anybody else. Last night he was talking to the people across the hall when Steve came to see if I wanted to go to the movies with him last nite. I had to refuse cuz I felt lousy + had missed school so much, but told him some other time would be better. Richard heard us + said—"Looks like I have competition." I said—yeh—I guess so. When R[ichard] came back after supper he had a very far away, sick, pained, distant look—was quiet + goofy. I asked what was wrong. It took all evening to get him to 'fess up'—the trouble was he's jealous + doesn't want me to go out with Steve. After much discussion I finally decided—I'm going anyway—if you don't like it—it's just tough! Being as I'm not in love with him (tho I do like him a lot) he has no right to tell me whether to go out with others or not. It's not that he doesn't trust me—he just doesn't want to share me with anyone! He's just to darn possessive. He knows it, but can't help it. He's always been that way.

Richard had become jealous of Donna's potential friendships with other men, even though they had only known each other a very short while. His attitude troubled her, but by the next day, Richard had "had a long discussion with himself and is a happier boy today." She explained that he had apologized for the previous night, and she assured her parents that "he's so sweet. He'd do anything for me," but added, "He'll never even let me date other fellows without pouting." She was frustrated, perhaps as much at herself as with him, "Sometimes I'm mad about him and other times I can't stand him." Mostly she did not like his attempt to dominate her life and she began to show some rebellion to his possessiveness, at least in letters home.

She also had a crush on another man in town named Gene Levine, an engineer working on the airport runway expansion, but nothing ever materialized. Even so, she reported that at least four people around Dillingham kept trying to fix her up on dates. Yet with all their efforts, she wrote, "Doesn't look like I'll be married before Jan. '59." Marriage and relationships had become a major preoccupation in her letters, shoving her stories about interaction with Alaska Natives and schoolchildren into the background.

Even though Richard upset her at times with his constant presence, Donna appreciated his assistance on many occasions. For example when Bill and Marie Andrews purchased the Opland Hotel in late October and forced Ann and Donna out of their apartment, Richard borrowed his friend Myron Moran's jeep truck and helped Donna and Ann move into the Dillingham Hotel. After the move, they all went to Myron's home to relax. While at the Myron's, Richard asked her out for the following Sunday. It would be their first official date, but almost every day until the following Sunday, Richard showed up at the Green Front Café, where he knew Donna took her meals. The night before their date, he met her in the lobby of the hotel where they talked late into the night. His constant presence seemed to put Donna on edge. In November, she stated bluntly, "He's in love with me—very muchly so." Yet she lamented, "This makes me very unhappy because I'm not in love with him. . . . I love to be with him and in his arms, but if he were to leave for TimBuck-Too tonite I don't think I'd be crushed. I'm so mixed up." While to Donna, Richard seemed at the time possessive and jealous, in turn Richard saw Donna as a wonderful friend and potential mate.

Donna tried to figure out how, or if, he would fit into her life. She did not love him and queried her twin sister, "How do I make myself fall in love?" Only her best friend Tressie truly understood Donna's frustration with what she perceived as Richard's possessiveness. On her visits to Tressie's house, Donna would plop onto the floor and spill her feelings about Richard's constant demands on her time. She tired of him stopping by to visit as late as 11:00 P.M. if he saw her light on. Richard sought her out at the Green Front Café, and would follow her back to her hotel. Donna's roommate, Ann, clearly tried to influence Donna's indecisiveness by introducing Richard to other potential suitors as

Dillingham Hotel is the white building in the middle of the image.
Few photographs of this building exist, as the hotel burned down a few
years later. Photograph taken by Donna McGladrey, courtesy of author.

Donna's fiancé, provoking Donna's temper in letters home. Richard's
visits had become more than just periodic, and Tressie wondered if her
own house became a refuge for Donna. Yet Richard ignored Donna's
indecisiveness about him, hoping that she would learn to love him. He
hauled her water from the community well, penned a dictated letter
home for Donna while she was ironing or doing dishes, ran errands for
her, and brought Dr. Libby to see her when she was ill. He also took her
on car rides to see the sights (on the seven miles of road that had been
built by the road department out of Dillingham toward Aleknagik). She
admitted that she took advantage of his kindness.

Her family worried terribly, because Donna reported often about
her recurring ailments. They also remembered her nervous condition,
which during her childhood had periodically resulted in uncontrollable
and violent tremors. Their fears were predicated on Donna's references
to her growing nervousness with Richard in her letters and her recurring
illnesses. Her family believed that the two were connected. As Donna

matured, she found herself torn between the need for someone to take care of her and her bourgeoning sense of independence. Both of her sisters had married, and her best friend in Illinois, June Swatosh, was planning her own upcoming nuptials. Donna felt society's pressure to marry. And while she enjoyed Richard's company, she still did not see him as a potential mate. Moreover, he impeded her ability to explore this new self-confidence. The stress of Richard's demands on her affection and time frustrated her, as did her unyielding schedule. Her twin Dorothy's physician husband postulated later that her illnesses were also likely linked to impurities or even parasites in the community well and sewage in the streets, something certainly corroborated by Muriel Speers's report just a dozen or so years before. In nearly every letter Donna wrote home about her illnesses, she also mentioned Richard's continued presence in her life.

Richard's intentions with Donna were sincere, albeit intense. His co-worker, Hermann Kroener, had only the kindest words about his longtime friend, Richard. (While Donna never wrote about Hermann in her letters home from Dillingham, they would share a unique experience the following year.) Hermann Kroener first flew to Dillingham in 1952, with Richard's brother Charles, to work on the new addition to the Dillingham Territorial School in 1952. On his way to Dillingham, however, Charles was forced to make an emergency landing. Hermann recalled that their plane went down south and a little east of Dillingham. Finding the plane stranded, Charles slogged across the tundra to the Nushagak River, flagged down a boat, and hitched a ride to Dillingham. Charles had heard that a Mr. Olson had a rather large commercial fishing boat. He found Mr. Olson, and then hired him to take them out to retrieve their downed Cessna. He explained that even if they fixed the plane where it sat, the tundra would not allow for taxiing and takeoff.

Mr. Olson took Charles back down the river in his boat, whereupon they slogged back across the tundra to the plane. Charles devised a plan in which they would employ rope to pull the aircraft with timber under the tires. Utilizing simple, brute force, they would drag the Cessna to the river, and then lift the plane onto the boat. When they finally got the plane safely to Dillingham, Mr. Olson told them how much they owed. Charles recalled to Mr. Olson's daughter Hilda years later, "You know, your dad only charged me a hundred dollars. I mean, that's all, a hundred dollars." A long friendship between the two men ensued. When Mr. Olson needed plumbing done on his new house, he called the Newton brothers, Richard and Charles. "Hermann came out with Richard a lot, because they were drilling a well." Hilda Olson, who would eventually become Hermann's wife, was in charge of plugging in and unplugging their power tools while they worked. She did not remember much about Richard, other than he was a nice guy. Hermann returned to work on the Olson's house again in 1960.[1]

Hermann and Hilda were both quick to express their deep fondness for the Newton family. Hilda also said that everyone around town liked the Newtons. Hilda remembered that the entire family attended church regularly, and that most of the boys were very well behaved. Charles and his older brother Royce's generosity and consideration for others transcended all expectations. Donna wrote about the Newton family's kindness, invitations to family outings, and the kindheartedness of Richard's two older brothers. Richard also had a generous and playful heart. He enjoyed spending time with Hermann, on and off the job. In fact, Hermann recalled eating his first hamburger at the Green Front Café with Richard one day in 1958. Hermann had no idea how to eat it because it was so thick. Richard told him how to simply mash it down, and then bite into it. Hermann enjoyed spending time with the Newton family, and was invited to their home for the holidays.

The days grew shorter and the snow began to fall, harkening the winter's dreary return. While her descriptions of the mountains, berry bushes, swans, and rivers no longer permeated her letters, she reiterated her love of Alaska and her plan to remain. Donna still enjoyed the outdoors, as she had so many summers during her childhood. After the first substantial snowfall, she and her friends Bobbie and Marty borrowed cross-country skis and explored the surrounding areas, skiing across the much-utilized trail from the Lily Pond west to "Bread Hill." After acquiring bloody blisters and falling down numerous times, she and her friends headed home. Her toes were "like ice," her cheeks windblown, her arms ached like the rest of her body, hunger overtook her, and she was thoroughly exhausted. But she wrote of her excitement to go again.

Donna also confronted nature alone. Feeling lonely and depressed without her family in December 1958, she decided to take matters into her own hands. She got an axe and trudged into the woods and chopped down her own Christmas tree. She dragged it back to the apartment that she shared with Ann. She had to decorate the tree alone, however, for Ann had gone to Seattle for the holidays to visit either family or friends.

Donna needed to create a home, and Christian tradition insisted that she have symbols of the season.

As that first semester came to an end, Donna was homesick, tired, and weak. She had been ill several times during the semester and it had sapped her energy. She desperately wanted to go home for Christmas, but could not afford it. She apologized to her family, then wrote, "As the song says, 'I'll be home for Christmas if only in my dreams.' Mentally I am home." She said she would think about them on the twenty-fourth and twenty-fifth, "shed a few tears and remember you in my prayers." It had to be hard, coming from a religious family, celebrating Christmas as the daughter of a minister, only to find herself alone without family and old, close friends, thousands of miles from home. Therefore, she relished the mail that she received from them. At Christmas, she seemed to get more mail than usual. She received numerous Christmas cards from college and high school friends, as well as the Women's Society of Christian Service (WSCS) in Waterman.[2] To the latter, she responded with a Christmas card in which she wrote:

> I thank you for remembering me at this wonderful Christmas season. Being away from my folks and sisters is not what I would choose and I've been subject to a bit of homesickness.
>
> I've been working terribly hard lately and will really appreciate the rest I hope to get during vacation. I'm flying to Anchorage for a change and to spend my money—goody!
>
> Alaska is truly one of the most beautiful lands in the Americas. God must have worked overtime up here.
>
> There is so much the churches could do for Alaska. I wish my Dad were here in Dillingham.

Donna plainly missed her family. While letters that her family sent to Donna have disappeared, she obviously enjoyed responding to their questions and concerns. Donna lived close to the post office and likely visited it often, itching for news from home. She must have realized quickly, however, that mail came only by plane, and sometimes only twice a month. Luckily, mail service had changed from the 1940s when mail arrived only monthly, and in the winter, sometimes not at all.

Even though living in this far-flung frontier forced Donna to relax a vital connection she had always had, or rather depended upon, with her family, Alaska truly called to her. And in Alaska, she had become confident, strong, and self-assured. In December 1958, Donna explained that she had come to Alaska for a purpose, but did not know what it was yet. In the meantime, she thoroughly enjoyed the beauty that surrounded her.

I wish you could live up here. There's a spirit in Alaska that can't be found anywhere else in the world. It's exciting, invigorating, and makes you see the mess the states are in—Chicago esp[ecially]. I wouldn't go back to Chgo for all the gold in Alaska. The scenery is spectacular everywhere up here. I remember when I used to be starved for a glimpse at Nawakwa and No[rthern] Wisc[consin]. I could hardly wait til summers—Now—I just have to peer out any window + there it is.

She loved Alaska, constantly trying to convince her family and friends to move up to either work at Elmendorf Air Force Base near Anchorage or to homestead. Whether or not her family planned to move to Alaska, Donna was there to stay.

While Donna and her friends and family exchanged Christmas greetings, residents around town began to decorate for the holiday season. Children became more unsettled and less attentive, and teachers began planning their holiday vacations away from the responsibilities of teaching, grading, and attending meetings. On Christmas Day 1958, Donna hoped to fly with Richard to Anchorage in his company plane to spend time with his family over the holidays. Even though Donna complained about Richard at times, she really missed being with her family at Christmas and perhaps she hoped that joining his would fill that void. The schoolchildren in Dillingham, particularly the boys, were devastated that she would not stay. She needed a break, however, and spending time with Richard's family and shopping in Anchorage would be a welcome change of pace. Unfortunately, the weather did not cooperate. Donna, Richard, Bill Lydic (Richard's nephew), and their pilot took off from Ball Air Strip just before 11:00 A.M., but had to land at Iliamna less than halfway to Anchorage, and wait out the weather at the Civil Aeronautics Administration (CAA) office. For hours they paced the floor. Finally, the CAA allowed them to depart. They flew over the mountains toward Cook Inlet and Kenai, but ran into fog once they crossed the mountains. In a letter describing the day, Donna's fear of flying was evident between the lines: "and daylight was leaving us."

Around 6:00 P.M., the trio landed in Kenai and looked for over two hours for a place to eat. Finally the CAA office found them something to eat. Once the fog lifted, they were finally cleared for takeoff. Shortly, they arrived in Anchorage where Donna looked forward to "rest and change" as well as "the opportunity to spend my money." After the long, unnerving journey, she was eager to put the trip behind her and enjoy her break.

While in Anchorage, she attended the First Baptist Church with Richard's family. A very religious family, the Newtons placed great emphasis on their relationship with God. This had to be comforting to Donna, who spent all of her prior Christmas holidays so closely connected with her family and the Methodist Church. Years later, Charles's son Rick remembered Donna and her interest in music. He recalled having taken his drum set out and playing for her during that Christmas visit. After Christmas, she expected to return to Dillingham on January 2 for school, but weather conditions had deteriorated. It had been terribly windy in Dillingham, with temperatures hovering around ten degrees below zero. Anchorage, Donna wrote, was far colder, "30 degrees below. Gales and tremendous winds have been blowing us to death here—makes it most uncomfortable to walk anyplace." For three days they remained weather-bound. She finally gave up on January 5 and flew back commercially to Dillingham with Richard, leaving the Newton's new Cessna in Anchorage. "Christmas of '58 is one I shall never forget."

Besides the difficulties of flying, as well as sharing a holiday with a boyfriend's family, she had another reason to remember that particular Christmas season. Even with a minister for a father, she had still questioned her life. "I have wondered, doubted + felt inadequate and wondered why I was ever born. I didn't enjoy life—I was unhappy and felt it would be better to be dead than to try to struggle thru this miserable life. I could see no purpose for my life." All that changed on January 4 when she became a born-again Christian and began an earnest search for her life's purpose. "But now I feel that a great burden has been lifted from me and I can see much more clearly many things that were dark to me before." While the rest of her life had not yet come into clear focus, she knew one thing for certain: she belonged in Alaska. She wrote, "Up until that Jan 4th when I accepted the Lord I had been thinking that there might not be a God—and the Bible was just a lot of nice stories and rules to follow. Now I have real peace in my heart—There is a God." Richard had urged her to attend his Baptist Church, where she could learn more about the Bible. Life did not become more simple, however, for now she had to decide whether to join the First Baptist Church, which brought her to Christ, or another church in Dillingham. Either way, she wrote that "It's a marvelous thing to know God. . . . I have no fear of death now—I did before. I can see a purpose to life—before I didn't know why I have been placed in this miserable life." She had finally begun to feel at home, not just in Alaska, but also in herself.

She had also lost some of her fear of flying by March 1959, as evidenced in a trip she took solely for enjoyment with the Newtons. At 7:25 A.M. on one Saturday in March, she left Dillingham for Bethel, just over an hour and a half west by plane and situated on the Kuskokwim River essentially to see another part of Alaska, purely for adventure. Charles and Richard Newton, along with Don Wagner (another Matanuska Plumbing and Heating employee) needed to look over a new school job they planned to bid on. They boarded the Cessna 175 and headed west. Donna joined them, taking photographs of the mountains that they flew over. At one point in their journey, heavy clouds shielded the mountains from view. Neither Charles nor Richard Newton were "instrument rated," the formal designation of having completed instrument training, and so could only navigate by sight. In order to see where they were going, Charles had to climb to six thousand feet above the cloud layer. Unfortunately, without visual contact with the topography, Charles flew off course and instead of landing at Bethel, they got lost. Charles proceeded to land the plane at a small village to ask someone where they were. The nearest village with a runway, they soon found out, was the Yup'ik village of Akiak on the Kuskokwim north of Bethel. After talking with locals, Charles realized that they were about twenty-five miles north of Bethel. So, they took off and followed the winding, snow-covered river, with its sharp switchbacks and turns.

They recognized the village of Akiachak as they flew over it, at which point Charles became disoriented, and fifteen minutes later they passed over the same village again. Once again they had to land, this time on the river's frozen surface, to determine their whereabouts for a second time. The Kuskokwim River splits into two forks, rejoining approximately a dozen miles farther south at Kwethluk, both forks shooting east or west at a 90–120 degree angle. This may have been the source of his confusion. Nevertheless, Donna wrote that they disembarked and walked from the river up to the village to ask directions. She reported that the village was a "very quaint and interesting place." She reported that caches and log huts surrounded them, just like in the pictures. The "Dogs were as lousy as fleas on a dogs back and kids were abundant. They all stood around staring at us queer ones." She snapped several photographs of them, but upon returning to the plane, her lens cover dropped off and she realized she had shot blanks. When she turned around to take some more pictures, she realized she was out of film. "I was just sick." Donna still found bush villagers somewhat of an oddity, hoping to save their image for posterity, and was devastated that she could not. In any case, they finally arrived at Bethel and the "boys got down to business."

Donna reported that Bethel was about three times larger than Dillingham, "but not nearly as nice. I thought Dillingham was shacky— but it isn't in comparison to Bethel." Confronted again by the reality

Scene on way to Bethel, Alaska, March 1959,
photograph by Donna McGladrey, courtesy of author.

of the bush, she once again found appreciation for her hometown of Dillingham. But she did not have time for a tour. Soon they were back in the air again with two and a half hours of fuel. The trip to Dillingham normally should have taken about an hour and forty minutes, but Charles "goofed and we got off course again and ended up at Togiak Bay rather than Nushagak Bay. About 30 minutes off course." Togiak was a small community located approximately seventy air miles west of Dillingham. Togiak grew from ten people in 1939 to 220 by 1960, but was still much smaller than Dillingham. After Charles realized his mistake, he reoriented himself and headed east, skirting the south side of the Ahklun Mountains and flying over the village of Manokotak with its small population of 149, and on to Dillingham, finally. Charles knew that he had used more fuel than expected, but no one realized how precarious their situation had actually become. As they landed, the engine cut. It had run out of fuel.

They did not have time to commiserate about the near disaster, because Dillingham's fire alarm began to ring! The road commission garage was on fire. Donna grabbed her movie camera and ran up the hill from the Lily Pond runway to get the whole event on film.[3] When she got up the hill, townsmen were frantically trying to save the heavy road machinery and equipment from the flaming building. Donna reported that she had twenty-five feet of movies, as well as snapshots of the fire. While the whole place was destroyed, the small canvas hut next to the garage with dynamite in it luckily was not.

In a hurry to get back to Anchorage, Charles began refueling the plane and Richard took Donna home. After about ten minutes, she realized she had left her regular glasses on the plane and began to run back to stop Charles before he left. Someone took pity on her and gave her a ride, allowing her to reach the Lily Pond just in time. She needed her glasses to play for the Easter church services in town the next day.

The following day, when she was playing the pump organ at the Moravian church Easter service, she began to feel a little ill. After the Moravian service, she and Richard headed over to the Seventh Day Adventist church for their 11:00 A.M. Easter service. As Donna sat down for the service, however, she began to feel more ill and lightheaded, and her stomach began to feel upset. She headed back to the Sunday school room to rest, but instead she fainted. When she fell, her head slammed against the organ and she landed squarely on her shoulder. Her nearly forgotten glasses flew halfway across the room. She wrote that she "rocked the whole building." Mary Carlson, the wife of school agent David Carlson, ended up playing the organ in her place that evening at the Moravian church.

Apparently, her fall prompted the church members to call Dr. Libby, who lived about 150 yards northwest of the church along the Ball Air Strip. The doctor gave her pills for pain in her chest, back, and head and told her that she had the flu. She headed to bed. The resurgence of illness coincided with the mild weather in Dillingham. One outcome of the comparatively milder weather, of course, included periodic balmy days resulting in short thaws. As March came to an end, the mild weather had started thawing the snow and ice around town, and as David Carlson reported, "The water is beginning to flow down the road now." The resulting water and other runoff from the residents' backyard pits began flowing freely down the unimproved roads to Main Street, past the Green Front Café and schoolhouse, and down to the river.[4] The stench of the spring melt, according to many who lived in Dillingham during those years, was unbearable. With Donna ill again, Richard stepped in to care for her that Easter holiday.

Her musical commitments at Easter were no different than the rest of the year. Donna had always participated in Sunday services in the numerous churches around town. At the time, Dillingham hosted a number of churches. Donna either attended or performed at most of them: Church of Christ, Seventh-Day Adventist, Catholic church, and Moravian church. Her interests reflected her "pure" moral character, for she thoroughly enjoyed attending Bible classes, singing, playing the organ and piano. Often she played the organ for the Seventh Day Adventist church and the Moravian church. On Wednesday night Bible study–prayer meetings, she played an old pump organ, which she described to her family, "You have to pump until you're panting + then press the keys which strain all your arm muscles. I'm exhausted after 5 hymns." Since no Methodist church existed in Dillingham, she had decided to attend primarily the Church of Christ with Reverend Franklin Smith presiding.

The Church of Christ, originally known as the Alaska Mission, was built in 1939 on Main Street across from the school. Reverend Franklin Smith served as pastor in the 1950s and periodically left services for the lay missionaries to perform (often with little or no notice). As an avid outdoorsman, he often went fishing and hunting and did not bother to return in time for Sunday services. Donna mentioned Rev. Smith's absence in letters, but enjoyed the lay missionaries that stood in for Rev. Smith, her close friends Bobbie and Marty.[5] Besides their friendship, she also enjoyed the camaraderie of friends who sang in a trio and a quartet with her at the local churches. By early March 1959, when temperatures hovered between ten and forty degrees below zero, they still performed every night.

Donna had a busy March. Besides the perilous trip to Bethel, the garage fire, and attending the March PTA meeting while suffering a nasty case of the flu, she also acquired a typewriter (to write longer letters more easily), ate her first ptarmigan, and succeeded in landing a teaching job in Chugiak for the upcoming school year. In response to her father's insinuation that she was moving to Chugiak to live closer to Richard, she responded, "Daddy, you guessed pretty close concerning the Chugiak move. I'm not too sure yet, but plans are to live in Anchorage next year with a new name. Nothing's definite yet so don't get excited. Even if you don't get a new son-in-law I'll be in Chugiak." Donna began to lean toward marrying Richard after their trip to Bethel. She had wavered for months in the relationship, not knowing if he was the right man for her. She calmly added, "There's still plenty of time to think about it. I'm in no hurry." If she tied herself down in marriage, as society and perhaps her parents expected, she would lose her newfound autonomy and the exhilaration of being self-sufficient.

At the same time, she clearly recognized Richard's intense love for her. He assisted her while she was sick, took her skiing, and spent every evening with her that she allowed. But Richard must have realized that his future with Donna depended upon not just Donna's response to him, but also her parents' approval as well. One evening as he stopped by to visit Donna, he found her busy ironing. Instead of leaving, he stayed and kept her company. Since she was behind in her letter writing, she decided to dictate a letter home to Richard while she ironed. Donna must have taken a short break from dictating, for he interjected his own message. Perhaps he wanted to convince her parents of his good intentions, for he knew that they did not approve of his divorce:

> I hope to meet you people. You must be real wonderful if Donna is any example. I have never met anyone quite like her. You can tell just by her life that she was brought up in [the] right kind of atmosphere—she is so different from anyone else I've known and whatever happens I'll always be thankful having known her.[6]

Donna obviously meant the world to Richard, but she could not reciprocate with the same intensity.

Even as she tried to sort out her feelings about Richard, she enjoyed talking with friends at the Green Front Café, singing and playing at the various churches, attending civic meetings, and participating in events around town. One of her favorite events was the Beaver Round-Up. In anticipation of the Round-Up, Donna scribbled to her family, "It'll probably turn into a drunken brawl and be a big mess. I'll be there to take pics of the dogs . . . But that's all I'll have to do with it." She did, however, say that she planned to have a "beaver dinner. I don't know whether I can eat that." She wanted to try it, as she had eaten ptarmigan and moose already. On April 3, 1959, David Carlson penned in his diary that Dillingham's first annual Beaver Roundup had begun, and it "consisted of dog races, snow shoe races, and billions of other things." As promised, Donna snapped several photographs of the dog teams, more than she should have, she admitted. She loved the dogs, stopping to enjoy them at every opportunity.

Starting line for dog race in front of Opland Hotel,
First Annual Beaver Round-Up, April 1959, Dillingham, Alaska,
photograph taken by Donna McGladrey, courtesy of author.

On April 19, Donna celebrated her twenty-fourth birthday. Her twin, Dorothy, would celebrate her birthday with her husband and brand new son, Daniel, born just a few weeks before. Donna had not had time to think about getting her twin sister a present, so she sent her parents ten dollars and told them to "get anything she needs." Dorothy was obviously occupied, too, because she forgot to send anything as well! But Donna did get some presents. Her best friend from Illinois, June Swatosh, sent her a card and some pajamas with a matching housecoat. June's mother sent a card, notes, and a hanky. Perhaps the biggest surprise was that Donna's piano students baked her a cake and brought it to her. Donna and Ann's neighbors from across the hall also baked her a cake. Her birthday celebrations had, in fact, begun a bit early. Ann Carr, who thought Donna's birthday was April 12, had already baked Donna a special roast chicken dinner and invited Richard over, who gave Donna a big knit cardigan. Richard also gave her mukluks, made in the traditional way by a local Dillingham resident. On April 13, Richard returned from Anchorage with a dozen red roses. They were not in the greatest condition, Donna reported, "but oh—the smell—dreamy—love roses. The first real flowers I've seen in ages." Later, Richard took Donna out to dinner in a peculiar way. He bought a couple of chickens and asked his friend Johnny Ball and his wife to cook them for her. They had dinner at Johnny Ball's house. Donna had a wonderful birthday week.

The semester was winding itself down quickly, and she felt pressured to complete her many tasks before the school year ended. As May approached, she grappled with continued bouts of illness, the teaching load, numerous programs to perform, her church performances, piano lessons before and after school, and choir practices at lunch. Nevertheless, Donna began the process of tying up loose ends before leaving Dillingham.

Donna clearly found Richard's company welcoming when she needed him the most. She remembered her lonely days in her Chicago apartment the summer before she arrived in Alaska. When she had nearly broken her ankle and had cleaning responsibilities without anyone to help, she had expressed her intense sadness at not having someone to take care of her, even stating that she could die and nobody would care. In Dillingham, Richard had cared for her. She liked his attention when it suited her. In fact, Donna reported to her sisters that in May and June, they might have to help her make dresses and plan for her upcoming nuptials. Yet she admonished them, "Nothing is settled for sure yet so don't get excited and don't tell anyone!" She felt a strong desire to marry, especially since Dorothy had married nearly a year before and had her first child that spring. "Rich and I have been trying to figure out when it would be possible to get married this summer." She reported that May was too early for the wedding and August too late. He was working in the summer on St. Lawrence Island, just off of the Seward Peninsula by Russia through June and July. They thought perhaps July 25, but she wanted the wedding to be on June 27. She planned to spend her summer making a wedding dress, while Richard had plans to build a house for his fiancé in Anchorage.[7] She planned to commute from Anchorage to teach at Chugiak Elementary School the upcoming school year. At the end of her letter, she told Jo that she had finished the sweater, booties, and cap that she had started for her nephew, Daniel. Proud of her work on the baby outfit, her letter hinted of her longing to start her own family, or at least get married as society dictated.

Three weeks passed before anybody heard from Donna again. This time, she wrote to her twin sister Dorothy. Donna had grave concerns. Even though they had planned the wedding for July 25, 1959, she began to worry, thinking that they should wait a little longer. Donna feared that her relationship with Richard was moving too fast. She told Dorothy that Richard was a terribly jealous type. She explained that another fellow in Dillingham had great "affections" for Donna, although she did not reciprocate. "If I even mention his name Richard turns green and starts spitting fire." She wondered about the summer." If I don't miss the goof then what? The last thing in the world I want to do is to hurt him." She worried intensely about hurting him, but realized that she would probably not marry him in the summer. She reported that "I've done a lot of growing up and feel I'm more prepared to face life than I was last fall." She had finally gained confidence in herself, and therefore felt stronger and more able to face challenges in the future—on her terms. And that included letting Richard down. At semester's end in a letter to her parents, she thanked them for her birthday present and the pictures they sent her of her new nephew, whom she was very excited to see. She then reported some difficult news, "Sorry to say Richard and I have decided to postpone a wedding indefinitely." She promised to tell them why later, but asked for her parents' prayers. Donna felt strongly about Richard, but they had some real difficulties and hurdles to overcome. She looked forward to returning home, but reported that

Opland Hotel is the two-story building on the right. Western Alaska Airlines building is on the left, street scene. "Dillingham, Opland Hotel and street view, 3 June 1955," McCutcheon Collection #8890, printed with permission of Anchorage Museum of History and Art, Anchorage, Alaska.

she would miss her many wonderful friends in Dillingham, like Tressie, Marty, Bobbie, and many others.

Donna was proud of her successes, teaching the children about classical music, rounds, harmony, and instrumentation. Hilda Kroener remembered that after Donna came, the kids got instruments and "the kids were playing pretty, pretty good really." Donna had succeeded in instilling a love of music into Dillingham's children. But Dillingham's school board had decided that they needed the music teacher to teach Physical Education and English also. Donna felt that she already had too many responsibilities and decided against returning to Dillingham for another year, even if they offered her twice the salary. She bade Dillingham goodbye, claiming that she would be the first one on the plane. Yet, she wrote longingly, "I'll miss Dillingham."

As the end of the semester neared, she looked forward to her trip home. "Only 24 more days and I'm through." She planned to spend time over the upcoming weekend packing and sending some of her belongings home to use in the summer, storing the rest in Anchorage to pick up in the fall when she returned to teach in Chugiak. She reported that she would arrive in Anchorage on May 22 or 23 to see the school agent in Chugiak. She planned to fly to Tacoma to see her Uncle Merlin for a bit, then return to Chicago on either the twenty-fourth or twenty-fifth.

Surprisingly, she had done well financially while in Dillingham; after all, there were few places to spend her money. She thought she would have over $1,700 saved up by June. She planned to buy a sewing machine and material for new clothes. She looked forward to taking a break. "M y nerves are a wreck and I can't stand the grind any more," she wrote. Even though she hoped to take it easy, she planned to see a dentist, a physician for a physical, an optometrist for new glasses, and a chiropractor for her back. "I'm about ready to expire," she complained. "Oh do I need a vacation." She even mentioned the possibility of taking classes toward a Master's degree, perhaps at the University of Minnesota or the University of Illinois.

CHAPTER EIGHT

Chicago and Chugiak
Going Home Again

Much to the dismay of her students in Dillingham, Donna packed her bags and left permanently in May 1959. They hated to see her go, especially the boys who would miss her attractive presence in their classrooms and around town. No more whistling at Donna during recess, or writing, "Gee, aren't you pretty!" on their homework. Donna regretted leaving the first teaching job where she truly felt valued, important, and needed, and where she had found success inspiring her students. Like many young teachers that moved to Dillingham, she left after a year. It was indeed a rare teacher arrived to a bush community from "outside" (the Lower 48) and remained for her entire career. Donna understood that, for some had written books about their experiences. While she did not plan to remain in the bush, she did plan to write a book about her life in Alaska.

In the meantime, she looked forward to the 1959–60 academic year teaching in one of the largest school districts—Chugiak.[1] Chugiak was a small and rather scattered community and did not even register on the census in 1950, but by 1960, it hosted a population of fifty-one as an unincorporated village. By 1970, it had almost five hundred people. Nearby Anchorage, on the other hand, had grown from a mere 1856 in 1920 to forty thousand by 1960 as a result of the military bases. It was a full-fledged city with every amenity a young music teacher desired, including at least two music stores, complete with instruments and sheet music! And Anchorage was only a twenty-minute drive from Chugiak.

Donna seemed pleased that her new job would require her to teach only elementary children—no high school students. Although she would earn about four hundred dollars less than when she taught in Dillingham, housing and food costs were lower. She planned to enjoy the amenities that being near a larger city offered. She looked forward to getting a car, and having the "conveniences so long denied me here [in Dillingham]." Yet while she excitedly awaited the following year nearer "civilization," she wrote in a letter to her sister Dorothy who lived in Evanston, a suburb north of Chicago, "I feel sorry for you—all you can see from your window is the 'L' [elevated train] + dumb city noise. Any window I gaze from lets my eyes feast on either the snow clad tundra speckled with spruce and the white ominous mountains or the bay with its icy tide. Alaska is gorgeous." She obviously loved Alaska, yet she still longed for the comforts of the city. In the meantime, she planned to spend her summer in Illinois and lead a "life of leisure." Earlier she had explained to her father that she planned to enroll in a Master of Arts program, but by the time she penned her last letter home in May, she had already changed her mind. The year had worn her out emotionally, physically, and mentally. Besides, she had developed yet another illness and did not think she could recover in time to devote herself to her studies. When she arrived home, however, her illness had miraculously disappeared.

In late May 1959, Donna moved in with her parents in Waterman, Illinois, and ended up enrolling for five credit hours at Northern Illinois University in DeKalb. Her father's encouragement helped her realize that further education would improve her pay and employment opportunities. She hoped to eventually complete a Masters degree in Music Education. Five hours of course work, including the musical practice that the courses required, demanded tremendous effort. At semester's end, her report card paid tribute to her hard work: an A in Keyboard Problems, a B in Foundations of Music Education, and a B in Techniques of Research in Music Education. With five hours out of the way, she had only a little more than twenty hours to take before completing her Master's degree. At this rate, attending school in the summers, she could be done in four years. Donna looked forward to honing her teaching, performance, orchestrating, and musicianship skills while continuing to work on her advanced degree. Perhaps she began the Masters program so she would have an excuse to return to Illinois every summer, and thus an excuse not to marry Richard so soon. The farther geographically Donna was from Richard, the more her independent spirit soared.

Donna had matured significantly during her first year in Alaska. In the new northern state, she learned how to make decisions about lodging, food, transportation, finances, life, and relationships, without the assistance of her family. She had learned to depend on herself. Even though Donna felt more mature and confident than the previous year, she still looked to her sisters for guidance and advice, as many sisters would. She particularly enjoyed having Joan nearby. Verna had arranged for Joan to watch over an elderly couple for a few weeks whose regular caregiver needed to have surgery. The timing could not have been better, for Joan's husband Malvin had gone to Norway to visit his parents. While Joan worked, her five-year-old daughter Karen stayed with Leslie and Verna. They loved having their daughters and grandchildren in such close proximity. Even though Leslie and Verna lived in Waterman, it was only one and a half hours by car from Jack and Dorothy's home in Evanston, but neither Donna nor Dorothy had a vehicle. To make the family complete again, even if only temporarily, Donna had come back from Alaska and moved in with her parents.

Donna frequently visited Joan after the elderly couple in her care turned in for the night. During their long, heartfelt conversations, Joan recalls Donna sharing some of her confusion about Richard. In the 1950s, most folks did not talk frankly about relationships, especially the physical aspects of them, yet Donna openly explained to Joan that she had approached a point in her relationship with Richard that confused her, particularly, in Joan's words, about issues of sexual "progressions and stuff." Donna did not report to what point their physical relationship had gone, but Joan remembered well that Donna "felt a great danger" about expanding the relationship into something more physical. Donna described their relationship as pretty intense, something that she had never previously experienced. In Dillingham, Richard had visited her nearly every evening. He found her at the coffee shop, spent time with her at Bible Studies and church services, and accompanied her on outings with Guy and Tressie. She did not know how to balance her personal needs with his constant desire to be faithfully (or jealously) at her side.

Donna's conversations with Joan continued. Over the course of the summer, they became more detailed, yet at the same time still restrained. Donna seemed more confident talking to Joan, who was alone without Malvin. Dorothy, with her new baby, was very busy at home. Donna complained to Joan that when she did try to call Dorothy, she always seemed busy. Jack worked at a feverish pace as an intern at Cook County Hospital on Chicago's South Side. While probably hurt, perhaps Donna's lack of assertiveness caused her to not impose on her sister's time. Even her best friend, June Swatosh, was preparing for her own wedding the upcoming year.

So many weddings made Donna think about her own future. Verna had been surprisingly open in the past about sex, menstruation, and other women's issues. Joan remembered how her mother "brought me a book [about menstruation] and she had a book about sex that she kept up in the attic and I would go up there once in a while when she was taking her nap and I would read, you know, I don't remember if it was a manual or what." Verna had celebrated the girls' coming of age, and both Joan and Dorothy recalled how their mother called family members to the dinner table, announcing that Donna was now a woman. But Joan reiterated that their mother wanted to make sure that they understood the world and would not be surprised by "that sort of thing," even though at times the information presented was rather vague. And, Joan remembered, once Verna proffered the information, she "completely ignored us . . . and you wouldn't go back and ask for more information. . . . She prepared us for a good number of things but we didn't get beyond the basic preparation, the rest of it was up to us." Verna's preparation of the girls for relationships with men, in all likelihood, followed the same track, making Donna more disposed to talk to her older sister about relationships and by innuendo about sex, rather than her own mother.

Donna feared that she would go "over the edge" with Richard if she continued to date him much longer. While Joan cannot be certain, it seemed that Donna implied that she would end up being stuck with him forever as his bride. Donna continued to waver that summer about whether or not she would remain with Richard. Perhaps as telling, no record exists of contact between Richard and Donna that summer.[2] By late August, Alaska once again beckoned Donna and she prepared to return—conceivably with a better understanding of sex and what that meant for two people in love. Joan reiterated, however, that she "didn't advise her, [I] mostly listened." Therefore, by listening to Donna talk through her relationship, Joan presumably helped Donna sort through her feelings.

Instead of flying to Alaska directly from Chicago, Donna's parents drove her from Chicago to Seattle, where she would catch her flight to Anchorage. The McGladrey trio planned to visit Leslie's brother, Air Force Chaplain Merlin McGladrey, at McChord Air Force Base in Tacoma, Washington, after a nice camping trip through some of the most beautiful national parks and monuments in the western United States, including Yellowstone. Donna described her trip with her parents to Joan, albeit in truncated form, on the back of several postcards that she sent en route. They drove through Wyoming, Montana, across Idaho and Oregon, until they arrived in Washington. On August 17, Donna mailed a postcard from Dayton, Wyoming. She thanked Joan for the wonderful accommodations the Friday before. She told Joan that she had a little nervous stomach and had to leave during church services in Wyoming. Perhaps it was the company. She described the country as beautiful, and the "company trying . . . Crabby, I guess." The heat and dry conditions of the open prairie in the summer sun caused tensions to flare.

Donna, Leslie, and Verna traveled through the Badlands, planning to stop in the Black Hills during the morning. Just three days later, her postcard from Pendleton, Oregon, mentioned the earthquake that they had just missed in the Yellowstone area. Donna explained that they had traveled some five hundred miles that Wednesday, but could find no camping place at Yellowstone, so they stayed in a motel instead. She enjoyed being inside that night since it rained (and continued raining for a few days). They relished the opportunity to take showers, wash their hair, and feel "real nice and clean." Apparently, they had heard about the earthquake and subsequent dam breakage and slide, for they called Merlin to let him know they were safe and would arrive soon. "He was real worried about us. He thought we were caught in slide for sure." The 1959 Yellowstone earthquake had measured a 7.5 on the Richter Scale, caused twenty-eight fatalities, and more than ten million dollars in damage to highways and the timber industry. Massive rockslides triggered by the earthquakes caused the majority of the fatalities. Donna later told Joan that "they were near Yellowstone and she was sitting on the 'throne' and it quaked. She thought she'd get swallowed!" Luckily, they had escaped that disaster, and the rest of their trip was delightfully uneventful. She enjoyed traveling across the country,

Leslie and Donna McGladrey at Craters of the Moon
National Monument, near Arco, Idaho, August 1959,
photograph taken by Verna McGladrey, courtesy of author.

and particularly enjoyed Washington, with its "large tall fat pines. Gorgeous—smells good." She told Joan that the ambiance reminded her of The Pines Trail at Camp Nawakwa.

After visiting Merlin and his family, the trio finally arrived in Seattle where Donna boarded a plane for Alaska. Donna had looked forward to moving to Chugiak, even though it was not much more than a few homes scattered up and down the Old Glenn Highway. Donna probably did not understand the layout of Chugiak, for in May she talked about going to Chugiak and being among "civilization" again. "I can't wait until I get back into civilization!—T.V.—phones—movies—restaurants—cars—trains—highways—sidewalks—stores—store windows—gee!" Either way, Donna knew that Anchorage was only a fifteen-mile drive down the highway. In the 1950s, at least two music stores existed in Anchorage, as well as a Singer Sewing Machine store, restaurants, sidewalks, but not all the streets were paved in the 1950s. Nevertheless, she wrote, "I've never been so excited in all my days."

The excitement and nervousness began to build, however, because in her first letter home, she reported that she had been sick the entire six hour trip to Anchorage. Upon landing, she began to have side aches and felt "doggy" with an upset stomach.

When she arrived in Anchorage, she learned that Richard was in Dillingham working on the new high school. Construction had progressed slowly due to a carpenter strike. Donna told her family that Charles, who had other construction contracts in the Anchorage area, had not gone to Dillingham for over a month, nor was he planning to go soon. Richard was running low on supplies and money at the job site, and therefore found it difficult to make progress or get supplies. Donna believed that Charles avoided going to Dillingham because people there had grown upset with him. Little did Donna know, however, that the general contractor for their work on the school had not paid the Matanuska Plumbing and Heating Company, and Charles simply did not have supplies or money to deliver to Richard. Either way, it meant that Charles would not fly round-trip to Dillingham and bring back Bobbie and Marty, therefore foiling Donna's plans to go traveling with the duo. Donna complained to her family that it looked like she would have three weeks alone. With all of the extra time on her hands, Donna got settled in her new home. She contacted Chugiak School Agent Paul Swanson to procure housing. Unfortunately, he had no place for her to stay at that moment, so he and his wife Margaret offered her a bed in their home located across from the school on the Old Glenn Highway. Swanson would soon haul trailers onto his land for the newly hired and homeless teachers. In the meantime, Donna took Paul and Margaret up on their offer and stayed with them for several days. Throughout her tenure at Chugiak, Donna lived across the highway from the school in various trailers rented from Paul Swanson.

Donna enjoyed Chugiak. In her first letter from Chugiak on August 26, she reported that she had already bought a beige Volkswagen Beetle, a mere $650 down payment (including insurance). She had an eighteen-month payment plan of $101 per month, "Not too bad." Soon she had use for her vehicle, other than going to town to purchase groceries. On August 27, Tressie Vander Hoek, who had moved to Anchorage that summer, surprised Donna when she arrived in Chugiak with Marty and Bobbie. They had flown in via commercial service at $120 apiece. Donna was elated! Since Richard was still in Dillingham, Donna and her friends moved into Richard's trailer and lean-to at the Matanuska

Plumbing and Heating shop in Mountain View, an area of Anchorage.[3] From this base, the girls went shopping and "gallivanted," then they packed Donna's car and drove down the Seward Highway to Homer. Even though it rained on them during their whole trip, they had a wonderful time. Donna reported that they drove through Kenai and visited the missionaries there. They visited the Alaskan Christian School, a Church of Christ Home for Kids, finding that seventeen of the twenty-two kids were from Dillingham! Donna and her friends stayed at the mission for one evening, sleeping on the floor. Donna loved the scenery of the Kenai Peninsula, taking photographs of Ninilchik and Portage Glacier on the way home. Wrapping up the trip, Donna drove Bobbie and Marty to the Anchorage airport, drove Tressie home, then headed to Mountain View to pick up the rest of her belongings. After the carefree sojourn with her friends, she learned that Paul Swanson had purchased a "used trailer. Not large—but not small. Real cute—I like it." She moved in to the rented pink and white trailer on Saturday, September 5, and began to fix up the place.

She had her own trailer, a new job, her own car. No longer would she

Ninilchik, September 1959, taken by Donna McGladrey during her trip with Bobbie and Marty, photograph courtesy of author.

receive daily, late, or unexpected visits from Richard. And even when he was back from the bush, he lived more than twenty minutes away in Mountain View. Donna enjoyed her single life without the constant intrusions by Richard. This carefree Donna also seemed quite healthy; that is, until Richard returned from Dillingham. In the meantime, she enjoyed her new job and treasured her new friendships with teachers, many of whom also lived across from the school on Paul Swanson's land, called "Swanny Slopes," in the rented trailers and cabins.

Swanny Slopes got its name from the Swansons, who had moved to the area in 1941. Paul managed to miss the military draft in 1941 for medical reasons. But as a result of Pearl Harbor, the June 1942 Japanese attacks on Dutch Harbor, and their subsequent occupation of Attu and Kiska Islands, Paul joined the Seabees and served from 1941 to 1945. He returned to Anchorage after the war in January 1946 with his new bride Margaret. Shortly thereafter, they moved to a 120-acre homestead in the Wasilla District until they proved up. When they heard that a school would be built in Chugiak, they moved back to Paul's original home. The community recognized Paul Swanson as a leader, and as Margaret recalled, "they appointed him school agent because he was one of the prominent go-getters that lived in the community. . . . [He] went to the bank and got a loan and started building."[4] He took his role as the school agent quite seriously and, by all accounts, served the community well.

Chugiak Elementary School opened in October of 1951 across the street from the store that Paul Swanson had built. During its first year, the school enrolled sixty-six children, twenty-one more than the building could handle. The school had electricity when it opened, but had outgrown its building before the first day of classes began. The original school agent, Vernon Haik, had acquired many of the necessary books and supplies from nearby Fort Richardson when the school first opened. Haik and his wife Alma, who had first come to Alaska in 1936 and moved there permanently in 1946, opened the Spring Creek Lodge, north along the Old Glenn Highway in 1949. A favorite stop for Anchorage travelers and locals, the Spring Creek Lodge was always busy on Sundays. They served Alma's banana cream pies, famous throughout the valley. South along the road were the other early homesteaders of Chugiak. Each family hoped to scratch a living from the western edge of the Chugach Mountains, but at the beginning, few found large-scale farming an option. Rather, the Haiks sold strawberries and other garden crops. Like the Swansons, they also raised hogs for a while. Life was not easy, but the breathtakingly beautiful location made up for the lack of economy. From their front yards, on a clear day, they could witness sunshine and shadows shifting across Mt. McKinley and Mt. Foraker. The Chugach Mountains against which they nestled rose to mighty peaks that shadowed them in the winter months. But with the spring thaw, they also had beautiful views of Knik Arm flowing into Cook Inlet and eventually out to the Pacific Ocean.

The postwar years saw rapid growth in Alaska's population, and Chugiak grew quickly, too, as more people moved to the area to take out homesteads or acquire land in the recently established community. By the end of the 1950s, the community of Chugiak had a fire department, elementary school, quonset huts to house the overflow student populations, a PTA, numerous stores, a diner, school busses, and nearly enough teacher housing.

Perhaps one of the greatest achievements for Chugiak's residents was the newly paved stretch of highway that reached Anchorage (as well as a far safer approach to Eagle River and a new steel bridge). This

"Chugiak School with kids, 18 September 1955,"
McCutcheon Collection #9-603555, printed with permission
of Anchorage Museum of History and Art, Anchorage, Alaska.

highway passed through the nearby community of Eagle River, which also grew throughout the 1950s and 1960s. Eagle River even hosted the Eagle River Shopping Center, the first "mall" in the community, in 1955. Donna likely shopped at its various stores, including the Knick Knack Shop that served the community with "gifts, magazines, drugstore products," and even dry cleaning. The mall also hosted a complete grocery store, the Market Basket, as well as Hendrick's Hardware and a dentist's office. As recorded in Marjorie Cochrane's history of the area, *Between Two Rivers*, resident Ruth Briggs recalled that before the highway was paved, driving to Anchorage was difficult, "like driving over a gigantic muffin tin. You couldn't always avoid the holes and you couldn't go over 20 miles an hour."[5] With the new pavement, travel became instantly safer and much faster.

When Paul Swanson took over as postmaster in 1955, he moved the post office to Swanny Slopes. Locals came to the store and post office, but according to Margaret Swanson, "half the people didn't buy anything, they just came in to talk."[6] As postmaster, he quickly met everyone in the area and could organize parties and get-togethers quite easily. She laughed as she recalled, "And so people would come to the post office and say, 'Where is Chugiak?' and Paul would say, right here! And that's about all there was. There was just a few, the house we were living in and . . . we had a store first, with a post office in the store." The combination store and post office, situated just down the road from the school, had great ambiance. An old cottage-type log cabin, the front of the store had pictures drawn by school children tacked up all over the walls and windows. Paul enjoyed hanging up posters that the local schoolchildren drew. Everyone frequented the post office, and many a neighborly conversation took place there. The building still sits on the original lot across from the school and south a few paces, although it is no longer utilized as a post office.

With the community's endorsement, School Agent Paul Swanson acted as a liaison with the teachers and assisted them in finding housing. He even built cabins for the teachers to rent on Swanny Slopes. Paul ended up hiring people to assist him because, Margaret recalled, "he just had too many jobs." Besides being the school agent, he was also the bus driver, the postmaster, country storeowner, and local builder. Margaret remembered that Paul ended up moving several trailers onto his property across from the school because construction simply could not keep up with demand.

Paul had a sense of humor and likely made Donna and the other teachers feel at ease. At one time, he built a "swaying bridge" between his house's back porch to a tree. Out on the tree he built a little deck for his family and visitors to enjoy. Margaret described him as loving to build things, and that "he loved life, he loved people." Paul and Margaret Swanson were Donna's first friends when she moved to Chugiak. And even more than forty years after her death, Margaret remembers her fondly, as well as Donna's penchant for cooking the best pea soup she ever had. Margaret and Paul had the pleasure of knowing the "new" Donna, significantly more mature than the previous year.

From Chugiak, Donna's letters reflected a new seriousness and fresh outlook on life. No longer did she complain about roommate troubles, or fret about her job, the children, food shortages, or transportation issues. She did continue to deal with periodic illnesses and housing difficulties, but generally her letters seemed more positive. Her sister Joan suggested later that the letters illustrated her growing maturity. Her friend Tressie, who had also left Dillingham and moved back to Anchorage with her husband Guy, remembered that "She seemed to be happier in Chugiak."[7] Her childhood had trained her to make friends quickly, and so she developed close friendships in Chugiak, as well as continued friendships with Bobbie, Marty, and Tressie from her year in Dillingham. Tressie and Guy lived close by in Anchorage, so Donna visited or called Tressie on her own telephone, a marked improvement over Dillingham. In Chugiak, she kept in touch by mail with her friends Bobbie and Marty, who continued to work as missionaries for the Church of Christ in Dillingham. Donna jumped at the chance to visit her two friends at any opportunity. She kept tabs on them as well through Charles, who flew periodically to Dillingham to take Richard supplies.

Overall, Donna's letters from Chugiak were upbeat, and more matter-of-fact about her life. She no longer regularly described the community nor the people around her as she had so diligently while in Dillingham. Most of her charges were non-Native, after all, so her experience there did not seem exceptional or unique. The few Alaska Natives that did attend the school came from nearby Eklutna Village, an old Athabascan community of Tanaina Indians. Conceivably Alaska had also lost some of its novelty when it became a state in January 1959, both for Donna as well as her friends and family in Illinois. Now she lived in a community, not in the bush. She did not have to haul her water, use an "ugh" bucket, or watch sewage flow through the streets during break-up. She no longer struggled as a new teacher, having worked out many kinks in her teaching during the first two years. She figured out what worked and what did not. She had activities planned, songs orchestrated, and lessons ready. Joan recalled that Donna did not seem as pressured in Chugiak. As a result, Donna no longer wrote about staying at school until nearly midnight, or orchestrating music by hand. Most of the children were from military families or homesteaders, and discipline did not seem as problematic. Since several single teachers lived in the area, she therefore was not the only single white female in town. She was no longer the novelty, for Chugiak had had a music teacher before she arrived. Chugiak proved a very different experience than Dillingham, full of promise and adventure.

CHAPTER NINE

The Chugiak Interlude

Donna quickly established friendships with many of the young teachers who, like her, lived in the valley and rented a trailer or cabin on Swanny Slopes. Donna quickly settled into the new routine of teaching and church activities on the weekends, and spending time with Richard when he returned from completing work on Dillingham High School.

On that first fall Sunday in 1959 after she returned to Alaska, she attended the First Baptist Church in Anchorage. On the second Sunday, Richard arrived with a new kitten for Donna and took her to the First Alaska State Fair in Palmer, so she did not attend church. Richard enjoyed spending time with Donna when he returned from Dillingham. And Donna, while conflicted, enjoyed his camaraderie as well. (On one occasion, she admonished him for being late returning to Chugiak.) When they went to the State Fair, she wrote about her disappointment, "The county fairs in Illinois can do rings around this one." The one exhibit that particularly piqued her interest was the Singer Sewing Machine display. Singer had a store in Anchorage, but apparently the exhibit offered far better deals than the store. She bought a $240.00 model for $199.50, with the balance to be paid off in ninety days, "no carrying charge." She should have it paid off by the middle of December, she reported to her parents.

On the third Sunday, she planned to go to the little Baptist church in Eagle River with a fellow teacher, but she hoped that the fourth Sunday she could attend the Methodist church. The Chugiak Methodist Church, now located eighteen miles north of Anchorage on the Old Glenn Highway, first began as a committee of Chugiak's locals. They held their first church services, led by the young Reverend David Blackburn, in the Chugiak Community Hall on September 20, 1953, with a dozen parishioners—mostly from the Fetrow family. Reverend Blackburn served the small church until his departure to join the Board of Missions in 1959, when Reverend Wayne Hull took over as pastor. The church needed a more permanent structure for regular services, so with the help of the National Division of Missions of the United Methodist church, they purchased the Swanny Slopes Store, where they continued to meet until their new building was opened in 1960. The Methodist church drew Donna in, mostly because they needed a pianist and choir director. Part of her decision to join the Methodist church was loyalty to her father.

Donna had not intended to join the Methodist church immediately. She agonized in a few letters about whether or not she should have started going to the Southern Baptist church instead of the Methodist church to appease Richard. After all, if she married him, she would have to "convert." Upon attending the Chugiak Methodist church on September 23, she was immediately drawn into its family. She wrote her parents that the minister's wife was ill, so "guess who got to pound the ivories?" At first, Reverend Hull, who did not seem too friendly, did not overly impress her. Whatever her hesitation, by October 7 she wrote, "I'm the new music director—or maybe only pianist at Chugiak Meth[odist]. Rev. Hull came from Kenai—4 years—+ after getting to know him—I find him wonderful to work with. I think I'll be happy there. Had to go tell him I wouldn't be there Sunday though! . . . Rev. Hull and Mrs. will take me to Anchorage soon to meet Don Ebright [the president of the Alaska Methodist University which was being built just outside of Anchorage (now Alaska Pacific University)]. I guess I'll meet him yet. I'm a coward to do it on my own!" The church choir had two tenors, three sopranos (including Donna), three altos, and three basses. They were pretty good, too, she reported. Her choir practiced and performed, "with me singing sop[rano]. They sound real good for amateurs and I'm real proud of them." She also found herself playing the piano for a Methodist Youth Fellowship (MYF) party. "They had 32 kids. What bedlam. They're real noisey. They have no sponsors yet." She was proud of her new duties in the church as the music director and pianist.

Her valued role as the pianist and choir director far outweighed her need for Richard's acceptance or approval. The physical and growing spiritual distance between the pair, as well as Donna's growing strength and resolve in the face of Richard's love, gave her more confidence to deny him. She gained that confidence in standing up for herself and breaking up with her boyfriend either from experience or from the example of her friend and fellow teacher Carol Witherell. She also had begun envisioning her life and setting goals for her future, independent of a quick marriage and family. But this became more difficult, for by October, Richard had arrived for another visit from Dillingham. His presence seemed to diminish her resolve. These sentiments appeared in almost every letter.

> I'm still indecisive about Richard. Things seemed to have worked out and I had even begun to think of marrying the ape. Then I started to think about him more seriously and talking to others about it and I really don't think I could be happy with him. It seems to me I'm in love with love even tho I do like him a great deal. We fight—make up—fight make up etc. We can't seem to have any real fun together. . . . There are so many little things that would get in the way of our happiness. It's at times like this when I need a mother and dad around to help me out. I know I have to make my own decisions, but I sure could use a little advice. I have been thinking of going to Rev. Hull to have a chit-chat. But then I feel funny discussing things like that with him or anybody else even tho I know that's one of the things we should go to a minister about. I remember the times people came to see daddy. I should talk to someone. I'm afraid to give Rich the boot cuz then I'd feel like a heel hurting him so. But then I should think of my own happiness. He's probably half my trouble. So now I've got that off my chest.

She wished she had Carol's courage and strength to dismiss Richard from her life, but instead she felt trapped. Yet when he left for Dillingham, she missed him. She did receive some solace from her television, however, which drew visitors. "It keeps me from getting too lonesome, too." And she also had a beloved companion in the kitten that Richard had given her. Donna's letters often reported on the progress of her pet:

My baby has been growing so fast. She's already developed a monstrous appetite + even yowls for her supper. I closed the frig on her once—she was inside—monster! Yesterday I decided on a name—"Chena" (chee—na) which is an Alaskan name (Chena Slough—and also the Spanish term of endearment)! Good choice—thot I! All along I've been bragging that my nylons had never been snagged by her claws! My good luck has passed—Chena did it today! She loves to play outside and usually stays within a close distance of the trailer. Twice she has been chewed by a big collie.

While Donna wrote about Chena numerous times in her letters, fellow teacher Zona Dahlmann remembered Chena in a different manner. "It was a terrible kitten," she muttered under her breath. "It was an attack kitten. And it would attack her, too. Not just us. But it would go for the neck. It was an awful thing." Zona remembers seeing scars on Donna's hands and neck. Regardless of Chena's wild behavior, Donna and Chena had great fun together.

And there were many other opportunities for fun in Chugiak as well. Donna learned that the teachers in Chugiak were far more social than those in Dillingham. They took time to relax and enjoy each other's

Chena on ledge behind couch with driftwood, Fall 1959,
photograph taken by Donna McGladrey in Chugiak, courtesy of author.

company and they utilized whatever resources were available nearby. On one occasion, the teachers took advantage of the sub-flooring of one of Swanson's unfinished cabins to use as a square dance floor.[1] Swanson and his wife had thrown a picnic with wonderful food for the teachers on a particularly beautiful day, and Margaret recalled that the whole staff was there. An old yellowed photograph shows several young teachers dancing, and Donna dancing with fellow teacher Andy Kirk. On October 7, Donna wrote her parents about her new comrades: "We've done square dancing together twice as a group. It's a very congenial group and we have lots of fun together. Saturday we're having a Halloween party which is going to be a scream. I'm really looking forward to it." She enjoyed her new friends and seemed to worry less about Richard, who spent a great deal of time in Dillingham.

Donna wrote about her fellow teachers, "They are so friendly, nice thoughtful,—so unlike Dillingham last year. They cooperate beautifully with my plans at school too. Socially they are friendly too. The younger ones of us are doing all sorts of things together." She obviously enjoyed their friendship, and the Swansons' brilliant plan to bring them together worked out beautifully to create a sense of community. Donna wrote in one letter about the different teachers that she met at the school:

> Carol Witherell—5th grade—she's 23 or 4 and my best friend. Kind of short, very attractive in many ways, pleasing personality—having the same men problems I'm having (she has the guts to kick him out tho). Real vivacious and fun to be with. From NY—2nd year here—I'm going to give her piano lessons—we're getting Spanish records to study—good cook—we have dinner together often—trying to get her into my choir.
>
> Elaine Eggleston and Zona Miles—4th grade—single—teacherish—nice—pal together. Love skiing and sq[uare] dancing.
>
> Lori Lensing—28—been in Fort Yukon 2 years—funny—catholic—1st teacher.
>
> Mary Schwalen—getting married—cute—vivacious—2nd grade t[eacher]—fun to be with—talks your arm off.
>
> 3rd grade t[eacher] Mrs. Knight from Homer just married, plumb attractive, older.
>
> Mrs. Veach from Kodiak Island, older
>
> 1st grade t[eacher] Mrs. Emmert (Sup's wife—miserable teacher).

Mrs. Emmons—young mother.

2nd g[rade] t[eacher] Mrs. Barr—young married.

Mrs. Thompson—young mother from Minneap.

5th Mrs. D'Spain older nice early 30's.

6th Andy Kirk, young fellow just married having baby in a month—real nice. Mrs! Howard D'Spain ? character

7th—Mr. Morse young father working on homestead too. Mr. Veach ? Character.

8th—Mr. Pierce the guy getting my trailer.

Mr. McKinley—only bachelor—young good looking—uninterested in girls. just arrived from a stretch in army.

The small, close knit group of teachers leaned on each other for support, gave each other rides to the grocery store, and helped each other out with various chores when someone took ill. Donna enjoyed coffee in the evenings with her friend Mary, and group hikes to Thunderbird Falls. She particularly enjoyed her new best friend Carol.

After being such an integral part of her life in Dillingham, Richard must have felt left out. He spent much time that fall completing work on the Dillingham high school. Donna's growing sense of independence and self-reliance must have weighed on Richard as well. On October 4, Richard again returned from Dillingham and immediately invited her to go to his mother's homestead on the Susitna River for the upcoming weekend. Mrs. Stella "Eva" Newton's homestead was on the east bank of the Susitna River, just north of Susitna Station, not even a mile from the original Iditarod Trail.[2] Donna agreed to go because she loved an adventure.

When Donna had first met Mrs. Newton in Anchorage a month before, she described the pioneer woman as "rough and tough like Mrs. Wicker, but older and not so lively." Donna learned about Mrs. Newton's prior experience as a homesteader; she gave birth to Richard on their homestead near Dulce, New Mexico, where they lived in a cave in 1931. All grown up now and proud of his adventuresome mother, Richard looked forward to taking Donna to visit Eva on her homestead, a twenty minute plane ride, and then an hour by boat. To this fairly remote location, Donna planned to travel with Richard Newton and his friend and co-worker, Hermann Kroener. After school ended on Friday, October 9, Donna rushed home to her little trailer before the last class was even finished to eat a quick meal and prepare her baggage for the weekend at the homestead. She also had to find a place for her kitten Chena to spend the weekend. After all, in the back of her mind, Donna knew that a delayed return was a very distinct possibility. Alaskan weather could be very unpredictable.

In her long descriptive letter home to her parents, she exclaimed that the trip was "such fun, so exciting and adventurous." She started the weekend excursion by hopping into her beige Volkswagen Beetle and driving to meet Richard. Together they drove out to Merrill Airfield in Anchorage where they met Hermann Kroener and the pilot. After waiting only thirty minutes for clearance, they headed north into the air in the Cessna 175. Within only twenty minutes, they began to circle over what Donna described as a small a sandbar, or island, upon which they would land. Donna describe that it was "just long enough, wide enough, and smooth enough to land on safely." Out on the long sandbar, they then had to find a way to the eastern shore of the river where Mrs. Newton's homestead sat. They took a "small, green speed boat with motor" and headed to the homestead where Mrs. Newton awaited them. Donna described the Susitna River, upon which the sandbar sat, as "a slow moving stream of perhaps 50 yards in width." Another adventure had begun!

Once on the east shore, the trio ambled up a rather rough bank and, once they breached the more-level tundra, Donna spied the cabin,

or should I call it a tent. It had a tent or canvas roof and windows on one side with a door and a window on another side. The remaining two sides were blank wall made of second hand [wood] boards, [taken from the abandoned cabins in the former town of Susitna], canvas and a small window, which we removed. The inside view was even more startling. The floor was sod, or dirt, the walls as discribed and the majority of the place in a bit of disorder. There were three rifles and a pistol hanging around + with clothes on nails all around the sides. One bed was a mattress on top of an old spring on top of an army cot. This was the place I slept with Richard's mother. The boys took the bunks. Richard's friend, Hermann [Kroener], was the other boy.

Always referring to her as "Mrs. Newton," Donna did not change her September impression of her: a tough woman, but one understood the finer points of talking with strangers. For immediately upon their

Richard Newton and Donna McGladrey on way to
Mrs. Newton's Susitna homestead. October 1959.
Photograph by Hermann Kroener, courtesy of author.

arrival, the foursome engaged in lively conversation. Mrs. Newton fixed the group a meal on her old wood-burning stove, and then continued feeding wood to the hungry stove to keep the cabin warm. Mrs. Newton told a news reporter a few years later that she chopped three trees a day to keep her cabin warm during the winter months. As she hauled the wood behind her on a sled, she lugged a rifle with her for protection and in case she spotted (or was spotted as) a good meal along the way.

By 7:00 P.M., they had finished their meal and fatigue overcame them. Hermann, Donna reported, "pooped out and hit the hay" not long after they finished their meal. By 8:30 P.M., everyone else was in their bunk beds. But before Donna retired, she needed to relieve herself and asked where the outhouse was. They obliged her with a response and she went outside into the cold, starry night to investigate.

I found, however, it shouldn't be called an outhouse being as it is not a house. The little beauty is situated 25 yards from the cabin out in the middle of the yard on a slight rise. It consists of a box with a seat on it on a plank floor. During the day I found it more convenient to "go over the hill." But at night I felt perfectly alone and private. It is an odd feeling.

The next morning came early. By 6:00 A.M., her cabin mates were up and about. While she tried to "sack in" a little longer, she realized that she had to get up or she would have no breakfast. The previous day's work had left a gnawing hunger inside her belly; "Guess which I did!" she wrote. As Richard and Hermann scurried down to Susitna Station "to pull up their boat onto high ground," she must have had a conversation with Mrs. Newton about the history of the area. She wrote that Susitna Station "many years ago happened to be a thriving metropolis with a couple of a thousand people. It was the gold rush then and has long since been deserted. Homesteaders have torn down and burned the wood or used the wood from those houses for their own cabins. There are only a few signs anywhere that show it used to be a town." Hermann and Richard were gone several hours trying to maneuver the fifteen-foot boat onto higher ground, so she and Mrs. Newton had ample time to learn about each other. When the "boys" finally did return, all of them enjoyed lunch together. Donna wrote that her appetite had returned and she ate twice what she normally would have eaten. Her illnesses did not plague her, at least during this glorious weekend adventure.

After lunch, Hermann began chopping down trees while Richard and Donna stayed at the cabin, taking everything out from the inside. Richard had planned to install 2 x 4 plank flooring for the cabin. Unfortunately, the sun disappeared behind the horizon around 6:00 P.M., as it did that time of year, long before they could complete the job. So they just threw some plywood onto the floor and she described that "the beds and food came in while the remainder stayed out with the dogs." That evening, Hermann left on a plane that came to get him at 5:00 P.M. The pilot, likely Charles or Royce, had come for Hermann so that he could return to Dillingham and finish work on the high school. This actually pleased Donna, because it meant that she could have the upper bunk bed to herself. No more sharing with Mrs. Newton.

While they were working the next day, the temperatures dropped and the river began to ice over. "We expected more," Donna wrote, "but <u>not</u> what we got." Donna continued in her letter, describing

Sunday morning as rather "dreary. Nevertheless, we continued ou[r] job of rebuilding the cabin." Before noon, they decided they needed more wood, so they trekked down to the Station "again to get some that Mrs. Newton had had [in] her cabin there." They piled up a large amount of wood that they found and stacked it "on the top of a sled and fastening it with coat hanger wire we could drag it over the tundra back 1 and $^1/_2$ miles to the cabin. It was rough going but we made it." Thus they improved Mrs. Newton's cabin, as required by Alaska homestead laws.

Ominous warnings from the icing river forced Richard to recheck its condition. He tried to go out on the water in the boat, but could not. The ice grew to three-quarters of an inch thick and was therefore impassable. Richard hoped that as the day passed, the sun would thin the ice and they might reach the sandbar when the plane arrived later to take them to Anchorage. Unfortunately, as they were hauling the wood back to Mrs. Newton's "tent," it began to snow—and then it continued snowing all day. By afternoon, all three knew that even if the plane could make it to the Susitna sandbar in the storm, Donna and Richard would never be able to get to the sandbar by boat. Donna had come to expect these uncertainties of living in Alaska, and continued to work on Mrs. Newton's abode without becoming uptight about their situation.

Donna wrote, "The cabin began to take shape with one window gone, but a beautiful floor to make it even, and more substantial walls etc." She obviously took pride in the work that she did on the cabin. After they finished putting in the floor, they began to move all of Mrs. Newton's belongings back inside. Before they were finished, however, "the snow was several inches thick." Richard continued chopping logs that Hermann previously had cut and hauled to the cabin, but Donna was worn out. She went inside and "sacked out from exhaustion." They would spend another night on the Susitna River.

The next morning, they decided to prepare for their departure and began to "pack a path to the river with snow shoes. Then we tried the boat again. We got out about 6 feet and couldn't budge the silly thing an inch more so had to claw our way back to shore. It was in doing this that Richard lost his footing and fell in the ice and water up to his waist. He had to wear his Ma's jeans the rest of the day." While Richard worked in his mother's jeans hunting game and chopping wood, Donna sculpted a cat out of snow "that later crashed to its death when the sun got warmer." She wrote that it was "just pla[i]n gorgeous out. The weather was so clear the mountains (Susitna) seemed close enough to touch." Around 2:00 P.M., they were eating when they heard a plane fly overhead. Donna wrote that the Cessna's pilot had never actually landed on the sandbar before in "good weather without snow much less in snow," and after circling for more than twenty minutes, he "finally flew away." So much for their backup ride, Donna thought. Donna wrote, "By this time I had nearly resolved that the next two weeks would be spent up there." Uncertainty no longer sent Donna into a panic. She understood the conditions of living as a pioneer and was with people who knew how to survive in the wild.

While the Cessna circled, Richard decided that he would try one more time to get the boat out into the river.

> He was doing fine until he had reahced [*sic*] about 25 feet from shore and could get no further. The motor was so hot it just conked out. Rich had carried the canoe to higher ground earlier that morning so the paddles were not in the boat. He had only a board to paddle his way back thru the ice to shore. To help after 15–20 minutes I went up the hill and got the canoe which I put in the water and tryed to paddle out to him. His mother had ahold of my rope and finally we got the two crafts close enough together so that I could catch his rope. Thus was we got to dry ground again. Both crafts were then stored away for the winter.

Donna's experience canoeing at summer camp paid off and Donna had saved Richard from a foolish experience, one that could have been dangerous and potentially life threatening. So, besides having to wear his mother's pants all day, his girlfriend rescued him from an icy river. No doubt his male ego needed stroking that day. Richard returned to chopping wood, stacking it neatly along the walls of his mother's cabin to provide firewood, as well as extra insulation for the coming winter.

About two and a half hours later, Richard's brother Royce arrived in a Cessna and circled for nearly a half hour. After two attempts, he finally landed. Richard shouted to Royce that he and Donna could not cross the river in the boat due to the ice. Royce responded that they should haul the canoe overland one and a half miles to the Station "and try to paddle across there." Donna explained, "We were game to try anything."

> We pack our things and carried–dragged the canoe (Rich did) up

the trail. The land is swampy–tundra gook. With the snow on it you can't tell where the water is. I went half way to my knee in icy cold water several times before we reached our destination. Finally on shore we tried the canoe. It went into the water with the same trouble as before, but it wasn't such piled up ice and snow as in our part of the river. It took 10 minutes before we could navigate the canoe into the slushy ice in deeper water. I know the good Lord was with us. If he hadn't been we wouldn't be here. The paddling was extremely difficult and swimming in that ice would have been impossible. If we had capsized–let's not think of that. !!!!

She had cheated death once more. Once they reached the sandbar, they had to haul the canoe another mile to where the plane had landed on the north side of the "runway." When they arrived, they found Royce walking back and forth across the runway, trying to pack the snow so that the Cessna would have a slightly more firm surface for taxiing. They joined him, and for nearly a half hour, they trudged back and forth, packing down the snow. After they loaded the plane, they made five attempts to take off, but unfortunately the snow was still too thick and soft. The snow stuck to the wheels and froze up the landing gear. For the next hour and a half, they utilized a gas stove to alternately heat and cool the tires to get the snow and ice off of them so they could take off. During this time, Donna sat inside the plane and tried to stay warm. She wrote that "I was freezing the whole time until they brot the heater inside." She had also worked up quite an appetite during that long and very tiring day. Knowing that all bush pilots in Alaska prepare for the worst, she headed to the back of the plane where the Newtons stored extra blankets, an axe, guns, fuel, matches, and other survival items. She found a can of chili and had a "bit to eat." In just the few days they were on the Susitna, they had already lost nearly a half hour of daylight, and when the sun lowered onto the horizon, she became more nervous: "the sun had set, the fog had rolled in, and the moon had risen in all its glory." At least Royce was an experienced pilot. In fact, he was the only of the three Newton brothers who actually had a pilot's license and instrument ratings. He knew how to fly in the dark, and could fly without the benefit of having to actually see the topography in order to navigate them safely home. But even experienced pilots can have difficulty landing and taking off on snowy sandbars in the middle of icy rivers in the darkness. In clear exhilaration and perhaps genuine relief that they had not ended up in the icy river, she wrote, "We tried again–nope–once more–HURRAH!!!! We were in the air. The flight was uneventful and enjoyable and beautiful. Anchorage from the air is really a sight to behold." She wrote that her "beautiful car was sitting there waiting for me and I was headed homeward in a very few minutes." But the harrowing tale was not yet over.

The roads from Anchorage to Eagle River and Chugiak had also felt the wrath of Mother Nature and were blanketed with snow and ice. Donna drove north out of Anchorage with relatively few problems along the Old Glenn Highway, but she described the roads farther north: "The road going down into Eagle River is a very treacherous road and hill in dry weather and was just deadly last night with that ice. I was only going 15 mph and had the engine in 2nd and still I slide. I thot I was heading for a stone wall once and then over the cliff another. I made the hill safely, but slide 7 more times in the next 10 miles." Donna's weekend had finally come to a close when she drove up the road to her little trailer. She had many close calls that weekend, and reconsidered her mortality several times. She explained that it was "about all my nerves could take. I swallowed two tranquilizers when I got home and sat down with Mary to talk with a hot cup of coffee." Donna was so tired when her head finally hit her pillow that she fell asleep immediately, forgetting to shut her window. She wrote that when she woke up at 7:00 A.M. the next morning, she was "in the same position with the window wide open. I have never slept so soundly."

She told her family and friends, "It was an experience that will stay with me the whole of my life." She lamented that she would be penalized a day's pay for missing school, but she wrote that she did not mind. In fact, she awoke that "morning wishing I was out at the homestead instead of in town knowing I had to go to work." She relished the memory of her experience, even though she was on the edge of disaster. It took her over an hour to construct her letter home, underscoring for her family and friends back in Illinois the importance of the trip in comparison with her plain life as a teacher in Chugiak. She finally had another unique frontier experience on Mrs. Newton's homestead. Apparent in her letters was her love of the "wilds." She later wrote about her desire to homestead herself some day, or to boat down the Yukon River from the Canadian border. But that would have to wait.

When she returned to the classroom, Donna continued to sharpen her skills as a music teacher. In Dillingham and Northbrook, she had tested techniques, lesson plans, and methods of reaching students. As she perfected her style, she rarely complained about her students, their lack of attention or experience with music, or her frustration in finding or hand-copying and orchestrating music. She had finally found her niche. Of the nearly five hundred students in the first to eighth grades, only a few of them were Eklutna Indians. Most of the children came from families in the surrounding valleys, many of whom lived on homesteads or worked for the military.

On rare occasions, she mentioned her progress with various classes. She told her parents that she taught forty-five classes per week (nine classes a day), ten of them being first- and second-grade P.E. She told her family that she would not spend much time on those classes at all, rather they would play games and do exercises. It turned out that the new job required her to teach more than just music, one of the very reasons that she left Dillingham months before. She described her worries about teaching the boys in the seventh and eighth grade. After all, they had caused her so much grief during the previous year in Dillingham. She was relieved considerably when Superintendent Emmert told her that she would not have to include those boys in music lessons. The previous teacher had far too many problems with the boys, he explained, so the music teachers no longer had to teach them. She therefore decided to combine the girls in seventh and eighth grade and then bragged in letters about their excitement to learn music and sing. Donna obviously enjoyed her students, "I'm writing songs for the first grade. They need songs that fit the subjects they talk about. Like being clean, brushing teeth, etc." She included the lyrics to one of the songs, which highlighted their classroom turtles.

Besides reporting less on the students than the previous year, she also did not seem as interested in recording residents' daily life, which she had found so interesting in Dillingham. Could it be that the Anglo-Americans that surrounded her simply did not provide as much of a counterpoint to her own experiences? Likely. Even though Chugiak's residents seemed far more "civilized" than her Dillingham students did, Donna's impression was partly due to the fact that she could not see their primitive living conditions; many of the children lived on homesteads that she never saw. Fourth-grade teacher Zona Dahlmann remembered how her class had a big celebration because "one little girl, well the Thompsons, they got water and she was able to take a bath in the bathtub. Probably her first real bath in a real bathtub. That was cute." The kids all lived pioneer lives, some of them raising goats and many of them living on homesteads.

Zona remembered how Donna came to her quonset hut to teach singing, for instead of having a music room, Donna visited each homeroom to teach music.[3] The teachers could participate if they wanted to do so. Zona described Donna as a beautiful blonde, but she did not remember too much about Donna socially. Zona remembered a lot of single teachers in Chugiak at the time, they had "a fun group . . . about five of us, and so we really had a good time together." While in Zona's classroom, Donna taught the children how to sing rounds and catchy tunes, and began to try to convince the children that their parents should purchase musical instruments. Superintendent Emmert later would tell Donna's father Leslie that she had been doing "an outstanding job in music." Mr. Emmert appreciated Donna's hard work and ability to engage the children.

Another difference that Donna noted between Dillingham and Chugiak was nature itself. While the weather did not seem as drastic as Dillingham, other aspects of the valley proved tiresome. They still received snow in Chugiak and, because they were located in the low mountains, they had to contend with snow and ice on the hilly roads leading in and out of Chugiak. The sparse settlement pattern along the Old Glenn Highway left much of nature to the moose and other wild animal populations. The highway wound its way from Anchorage to Palmer and beyond. But in the Eagle River and Chugiak area, the Old Glenn Highway snaked through narrow valleys, along beautiful lakes like Mirror Lake and Fire Lakes, and past dirt and rock driveways that disappeared into the thick forests of birch and pine. The houses, often located above the road a few yards or several hundred, were hidden completely by the dense forests that blanketed the mountains and hills.

Odd looking but beautiful spindly-legged creatures, moose were prolific in the area. In one letter, Donna reported that she saw five moose, and while driving her car almost hit a cow with its calf. Moose could be particularly dangerous if challenged. They had been known to trample and even kill adults, as well as charge and damage vehicles. Probably the most common excuse for missing school was illness, but another excuse was moose. Schoolchildren would walk down their winding driveways, through rain or snow or shine, and wait for the school bus to pick them up along the highway. Sometimes, however, the bus driver arrived at a driveway and no child appeared from behind the thickets. Without worrying too much, the driver waited a few moments, then continued along the rest of his route. Parents taught their children that if they spotted a moose they should turn quickly around and return home—catching the school bus was not worth risking a moose charge.

Although Donna luckily never hit a moose, she did worry about driving on the steep grades, narrow bridges, and slippery, icy, and snowy roads in the winter. And she loved to drive; in the first twelve days that she had her car, she had already put 1,050 miles on it. By October 13, after she returned from Susitna, more than 1,700 miles: "my car is gorgeous and does a good job." She began to plan more car trips, to Homer and Valdez, before the weather turned. Always up for an adventure, she looked back at her days on the Susitna homestead with longing, planning for new adventures where time and weather would allow.

Having a car and being so near Anchorage also gave her opportunities to spend her well-earned money. In Dillingham she made money, but she had no place to spend it. In Chugiak, she had caught up on her bills and had money to spare. She guiltily confessed to her parents that she had purchased an eighteen-dollar beautiful sterling silver bracelet with a large hematite stone in it. "It is finely carved—intricate and gorgeous." She planned to buy earrings and a ring to match. She had a chance to enjoy her money; however, she also learned the reverse side of buying too much: "My trailer seems to be getting smaller and smaller. All the junk I have just won't fit in. With sewing machines, typewriter, record players (Rich's), records, box of knitting, box of materials, etc. there's no room to walk." She further explained that her living room served also as the kitchen. Her bed folded up into a couch, she had a table with leaves, a refrigerator with a large freezer. She had a sink, a gas stove with an oven and broiler, and a long shelf for books behind the sofa, on which she placed one of her prized possessions, a really unique piece of driftwood she had found on the beach.

Excited about her sewing machine she had purchased at the fair and her ever-more-crowded pink and white trailer, she told her family about other big changes in her life. She wrote that she moved into a bigger trailer on October 15, something that she had looked forward to greatly! She described it in detail. "It has a lean-to on it and has so much closet space I can't use it all. There is a big front room with a large kitchen–huge frig–a middle room with bunks–a bath with tub–and the bedroom. . . . A deep freeze, TV, washing machine, and vacuum cleaner are also mine to use." In the same letter, she also wrote that Mr. Pierce, the eighth-grade teacher, and his family had been living in a dreadful quonset hut, and now wanted her new trailer. She seemed frustrated with him, for he previously had the opportunity to claim the trailer, but did not. Because he had a family, she learned that he had priority and she soon found herself removed from her home. She had no choice, but luckily the alternative trailer was a good one. It had belonged to her friend Mary who was getting married in two weeks, or early November. After Donna finished sewing a new dress, she held a shower for Mary, complained about having no time, then prepared for the move.

She could not seem to release her anger about being forced to move. In late October, she described the tension regarding the move: "Everybody expects me to and I'd feel like a heel if I didn't. I'm finally settled too. I'm so tired. I'm tired of being unsettled, I'm tired of living alone, I'm tired of so many things, I'm homesick, I'm lonely, I feel ghastly, I want to come home for Christmas and I can't, etc." Frustrated by her incapacity to stand up for herself and the uncertainties that brought, Donna developed insomnia. Even worse, she told her family that she had developed hives on her arms, face, eyelids, and lips, as well as places where elastic or tight clothing pressed against her body. She bought Calamine lotion, but it did not seem to help. She reported that she suffered through the night itching, for her hives seemed to be getting worse. As if life had not dealt her enough blows, Donna was told that Chena likely caused her allergies.

Donna's adoration of her pet was evident in the attention she gave Chena in her letters. "She's a calico . . . and the cutest, most loveable, playfullest, sweetest, gee she's cute!" Donna described Chena as a very good kitten who was already housebroken. Chena greeted her at the door with a cry, then "won't stop crying until I pick her up and give her sufficient loving. My face, nose, ears, etc. get a thorough bath with a pink tongue every day." Regardless of the happiness that Chena brought to Donna, however, her doctor suggested that she find a temporary home for Chena, as well as give up coffee and chocolate from her diet. She had already been off of chocolate due to the canker sores that broke out in her mouth. The cankers remained though, because as she admitted, "I couldn't keep my grubby mits off the chocolate." She feared, however, that the doctor was correct. "Now isn't that awful. . . . Me–the one who loves cats and especially Chena more than anything and I get allergic to her. How ironic."

With Richard in Dillingham, Donna did not have him available to care for her. And when Richard did not return as scheduled to Anchorage in early November, she worried. He did not call or write her either. She loved her independence and thought she wanted to break up, but once without him, she became anxious and worried, "I don't know what to do about Rich. . . . I think often that I do want to get married, but then I have my doubts about him. The more I think about it the more I'm afraid that because he was divorced that maybe part of it was his fault and I'm afraid that if I married him it might happen again." She told her parents that when he returned, she would hash it out with him. Richard must have asked Donna to marry him, or she would not have added that if they decided to marry, it would be in Illinois at Christmas. She decided that her father would perform the ceremony, which she had to know would be unacceptable to Richard, who was very devoted to the Baptist church in Anchorage, thereby dooming the very idea of a wedding to certain failure.

By mid-November, her life became more frustrating and complicated. She began to worry about completing the eleven school programs before Christmas, adding that she could not seem to get everything done. She still had to orchestrate all of the pieces, as well as train the children to play their parts. She lamented that she had finally gotten around to washing clothes, a chore long overdue, she reported, but now had to iron the clothes before she could wear them. By November 18, she had to move again so that the Pierce family could occupy her trailer. Once she vacated her larger trailer for a much cuter place with a TV, washing machine, and lower rent, the Pierces decided they did not want the other trailer. After a few days, they moved back out of the trailer they had forced her to evacuate. She was "just plain furious. . . . I got not one word of thanks from them or help. Grrr." Even more, when she retrieved Chena from the boarders, her hives almost instantly returned. To add injury to insult, she slipped on the stairs at school going down to visit her friend Carol in the cafeteria and bruised her tailbone badly. So that Friday, she headed to Anchorage to see an osteopath, but had to settle for a chiropractor because of an unreasonable two-hour wait. She felt better for a few days, but by the following Tuesday, her back caused her great pain again. After another visit to the chiropractor, she was worse off. Luckily, the school insurance paid for her treatments, but it took many more days to get over the pain. This series of bad events did not seem to dampen her spirits. Donna seemed able to find the silver lining to any cloud of misery. On her way back to Chugiak from treatment, she marveled at the beauty of the northern lights whose green luminescence was "absolutely dancing all over," including that she had become a pro driving on ice. She also added that her Methodist church choir had done a wonderful job the previous Sunday, their debut. They were "scared to death. They sure are a nice bunch. We have lots of fun." The key to understanding Donna during the last months of 1959, lay in her frustrations and hardships with health and her uncanny ability to find real joy and happiness in her daily activities and the land and people around her.

More importantly, she told Richard that she was not ready to get married. "There didn't seem to be any hope. As far as I was concerned it is off. It nearly killed him." She conceded that they could still go out together as friends, "He knows where he stands and it'll be a lot easier on me." Then she moved on to talk about the upcoming holiday season. She and four other teachers had been invited to spend Thanksgiving at the home of her friends Jim and Bea at The Lakes. Before dinner, she had her Thanksgiving Programs. She had the first through fourth grades perform together. The older kids, whose former "old school" teacher had used fear tactics to make the children behave, decided that they would "show him [their former teacher] up. They were all so perfect I nearly dropped my teeth! That program went so well! Just a pure Utopia! I was tickled to death." The kids loved Donna, and they enjoyed music, and this combination of performance and stellar behavior boosted Donna's confidence. After the program, she stopped at the store and then continued on to the Thanksgiving dinner with Jim, Bea, and the other teachers. "I'll feel like I'm home maybe." The photographs from The Lakes on Thanksgiving show a happy Donna surrounded by friends.

After Thanksgiving, the pace of her life quickened. On November 30 she jotted a few hurried lines to her family. Her back was better, her hives were nasty, she got paid, she and her friends planned to go skiing, and she had three programs to get ready by the upcoming Friday. Donna fretted that the kids would not be ready! On Thursday, Mrs. Don Ebright would speak at the WSCS and at PTA on Tuesday night. Then the Hulls would take Donna into Anchorage and she hoped that she

Thanksgiving at The Lakes near Chugiak, Donna is on the far right, photograph courtesy of author.

would be invited to see the Ebright's "museum house." She ended her letter home by promising that she would try to send a tape for Christmas, and perhaps even call if her whole family gathered together at Christmas.

The fevered pitch of semester's end began to wear Donna down. By December 9, she had developed the flu. She was terribly sick and missed school that day and, unlike in Dillingham, regretted it terribly. "I'm crying for more time anyway–then I have to miss a day." She was terribly nervous about the programs on December 17 and 18. Perhaps some of her illness was due to her expedition to the Military Ski Bowl with some of her gal pals. Four of them had rented skis and hired an instructor. They learned all about climbing up a hill and skiing down. She said that she fell a thousand times and her muscles were so weak that she did not do well. The ski bowl had seven different towlines on the hills, she wrote, and she looked forward to skiing again really soon.

Recovering from her ski trip and in bed with the flu, Donna began thinking about Christmas. She had already received packages from family members and sent to them the gifts she had purchased. She looked forward to the Christmas party that would be held on the seventeenth at school. She became anxious about money again, and talked about refinancing her VW car at twenty-four months after Christmas. On Christmas Eve, she penned a letter to her family. She opened her gifts that night, and immediately sat down to write thank-you notes. Her parents had sent her a check for eighteen dollars, which she planned to use to help pay for medical costs for Chena. Donna reported that at lunch the day before, she had found a seriously wounded Chena, apparently hit by a truck on the highway. She ran to her trailer and called Richard, begging him to take her to a "Dr. and he told Rich she would be okay, but he would take xrays. Her insides were not working well–no control over certain organs–and she dragged her right hind leg. She was in pretty bad shape." Unfortunately, she had to go back to school that afternoon, where she had "a terrific time controlling my tears . . . I've never loved a pussy so much." Even as her Chena suffered at the doctor's office with severe injuries, Donna did receive a tidbit of good news on that tragic day: eggs, not Chena, were the cause of her hives. Nevertheless, the good news was tempered by the fear she would lose her beloved Chena.

Besides the check from her parents, Donna received a beautifully decorated handmade parka from Richard. The Dillingham seamstress who had made her mukluks also made the parka, with matching mouton and wolf fur trim. Her parka would keep her warm in the frigid Alaska winter. And that winter had been particularly harsh, with a large amount of snow. Several times drifts had buried her car, and the snow was so deep that mountainside snowdrifts slid onto the highway. Her electricity had even gone off a few times. But the snow and lack of electricity did not keep her from celebrating Christmas. On Christmas Eve, she went Christmas caroling with a group from church, being drawn about town in a horse-drawn wagon—her mukluks and new "parkie" keeping her toasty warm.

She explained to her family that although church began at 6:00 A.M. on Christmas morning, it technically was not a sunrise service. After all, the sun did not come up until 9:30 A.M. that time of year. Her solo, "O Holy Night," was a repeat of her previous week's performance. Just like her seventh- and eighth-grade classes did in their Christmas program, she sang it in both French and English. After the service, she planned to have breakfast at her house with Richard, then drive with him to visit with his oldest sister Grace for the day. Joe, Grace's husband, and her son Bill and his wife Audie would be there with their two kids. She expected that Royce and his wife Ruby and their daughter would come as well, along with Charles, Mary, and their five kids. Donna also heard that Mrs. Stella Eva Newton would fly in from her homestead to spend Christmas with her family. Donna had laid down the new platonic boundaries for Richard, and even though she told her family that he wanted to buy her an Art Carved "Evening Star" ring, it was unclear in her letter if he ever did. Surprisingly, she lamented that as much as she wanted to have the ring, she would rather take the money and send it to her parents for plane tickets to visit her in Alaska. She insinuated that she and Richard were talking about getting together again, perhaps even getting married. She wrote, "Would you be terribly disappointed if I decided to get married up here some time this spring without you here? There is a chance, we hope." He had wiggled his way back into her life again, but then in an afterthought, as if she was once again struck by reality, "Well, we'll see how things turn out later."

CHAPTER TEN

Disappeared

Donna finished the semester and once again began to feel the lone-liness of frontier life. While she loved Alaska, she missed her family—even her kitten could provide no solace. With Chena still recovering at the veterinarian's clinic, her trailer seemed so empty and she wondered how she could fill her days until the next semester began and Chena returned. Then she learned that Richard would soon fly to Dillingham to repair various heating and plumbing items at the high school tagged by building inspectors. It would be a quick trip, for the school needed to open in early January. Richard knew that Donna missed her family, and he could alleviate her loneliness by taking her to Dillingham to visit Bobbie and Marty. The hours during the flight would give them an opportunity to spend quality time together. Even though he was a student pilot without permission to fly with passengers, Richard took pity on Donna and invited her to fly with him to Dillingham.

Although nervous about flying over so much uninhabited territory and through such steep mountain passes in the winter, on Wednesday, December 30, 1959, Donna drove her little beige Volkswagen Beetle from her Chugiak trailer down the Glenn Highway, taking Airport Road to the main entrance of Merrill Field. She parked her beloved car at Barton Air Service, where she met Richard. Richard had come from his brother Charles and sister-in-law Mary's house earlier that day. His brothers, Charles and Royce Newton, attempted to convince Richard not to fly that day. After all, the CAA had issued warnings about weather conditions farther west, grounding planes at Merrill Field. Richard was undeterred because he needed to make the necessary repairs before school was to open a week later, and he wanted to spend time with Donna. So Richard and Donna waited out the warnings at Peggy's Diner across the street, frequented for years by waylaid pilots. The two sat and enjoyed conversation and coffee from after 10:00 A.M. until just after 2:00 P.M. when the CAA cleared Richard to depart.

While Richard and Donna waited at Peggy's, Richard called his friend and co-worker Don Wagner and reported that they were grounded and awaiting clearance. Don remembered that cold day where only a few hours of sunlight would guide them to Dillingham, knowing that a few hours delay could spell disaster for Richard and his unreported passenger.[1] Don urged Richard not to fly, rather to wait until the next day when he would have more hours of light and less possibility of hitting bad weather. Both Mary and Ruby Newton, who had by then joined Grace's family in Anchorage for Christmas, recalled Royce and Charles trying to get Richard to come back to the house and leave the next day. They insisted that he would have, at most, two and a half hours of sunlight left, meaning that even with favorable conditions, Donna and Richard would still be flying well after sunset. If the pair encountered a strong headwind, the trip could take more than four hours. With the sun rapidly approaching the horizon, Richard would be stuck over the inhospitable tundra in the dark. But he likely had "get homitis," according to local Dillingham pilot John Paul Bouker, and undeterred by his family and friends, the two headed back to Merrill Field. Why Donna would have flown with him that day is a mystery, but it possibly could have been a combination of her being desensitized to the near-death excursions she had already survived, the potential loss of Chena, and the opportunity to see her beloved friends Bobbie and Marty.

After checking their aircraft for fuel and necessary supplies, Richard and Donna boarded the family company's cream, silver, and red Cessna 175 and taxied toward the runway. Waiting for other planes that had also heeded CAA warnings, they sat patiently on the tarmac for the traffic to clear. When they hit the runway, Richard opened up the throttle and soon they soared above Anchorage and headed west across Knik Arm just outside of Elmendorf Air Force Base's controlled air space, toward Figure Eight Lakes. While crossing the Susitna Flats (River), Donna peered north to see if she could find the sandbar upon which they had landed to visit Mrs. Newton only a few weeks before. Then Richard angled the plane southwest, flying parallel to Cook Inlet's shoreline, passing Tyonek, an old Alaska Native village. Tyonek signaled that they were halfway to Lake Clark Pass. They continued flying over mostly flats, which McArthur River, Kustatan River, Bachatna Creek, and a myriad of other creeks and streams crossed before dumping into Redoubt Bay.

After spotting Black Peak off the right wing and Big River Lakes to the left, he followed the North Fork past Double Peak which sat at 6,818 feet, looming silently from the low clouds on his left. Shortly thereafter they navigated Lake Clark Pass, where Tanaina Glacier dropped down out of the mountains, meeting another glacier that wound its way precariously north from the higher reaches of Double Glacier, beyond which Redoubt Glacier majestically sat. Immediately past Lake Clark Pass rested Summit Lake, covered by snow. Once safely through the Chigmit Mountain range, which hosted the 10,197-foot Redoubt Volcano, and 10,016-foot Iliamna Volcano farther south, Richard picked up the Tlikakila River, which guided him south and west to Lake Clark, a long and narrow lake shouldered by majestic mountain ranges on either side. With Port Alsworth in view on the south lakeshore, he knew he was halfway to Dillingham. So far, the flight had taken them nearly two hours, for they fought a steady wind, slowing their progress.

The amazing vistas, as Donna had described them on past flights, must have been incredible. As the Cessna 175 followed the south side of Lake Clark, they flew near Kontrashibuna Lake, near Port Alsworth, where they could have peered out their left windows to see Lake Iliamna and the communities of Nondalton, Iliamna, and Newhalen. They likely then followed the north shore of the lake, skirting the tiny village of Igiugig, situated on the southeast shore of Lake Iliamna and at the headwaters of the Kvichak River.[2] Richard could fly, but only if guided by the geographic features below him. He had flown across this tundra numerous times hauling equipment, workers, and fuel to Dillingham between 1958 and 1959. This trip should have presented no new challenges, but both understood Alaska's unpredictability. Besides confronting headwinds, Richard realized that since he and Donna had started so late in the day, he had run out of daylight. About the time Richard realized that he would soon lose visuals of the terrain to darkness, they entered a blinding snowstorm.

Richard and Donna had left Merrill Field shortly after 2:00 P.M. The

Lake Clark Pass near Lake Clark, Alaska,
photograph taken by Donna McGladrey, courtesy of author.

trip could take up to four hours, depending upon the weather conditions, which would force Richard to fly the last hour or so without the
benefit of daylight. If Richard did get blown off course, or just simply
a little disoriented because of the storm, he would have searched to
establish visual contact with Nushagak River near Ekwok, on the regular flight plan. If he could see neither, he might have looked instead to
find the next closest river, potentially the Kvichak River. If he had established sight with the Kvichak River, he might have followed it, hoping to
find Kvichak Bay, then skirt the coastline west until he found the mouth
of the Nushagak, which he could then follow north to Dillingham. He
likely also hoped to establish radio contact with King Salmon whose
equipment supported a range of forty miles in clear weather. The strong
winds had blown him off course, but he had not realized it because of
the storm and darkness. Richard's maps with the established flight pat-
terns clearly marked would not have helped him. As soon as he could,
Richard established radio contact with CAA's Lt. Earl Gay at King
Salmon (later of the Federal Aviation Administration, or the FAA) and

reported the dangerous situation into which he had flown his Cessna 175. Richard reported that he was lost, identifying himself by his plane's N-number, "9332–Bravo."

In Donna's album, Verna McGladrey carefully pasted a report that included information about Richard's last transmission from the Cessna 175. The summary below was FAA Lt. Earl Gay's report, referring to Greenwich Mean Time (GMT) beginning at 310250, or 4:50 P.M. local Dillingham time, just six minutes after the sun had set:

0250   Received a call from N9332 stating that he was lost and requested radar bearing.

0251   Advised radar. Radar very dubious of results due to snow storm.

0254   Requested heading and signal being received.

0257   Pilot advised 030 degrees. Receiving dot-dash signal.

0258   Gave pilot King Salmon altimeter (Air Force base) and requested he fly heading of 250 degrees and determine if getting gain or fade on a signal. Also instructed pilot to turn receiver low so that gain or fade would be easily discernible.

0301   Pilot advised dot-dash gaining in volume. Requested hold heading 250 to further orientate. Requested if in visual contact with ground. Reply negative.

0305   Pilot reported signal increasing; Aircraft now believed to be in east A quadrant of King Salmon Range.

0307   Requested altitude and inquired if pilot could fly straight and level on gyron. Explained use might be necessary if unable to fly visual contact. Pilot advised artificial horizon and gyro available but that he was not familiar with use. Pilot reported signal increasing in volume.

0310   Pilot advised at 600 ft. and passing over lake shore. Country appeared to be flat. Forward visibility 1/4 mile due to snow.

0315   Suggested change course to 295 degrees believing aircraft was approaching Sugar Loaf Mt. Lack of altitude immediate danger.

0317   Suggested change course to 360 degrees and standby to intercept northeast leg of King Salmon Range. Explained signals that would be received crossing leg.

0319   Pilot advised to climb to 1000–1500 ft. if possible. Explained altitude would assist radar in obtaining bearing.

0321   Pilot reported 1500 ft. maximum due to overcast.

0322   Pilot reported compass gyrating. Advised pilot to observe artificial horizon and to bring wings level and up to bar. Assumed aircraft in spiral!

0323   Pilot reported aircraft straight and level. Heading 240 degrees. (Note. Although calls were repeated for the next 10 minutes, no further contacts were made by King Salmon radio.)

They had maintained radio contact for more than a half hour.

The transcript tells a harrowing tale of Lt. Gay trying to guide a confused pilot safely home. At 4:50 P.M., Richard reported he was lost. The sun had set in Dillingham at 4:44 P.M.; therefore, Richard would have had a difficult time reestablishing visual contact with geographic features, especially in the storm. By 4:57 P.M., Richard reported a heading in relation to the signal from King Salmon that indicated he was headed back toward Anchorage, or perhaps more accurately, the Kenai Peninsula.[3] Since he was not trained to fly using the navigational instruments, he likely had no idea whether his 030 degree heading would or would not take him to Dillingham. Perhaps Lt. Gay thought Richard had overshot Dillingham, and he thought he needed to return on an eastern heading. Even if the pilot could find his way in the dark, he also would be running low on fuel if he had overshot Dillingham by any great length. By this point Richard and Donna had already been in the air approximately three hours. Lt. Gay requested that Richard change headings by 220 degrees, turning the aircraft in nearly the opposite direction, to see if the radar would become stronger or weaker. The signal did become much stronger, but this was of little comfort as Richard still could not make visual contact with the ground. Donna must have been squirming in her seat by this point, knowing that the approaching darkness had caused Richard to become disoriented, that the storm likely would not weaken, and that they were running out of fuel. Like other bush pilots, they carried a supply of fuel with them—since fuel service stations in Dillingham charged exorbitant amounts for their supply. But they would have to land safely to add fuel—an unlikely proposition if Richard was indeed lost. Donna and Richard probably quietly, but fervently prayed that God would help them find their way safely. If the storm would just let up, Richard could make visual contact with the ground and regain his bearings.

At 5:10 P.M., Richard advised Lt. Gay that he saw the shore of a lake.

Fairly certain of Richard's location, Gay had immediate concern that his altitude of six hundred feet placed the plane in imminent danger of slamming into the side of Sugar Loaf Mountain just northeast of King Salmon, and he advised Richard to adjust his flight path to a northeastern direction. A few moments later at 5:15 P.M., Gay again advised a change to due north to keep Richard from potentially flying over Kvichak Bay and putting himself in further peril. At this new heading, Gay explained how the signals would change as he passed west and north of King Salmon. Gay also suggested that Richard climb altitude in order for the radar to continue carrying the signal, and Richard climbed as high as conditions allowed him. Within a moment, Richard reported his compass gyrating. Gay's instruction to "observe the artificial horizon," an instrument that indicates the plane's attitude in relation to the ground, and to bring the wings level and "up to bar," indicated that he suspected that the plane was in a spin and he was attempting to help Richard level the plane. At 5:23 P.M., Richard reported he had recovered and was headed west. No further communications occurred after this, regardless of ten desperate attempts by Gay. He was sure the plane had crashed, but did not know the condition of the pilot. He had no idea that Donna was in the plane, for student pilots were not supposed to carry passengers (although many Alaskans did during those years). Due to darkness and weather conditions, he knew that recovery efforts could not begin until daylight, some sixteen hours away. This experience had to be emotionally and psychologically devastating for Gay, who tried throughout the evening to communicate with the plane.

Not long after Richard's last transmission, news of their disappearance reached Dillingham. Bobbie and Marty had hoped that their dear friend would arrive soon to share the New Year's celebration with them, attend the Church of Christ, and perhaps participate musically in services, as Donna regularly had when she lived in Dillingham. But as a deep fog developed on the horizon and swept into Dillingham, followed by a dizzying snowstorm, Bobbie and Marty in all likelihood began to worry. On that cold, blustery Wednesday evening, Bobbie and Marty likely prayed that Donna and Richard had changed their minds and decided not to travel on such a dangerous day. But without the Weather Channel, the internet, GPS, and accurate and updated storm reports, conceivably Richard had no idea what kind of storm he would encounter. As women began to prepare their evening meals, the men fired up the sweat baths. Children tangled underfoot, refusing to do their chores, and Bobbie and Marty prayed for their community and their young friend.

When Bobbie and Marty learned that Donna and Richard had indeed left Merrill Field, they feared the worst. Looking out their windows, they saw what other Dillingham residents later recalled: the snowstorm was howling and the snow created nearly whiteout conditions. Marie Andrews remembered that it was a very "foggy stormy" day. They prayed, however, that if the plane had gone down, Richard and Donna somehow survived and could utilize the tools, fuel, food, and other supplies on board to survive. In the back of the Cessna, the Newtons had stashed large containers of fuel, a tent, food for a week, rifle, shotgun, pistol, ammunition, axe, matches, tent, and sleeping bags, according to one newspaper report. Both were dressed in clothing for the Arctic conditions; Donna likely sported her new winter parka and matching mukluks. With the survival supplies and ammunition for hunting, Richard and Donna theoretically could have survived for several weeks—if indeed they had survived the crash.

The little Cessna disappeared on Wednesday evening, and on Thursday morning (New Year's Eve, 1959) friends and family began frantically, but methodically, to organize a search—something Dillingham had done dozens of times before for friends, neighbors, and complete strangers. The search concentrated on an area including Dillingham, King Salmon, and Cape Constantine on Bristol Bay west of Dillingham, north along the east side of the Ahklun Mountains (where Wood-Tikchik State Park is located now). The parameters ran as far north as Nuyakuk Lake and ran east along the river that bears the same name. The search boundary turned south at approximately Stuyahok, where the Stuyahok River empties into the Mulchatna River. The boundary continued south to where a vector west would bring a pilot south of Egegik by about ten or so miles.

The *Bristol Bay News* reported that on December 30 Donna and Richard disappeared. "It was snowing and a strong southeast wind cut visibility to less than one-eighth of a mile in King Salmon. Dillingham, where the pair was destined, had comparable weather, while Iliamna was giving a 7000-ft. ceiling. It is presumed that Newton flew into the snowstorm area and in an attempt to find Dillingham became disoriented." Richard could not have realized how intense the snowstorm had actually become beyond Iliamna. Even though Richard had maintained extended contact with the King Salmon CAA radio operating with a VHF frequency that had a forty-mile range, their downed plane would not be found easily.

By the day following the plane's disappearance, the storm subsided slightly. The ensuing search concentrated in the radius of King Salmon's radio range, but the searchers found nothing on the icy tundra—the fresh blanket of snow might have enshrouded its prisoners, entombing them in a mass of twisted and melted metal. But the same day, the radio station at Cape Newenham reported hearing a faint SOS. The message was "faint and garbled," and on VHF radio. The message said only "—33— Bravo." Richard's call sign was N9332 Bravo. As soon as the weather cleared, some of the search aircraft was diverted to the Togiak—Point Newenham—Hagemeister Island region farther west to investigate the faint radio message. This extended search contradicted Lt. Gay's perception of where Richard might have been when he called in to the FAA radio operator, but searchers were willing to follow any lead. Meanwhile, others continued to concentrate near Ekwok, northeast of Dillingham, after some residents reported that an airplane had circled the village around 5:00 P.M. the evening that Richard's plane disappeared. This would correspond to Richard's change of direction (from 30 degrees to 250 degrees) at approximately the same time. After the search was underway, two trappers reported that a plane had circled their cabin around 7:00 P.M. in the Togiak area. Therefore, the search boundaries expanded to include a region south of Egegik village in the south, as far east as Kulik Lodge on Nonvianuk Lake to the east, up to Lake Iliamna and Iliamna village in the northeast, west including and beyond what is now Wood-Tikchik State Park and as far north as Chauekuktuli Lake (north of Aleknagik) and west to Togiak Lake, out to the Kanektok River, and down the eastern half of the peninsula to Cape Newenham.

Because Richard had not reported Donna as a passenger, the searchers thought the plane only carried the pilot. Donna's good friend Tressie Vander Hoek, however, knew that Donna had planned to go with Richard to Dillingham to visit Bobbie and Marty. When she heard that Richard's plane had disappeared, Tressie feared the worst. Her unease increased after numerous telephone calls to Donna went unanswered. She called the school to find out if anyone had seen Donna—no one had. Fourth-grade teacher Zona Dahlmann also suspected that Donna was on that flight. Zona and the school authorities "told the [CAA] authorities that we knew that she was on the plane with him, and they said oh no, he was

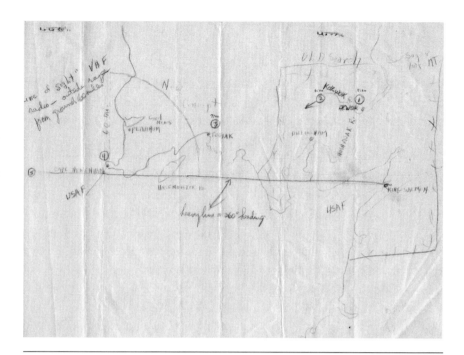

Map indicating new search area drawn by Merlin McGladrey, courtesy of author.

alone, it's not in the flight plan or anything, and besides, he can't have a passenger." For three days Zona and Tressie tried to convince the CAA that Donna was on the plane. They learned that Donna's Volkswagen Beetle had been parked at the airport for three days. By January 5, the Civil Air Patrol (CAP) expanded the search to include a passenger, and by January 9, it was certain that Donna was aboard the plane. The search widened to include Donna, the beloved first band instructor of Dillingham, the daughter of a Chicago-area Methodist minister, and the sister of twin Dorothy and older sister Joan.

While the flurry of activity approached a feverish pitch in the Bristol Bay region, news of Donna's disappearance was only just arriving at her parent's home. When it appeared that the search would continue after that first day, Reverend H. Wayne Hull of Chugiak, as a CAP chaplain and pastor of the church where Donna directed the music program, was notified of Donna and Richard's disappearance. At 10:30 P.M. on January 1, 1960, the telephone rang at the Methodist parsonage in Waterman, Illinois. The family did not usually receive calls so late, unless it was some sort of church emergency, so the Reverend Leslie D. McGladrey ran downstairs to answer the phone. He listened quietly as Reverend Wayne Hull explained to a fellow pastor the tragedy that had likely befallen their daughter. "The plane carrying Donna and Richard to Dillingham on December 30 has disappeared. They have not been seen since their departure from Anchorage. We were so sure yesterday that they would be found that I hesitated calling you until now. But there is no sign of them." Verna wrote many years later of her memories of that moment, "The parents held each other tightly, each trying to comfort the other. And together they placed the fate of their daughter in God's hands. 'Oh, God, Let this cup pass from us, but nevertheless, not our will but thine be done. . . .' And a feeling of trust and peace filled their hearts."[4] Leslie then had to explain to his other daughters that the plane carrying their beloved sister had disappeared.

Joan, Malvin, and daughter Karen had just returned from spending Christmas in Illinois with her parents, Dorothy, Jack, and son Danny. While in Illinois, they had joined each other around a microphone into which they recorded a reel-to-reel tape for Donna, a special Christmas message that they mailed to her so that she could hear her family's voices and thus feel closer to home. But when Joan and Malvin returned home to Minneapolis, they found a telegram that informed Malvin that his mother had just passed away in Norway. Three days later, Joan got the call from her father that Donna had "gone missing." The family's fear was intense, but their whole lives they had heard Leslie's messages of love and faith. They had called upon God for guidance, and strength and protection for Donna and Richard.

On Saturday, January 2, Leslie borrowed money from a banker for plane fare and headed to Seattle. Upon his arrival in Seattle, his brother, Air Force Lt. Col. Merlin McGladrey, met him and whisked Leslie to his home. Merlin coordinated Leslie's connections to Anchorage. Due to his many years of military service stretching back to World War II, Merlin had many influential friends and offered his assistance to his distraught brother. Merlin gave his brother a small sheet of paper, about three inches by seven inches, "Special Orders, Number B-2." The heading: "Headquarters, Alaskan Air Command, United States Air Force, APO 942, Seattle, Washington," the date, January 4, 1960, "1. REVEREND LESLIE D MCGLADREY, Waterman, Illinois, is authorized to proceed on or about 4 JAN 60 to King Salmon & return to this station via MILITARY ACFT [aircraft] in connection with chaplain activities in Air

Rescue Operations. Authority: AFR 76–6 & AFR 76–15 as applicable. Travel is authorized with no expense to US GOVT." Some of Merlin's friends were currently stationed at Elmendorf Air Force Base. Merlin had already informed the chaplain at Elmendorf about Leslie's impending arrival. When Leslie arrived in Anchorage at 5:00 A.M. (after sleeping about six hours en route), he learned the details about the previous five days of intense searching by the CAP and private pilots. Merlin's assistance with Leslie's expensive and unexpected search costs provided him with the ability to stay longer in Alaska, whereupon he would later travel from Anchorage to Chugiak, then to King Salmon, and Dillingham. Leslie's "seat-mate" on the flight from Seattle, an Anchorage pilot who did quite a bit of commercial hauling with his private plane, took Leslie to his Anchorage apartment where he spent the night. Leslie reported to his wife that this particular pilot flew to Dillingham regularly, and that he "held out more hope than I had even thought of." No doubt Leslie had experienced many deep and painful emotions, so any tidbit of hope lifted his spirits.

After spending the evening at the pilot's home, Leslie went to the chapel at Elmendorf Air Force Base where he attended services at 11:00 A.M. Two very good friends of Merlin's and their wives took Leslie to lunch after church. One of them was Chaplain (Lieutenant Colonel) John Smeltzer. Leslie told the small group that he hoped to get back on a plane at 3:30 P.M. to head to King Salmon, then on to Dillingham. After lunch, Leslie went to the search headquarters to receive updates. From Anchorage, Leslie sent a Western Union Telegram to his wife. In it he wrote encouragingly that "there still is hope for they [Donna and Richard] have ample food and clothing." He continued, "Ten thousand square miles have been searched and intensive observation is planned for tomorrow." He concluded by saying that he planned to join the search at King Salmon the following day, and to talk to the "radio man who received their message of being lost." He then wrote two letters to his wife that day.

By the following morning, Leslie had secured passage to King Salmon to help with the search. "Extra 'eyes' are welcome in searching," he wrote, and added that "Everyone here still talks of 'good chance of survival,' and tell tales of things fully as bad as this that have turned out OK." Leslie's letters reassured Verna, as well as Dorothy and Danny who had come to stay with Verna. Not even ten months old, Danny's unknowing smiles, cooing, and youthful silliness helped them escape the constant anxiety of Donna's disappearance somewhere out on the Arctic tundra. Dorothy also recalled that they never spent an evening alone. Members of the Waterman Methodist Church, which Leslie had served, invited them to dinner at their homes every single night. These constant visitors and activities helped them cope, and Dorothy remembered vividly and with endearment all of their efforts, concern, and assistance on their behalf. She has never forgotten the grace they showered on Verna and herself during those trying times.

In a January 4 letter to his daughter Joan, Leslie conveyed what news he had regarding the disappearance and the search. He told of how Merlin's connections gave him special access to staff at Elmendorf Air Force Base and soon, with Colonel Carriker's assistance, "got to top sources." Leslie explained how "over 10,000 sq. miles have been searched + intensive work is going on today. Merlin + I have passage at 1 P.M. to King Salmon. Richard radioed he was lost so search is concentrated where they got the report. He was in contact for over $1/2$ hr. before radio quit. He should have had time to pick some kind of a decent landing place." Leslie obviously had learned that pilots in distress immediately begin looking for bush runways to land on if necessary. Perhaps Richard had asked Donna to keep a lookout for such a runway, but with increasing darkness and blackout conditions, it became more difficult to see. Leslie believed that they would be found alive, for they had "adequate food + clothing for any weather." He reported that the weather was quite mild. Even though the weather did not completely hamper their search, Leslie reported that the military issued him a "duffle bag of artic clothing. You can't fly from Anchorage this time of year without survival gear." Finally, he reported that fourteen planes flew on January 3, and that more would be up today "if weather permits flights of small craft from here. There's still hope." Ruby and Mary Newton remembered that during the previous year, another small aircraft had gone down in a Canadian storm. The older gentleman and a female missionary survived the crash, and four days later the pair finally flagged down another plane and got out alive. This story of survival gave the Newtons great hope that the same fate would befall Richard and Donna. Charles had been searching for his lost brother since the day of his disappearance. In the meantime, Leslie's cautious words of hope soothed the hearts of his family that sat and waited, so far away, for any morsel of news about the search.

The painful waiting game was underway, and her parents prayed for some positive word about the daughter that they loved so dearly.

CHAPTER ELEVEN

A Father's Desperate Search

On Officer's Open Mess stationery from Elmendorf AFB, Leslie D. McGladrey wrote to his wife that a Col. Carriker had arranged for him to leave for King Salmon at 1:00 P.M. on January 4, 1960. While the temperature was forty degrees in Anchorage, it would warm up after 10:00 A.M. when the winter sun finally came up.[1] In an attempt to learn as much as he could from all sources, Leslie contacted Reverend Hull, who unfortunately had no fresh news. Undeterred, Leslie called Royce and Charles Newton, but his several attempts went unanswered. He assumed that the Newtons had headed west and he expected to meet up with Charles in King Salmon later that day.

When he arrived in King Salmon en route to Dillingham, he learned firsthand about the small community and their willingness to give up precious time, energy, and resources to assist the missing couple. In a letter to Verna, Merlin described his impression of King Salmon in January 1960, "This metropolis of 18 reisdents [sic] is the jumping off place to isolated Newenham Peninsula. King Salmon has an air base a few miles from 'town' where we slept and ate during the past week."

On the evening of January 5, Leslie penned another letter to Verna and Dorothy. Everyone believed that Richard and Donna survived. Hope soared when Charles and Royce heard that Richard's plane had been seen over the village of Ekwok, as well as other "tips" that located the plane in a straight line from Ekwok toward Dillingham, Leslie wrote. Royce and Charles borrowed a plane from a friend and spent all day Tuesday, January 5, intensively searching the line between Ekwok and Dillingham. Leslie had great concern for the brothers; not just for the loss they suffered, but because they had "worked almost continuously ever since, 2 or 3 hrs. sleep is all they get. They were out yesterday when no flying was really allowed." Little clues reported by various sources from Lake Iliamna down to Egegik, west across the Nushagak Bay and out to Togiak and Cape Newenham continued to give the searchers hope.

Leslie learned of the reports of Ekwok and Togiak residents hearing aircraft overhead in the storm, and of the Cape Newenham radioed SOS. In Togiak, at approximated 7:00 P.M., "the night we had church," villagers heard a plane sputtering north of town and they reported hearing an "uneven engine." Apparently three people from different parts of town reported the same sounds. According to Merlin's sources, at 5:45 the next morning, Newenham radio believed that the plane had "landed alive and soft enough for the radio to work. Range, crevices, battery run down ended communication." Newenham's radio operator obviously believed they had survived. After these hopeful reports from Cape Newenham, the search shifted away from the Dillingham and King Salmon region west to include, as Merlin described it, "a piece of pie." They began an intensive search from Cape Newenham north sixty miles, then curving east and south to sixty miles east of Cape Newenham, including Hagemeister Island. As Merlin wrote, "Leslie and I and the Newton brothers were feeling a strong 'hunch' in the Newenham direction all the time. The Newtons even flew in and were kept down a full day by weather in Togiak. With increasing evidence the CAP commander buys the new search area." Merlin again offered hope, "Yesterday I called the 'bush pilot's bush pilot'—best in Alaska—Bud Rude (now in Anchorage). He's a specialist on the Newenham peninsula. Said he'd get a twin engine and have a go at it. He knows every walrus and rock. The narrowed search, the expert help and—maybe a lift in the weather and I feel confident they'll have their spring wedding after all." Obviously, the family would not give up hope easily. They quickly learned the names and reputations of numerous bush pilots and, if they had not already volunteered, enlisted their aid in the search for Donna and Richard.

In order to monitor the search, Leslie D. McGladrey carried a

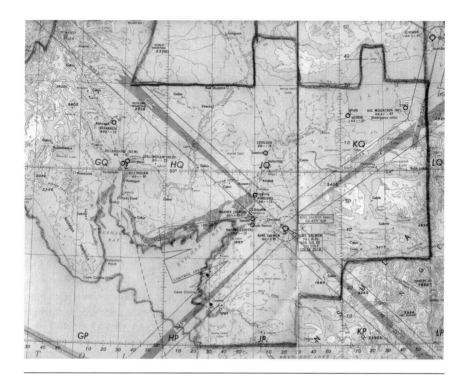

Search map utilized by Merlin and Leslie McGladrey, hand-drawn lines indicate search areas, the four long triple lines are flight vectors. Kodiak Island (136), World Aeronautical Chart, compiled and printed at Washington, D.C., by the U.S. Coast and Geodetic Survey under the authority of the Secretary of Commerce, March 1952, and revised July 1959, courtesy of author.

carefully marked U.S. Air Force Edition World Aeronautical Chart of the Kodiak Island quadrant with him, which he eventually carried back to Waterman, likely to illustrate to his wife all the places that volunteers had searched at their own expense. On it, he tracked where he and the others had searched for the downed plane. Later, Verna gently tucked it away in Donna's photograph album. Conceivably the most uplifting and encouraging experience of Leslie's while in Alaska was the response of bush pilots to the potential loss of one of their own. Besides Royce and Charles Newton, who flew in borrowed planes as they searched for Richard and Donna, Leslie learned about all of the other pilots who took to the air. In his notes, he listed many of them by name:

- Jim McGlasson and Burt James (both of Aero Marine)
- C. R. Lewis (Royce Newton's employer) and Ross Lewis
- Myron Moran (22 hours), George Krause (23:40 hours), Pete Heyano (13 hours), Jay Stovall (38:30 hours), Clarence Wren, and Dr. J. Libby of Dillingham
- Roy Smith (15 hours)
- E. C. Chron (5:15 hours) and Rev. Wayne Hull of Chugiak
- Al Lee of Anchorage (7:30 hours)
- Bob Harris (20 hours)
- Warren Ramsdell (15 hours)
- Ben Bockford (21 hours)
- Ebert Smith (10 hours)
- Elmer Smith (9 hours)
- Andy Anderson (14:20 hours)
- Bob Shelton (124 hours)
- Gene McGlasson (30 trips)
- Ros Lewis (5 trips)
- F. H. Griffin (6 trips)
- Alaska Aeromarine (6 trips, Barnhill)

Leslie kept a list of the people, at least those about whom he was aware, that helped with the search. When he could, he recorded the number of flight hours or the number of search trips they took. Donna's close friends Martha Jay and Roberta Tew (Marty and Bobbie), as well as many other unnamed friends, also served as extra eyes on the many searches. By early January, Leslie recorded that more than 278 hours of total air search time had been exhausted looking for his daughter. These hours, incidentally, did not include those expended by Reverend Hull, the Newtons, the CAA, the CAP, the Coast Guard, and numerous others who did not report their totals. Leslie's appreciation for the pilots showed. He also recorded addresses and phone numbers of these generous people whenever he could find the information and gave instructions to Verna to thank them. He continued to keep his wife informed, writing her often from Anchorage, King Salmon, or Dillingham, wherever he could find paper, postage, and a mailbox.

Merlin also expressed gratitude for the support he received from others in the search effort. He prompted Leslie's family members to send "letters of appreciation and encouragement" to them to "keep the pot boiling." Key individuals he identified included Lt. Col. Carleton

(King Salmon Air Force Station), Myron Moran, Airman White (King Salmon HDS Motor Pool), Lt. Earl Gay, Superintendent Emmert, Reverend Wayne Hull, Chaplain E. I. Carriker (Alaskan Air Command at Elmendorf Air Force Base), Chaplain John Smeltzer, and finally, Betty Wolverton (ISO CAP Squadron at Elmendorf AFB). Merlin believed that these individuals needed encouragement if they were to keep the search active.[2]

But the search was difficult, frustrating, and time consuming. Although the pilots flew in predetermined quadrants, they had to watch out for extreme and unsafe winter weather conditions, as well as other aircraft. With his own hand-drawn search map, Merlin explained that "What doesn't meet the eye on any map is the fact that this peninsula breeds the worst weather in Alaska—and that's competition! Contrary to my preconceived notion, southern Alaska weather is not (these two weeks anyway) terribly cold. But fog, clouds, snow, and general atmospheric GUNK keeps airplanes on the ground." They strained their eyes in the often-blinding snow or patchy fog and clouds to find the white and silver Cessna, perhaps buried by the very storm that had disoriented Richard. They fought fatigue, hunger, and disagreeable weather conditions to stay airborne, hoping to catch a glimmer of sunlight reflecting off of the Cessna's wing or rudder sticking up through the snow-covered tundra below.

Luckily at the end of the week, the weather cleared. A Western Union Telegram arrived in Verna's hands in the afternoon of January 11. Leslie reported that he and Charles had left King Salmon on Friday, January 8, and searched the hills north and west of Togiak. Weather had thwarted their efforts to search on Saturday, but by Sunday, they returned north and searched Togiak River and Togiak Lake, landing in Dillingham at the end of the day. He reported that over fifty thousand square miles had been covered and that weather conditions favored flying the following day. No doubt their eyes tired of peering into the snow covered tundra through trees, frozen inland ponds, low lying hills, remote and uninhabited cabins, fishing boats in dry dock, and snow and ice covered hills. During the sunny days, the sun's strong glare must have stung their already weary eyes.

The next day, Charles and Leslie got a late start, but flew at two hundred feet over a fairly heavily wooded area in the direction of Manokotak. The region, well irrigated by the Igushik River, which meanders tirelessly from its mouth at the Nushagak Bay inland west, and north from Amanka Lake, has tidal flats in the summer that freeze during winter. Upon these tidal flats, the winter mushing trail reached from Dillingham through Kanakanak where the Alaska Native hospital and tuberculosis sanitarium sat upon the hill. The trail then headed across the Igushik to Kulukak and farther west along Togiak Bay to Togiak, then west to Goodnews, then points farther north. In the winter, Leslie would have seen the trail wind through the blanket of white covering the river, tidal flats, and low hills that surrounded Amanka Lake and the community of Nunavakamut. Leslie learned later that mushers taking that very trail kept an eye out for the downed craft.

Leslie realized how important his brother's connections to top brass in the Air Force were. He wrote that "they have put several things in motion. A plane here is loading 10 barrels of gasoline to take to Newenham as a supply base. CAP—Civil Air Patrol—is intensifying operations. A plane from Anchorage is due here in an hour with added pilots + special technical men—radio equipment etc." He continued to report that his brother Merlin spent most of his time on the telephone and knew more about the search than anyone else, except perhaps the radio operator who first heard the distress call. "Lt. Gay is really on the ball," Leslie remarked. Leslie felt recharged daily, refreshed in hope by the many volunteers searching for his daughter. He reported that one day was the best day so far during his trip. "Yesterday was impossible," he wrote. "Our trip was entirely instrument flying + we came through snow + ice + bumpy weather." Waiting for clear weather or flying in difficult and even dangerous conditions caused frustration to mount. But Leslie had good news for his wife, too. Thanks to Merlin, he needed only spend one dollar per day for lodging and as little as twenty-five cents per meal. Merlin even had a jeep at his disposal to take his anxious brother around the base at King Salmon to talk to people and acquire as much information as possible about the lost Cessna and the search. Completely out of his element, Leslie persisted daily only by the kindness of people he never knew until that tragic time.

Worried or not, Leslie felt reassured with all the assistance that he received from every quarter. He reported that "people at Dillingham are out on the search in as great numbers as they can get planes." In a conversation with Leslie, Charles described with heartfelt gratitude the great lengths that Dillingham's population went to on behalf of his own brother and Leslie's daughter. Also important to Leslie was the knowledge that even as far away as Anchorage, hope continued that the two would be found alive. Leslie reported that the *Anchorage Daily Times* carried "quite a story including pictures of Richard + Donna." He reported that he hoped to hear good news soon, yet he cautioned that the "results today are negative. Weather turned foggy before daylight was over. Forecast is not too good for tomorrow." His short sentences only hinted at the growing frustration and fear that mounted within his heart. While sunlight continued to expand during the day, even if only a minute or two, January's weather brought storms, overcast skies, and high winds. Indeed tenuous conditions for searching. The searchers found themselves grounded for days at a time.

While grounded, Leslie had other duties to complete. He spoke at local churches and schools. He wrote that as the recently appointed national executive of Temperance Education, Incorporated (TEI), he felt inclined to speak at the Dillingham high school. When he arrived at the school just after lunch Tuesday, January 12, he heard that the students had gone on strike the previous Friday. They had only just returned to school. Leslie explained, "There was quite a squabble about a row between the Supt [Superintendent] + a teacher + the teacher resigned." He did not know that it was the music teacher that had resigned, nor did he expand upon the recent strike. During his speech, he described his daughter's admiration for the students, his appreciation for the community's assistance, and thanked them for their acceptance of his daughter. Most important, he spoke about the importance of abstaining from alcohol, for Donna wrote about the abundance of drunks on the streets "any time of day."

He planned to make reservations to return to Anchorage the following morning, whereupon he would spend the evening with the Newtons and go to Chugiak on Thursday. He planned to spend all day Thursday "fixing things," such as selling her car and the unenviable task of emptying out her trailer. Then he planned to talk to Chaplain Smeltzer about his interest in buying Donna's VW Beetle. He then had to see about Donna's cat, "I'll see to it that the cat is disposed of." Whether he meant that the cat simply needed to be released from the veterinarian, a home found, or her suffering ended, is unclear. Nobody seemed to remember. While Leslie still held out hope, perhaps he realized that by this time, if they had survived, he would need to bring Donna back to Illinois with him to nurse her back to health. He also could not afford to continue paying her rent on the trailer on Swanny Slopes in hopes that searchers might eventually find the plane.

On January 13, local Anchorage newspapers ran a story about how the weather had cleared in Dillingham on January 12 and that twelve pilots had taken to the skies, flying more than thirty-two hours total in the search for the missing couple. The newspapers continued to carry information about the search, but less and less frequently as the days passed. Surely the Newton family worried about lagging interest in community support for finding Donna and Richard. By January 15, 1960, the search began to slow down due to snow, fog, sub-zero temperatures, and the days that now contained nearly six hours of sunlight. Even with interest diminishing and weather conditions worsening, Leslie reassured his wife that the search would continue, and that the CAP would search each mapped area three times before they abandoned the area. He reported to *The Chronicle* of Waterman that four Alaska National Guard C47 planes, under the direction of Lt. Col Melvin Witham, had covered "over 3600 square miles between King Salmon to Togiak."

When Leslie arrived at Donna's little trailer in Chugiak filled with her smells, her belongings, and her music, he was overcome with an intense sadness and, at the same time, an odd sense of comfort. At least he could have some physical connection with items, which at the very least, belonged to her. But Leslie knew that he had to clear out her belongings. Besides finding a freezer filled with pea soup, Leslie also found her typewriter, Singer sewing machine, dishes, clothes, books, cat food, a litter box, toiletries, a hairbrush, sheet music, even the pieces that she had composed and copied by hand for the children, and her lovely piece of driftwood that sat so proudly on her window ledge. Cleaning out his daughter's personal belongings and trying to decide what to do with them shook him to his very soul. Maybe then he sensed deep in his heart that he would never see his daughter again, and touching the belongings that meant so much to her was the last physical connection he would ever have with his beloved Donna. Certainly, he sat on her couch, looking longingly out of her window, head in his big strong hands, and wept quietly to himself. But he had a job to do, and in the land of expensive foods, he would have to find a home for Donna's soup. Margaret Swanson gladly accepted: "It was the best pea soup I've ever had," she recalled.

When remembering Donna's disappearance, Zona Dahlmann recalled that same freezer full of pea soup. But she also recounted her fears about Donna flying with Richard, which related to her own experience. "I was concerned about her flying with him . . . because he didn't have his license. He was just a student pilot. 'Course, in Alaska a lot of people fly." She had her reasons to worry about her friend: "I had lost my best friend that I came up here with a year before the same way in a plane crash and so I was really very careful. You know, you first come up here and you think, oh well, everybody can fly a plane and there's nothing to it and then you realize that there's a lot to it. You really have to pick who you fly with." In Alaska, Zona said, snowstorms and high winds can arrive with no warning.

While in Chugiak, Leslie spoke at the Chugiak Methodist Church at the request of Reverend Hull. The hushed group of around a dozen waited with bated breath to hear what the Chicago father of a missing daughter might say. Leslie quietly rose to his feet, after being introduced by Reverend Hull, and spoke to the small congregation at Swanny Slopes. Those who heard him speak said they would never forget him, nor how he brought the group to tears that day. In his message, he spoke of his daughter, the search, and the intense pain that his family suffered back home not knowing if Donna had survived

Chugiak Methodist Church, July 1958,
photograph by Verna McGladrey, courtesy of author.

or died. As hope began to fade, he spoke of God's love for his children and the possibility that God had called Donna to him. Years later, Margaret Swanson recalled that the sermon was "a tear-jerking time for us because we, everybody loved her. She was [a] sweet, vivacious young woman." She commented that it "was a terrible shock to the community when they heard of her plane downed, and nowhere, and they couldn't find her."

Longtime Chugiak residents and Chugiak Methodist Church members Les and Dorothy Fetrow remember those awful days after Donna and Richard disappeared, as well as Leslie's sermon that Sunday. Les and Dorothy have been married for nearly sixty years "almost all of those sixty years in Alaska. I came to Alaska in 1940," Les Fetrow proudly announced. His wife Dorothy, recalled "well, Donna McGladrey was not with us too long. She was [here] a very short time. An excellent pianist and, while we didn't have a choir, she did give us some little direction. She was a lovely lady." She remembered that Donna had a boyfriend, "and he did some flying, and she liked to fly too. One day they just took off . . . and they never came back, and nothing, no evidence of what happened." She continued, "The rest of it is our acquaintance with her father." And they remembered Leslie McGladrey well. He came up to search for Donna and take care of other arrangements. He recalled that Leslie was tall and slender and great to talk with; "we kind of enjoyed ourselves." They talked about farming, among other things, for Les learned that the Reverend also spent time as a hail adjuster and was familiar with farming throughout the upper Midwest.[3]

Both Les and Dorothy remembered Leslie better than Donna, but they did remember that she attended church regularly. They also remembered that Donna played piano exceptionally well. "She always had something ready for Sunday morning. She had the congregation pretty well in hand. . . . She was a beautiful woman, yeah, a beautiful woman." She was the first choir director that the little church had. Although she was not the first musician, she certainly made a huge impression upon the church. And at that time, the church was not very big. "You get a congregation of ten people and that was it. . . . She played that upright piano. . . . It really wasn't a concert piano, but Donna did her best." The community would miss her dearly, and soon they began to ask questions, as Margaret Swanson recalled. Besides the unbearable shock of having lost such a young and vivacious person, "People were trying to figure out why it would happen that a pilot was unlicensed and not supposed to carry passengers." Why would Donna have flown with an unlicensed pilot? they pondered. Had she not heard about all of the accidents and deaths caused by pilot error? Margaret must have wondered if Leslie shared the same questions.

In the meantime, the *Bristol Bay News* of Naknek reported that the search planes "are in the air with observers scanning the seemingly endless tundra in hopes of spotting the downed airplane." The article continued, describing the tremendous sense of disappointment that the searchers must have felt daily, "It is disheartening for the searchers to spot a dark object on the tundra only to find on closer inspection that it is nothing more than a lonely spruce tree. However monotonous or discouraging each day's fruitless search turns out to be, the dogged determination of those involved has not diminished."[4] Truly frustrated, disappointed, and exhausted, Charles and Royce continued to look for their lost brother and Donna with the help of a diminished number of volunteers.

Meanwhile, back home in Illinois, Verna had received hundreds of cards and letters from concerned friends and family. Many of them had included monetary donations to help the family with their search expenses. Verna carefully recorded all of these expenses and pasted the list onto Donna's now yellowed and brittle photograph album. She also saved and pasted portions of the personal messages, as well as the Alaska newspaper articles that Leslie dutifully cut out and saved to take home. And she wondered when Leslie would return.

On January 15, Reverend Hull wrote about Donna and Richard in the *Mukluk Tell-Ya-Gram, An Alaskan Methodist Newspaper*:

> For 11 days I was taking part in a search for a young couple who became lost in their plane while flying there Dec. 30th. The young lady was our Church organist and choir director. She was also the music teacher at the school and the daughter of a Methodist minister of Waterman, Ill. At this time of the year, in Dillingham, you may travel by car on about 10 of its 30 mi. road system. Otherwise only by air or dog team. . . .
>
> Here is a vast expanse of country with streams and lakes untold; some timber some brush; some bog. Around the edges, mountains rising abruptly to two or four thousand snow covered feet. The Eskimo villages near here are much as they have been for generations, except now airplanes carry supplies and people in and out.

Of recent months the government has built schools in most of the villages which are situated along the banks of rivers or lakes with no streets or sanitation. . . .

On the search we have been plagued with fog, snow, rain & bad winds. We have searched an area over half the size of Kansas in strict search pattern. There has been thirty some pilots flying over 500 hours in the air—and it is still going on although there is only fair hope the lost will be found. . . . One of the hardest questions as I thought of coming home where Esther and others were trying to keep the Church and home going, was this—On what basis do you decide when to abandon search when there is still some hope, but duties call and you have looked but don't know just where they are, or *if* they are alive? Then ask this, friend.—How much effort and expense and time should be given to save a home, a Faith, a youth's dream, an alcoholic, a reputation; before abandonment to the destructive elements? C'mon Christians let's look to see what our answer is. The world is waiting . . and waiting . . .

Leslie left Alaska the next day. Verna explained to Joan that he arrived January 16, several hours late. He had returned to Illinois to attend TEI's annual board meeting and to make a first official appearance as its new national executive in mid-January. He took the opportunity to witness about his lost daughter, knowing that her frustration at the alcoholism in Dillingham might give him strength to carry out his duties. They moved the very next day to a new home on Sherman Avenue. On the following Sunday, Leslie led church services and on Monday, he did his temperance radio show in Chicago. The stress tore at the foundations of Leslie's strength, for as Verna reported, "Daddy is up + ready to go by 8AM. Last night, tho we woke 4 or 5 times, was 1st full night's sleep without pills. Daddy is very nervous but standing up well. He made up his mind to return Wed. since Waterman [United Methodist Church] gave him 'McGladrey Search Fund' of $500 . . . Weather so bad up there, he flew only 3 out of 10 days. Crashed once + was grounded in Eskimo Village 2 days." He would return shortly, but it must have been very difficult for him to leave.

He planned to return to Anchorage, King Salmon, and then Dillingham, praying that this time he would find his daughter, but expecting the worst.

CHAPTER TWELVE

"Death Was Between Breaths, Instantaneous, and Merciful"

While the searchers battled frustration and anxiety, tension mounted among family members at home in Illinois and Minnesota. As with any tragedy or great uncertainty, individuals dealt with their emotions in very different ways. Verna, who had kept a very detailed financial ledger of her honeymoon in 1930 and continued to keep detailed accountings of the family's finances (down to pennies she found on the sidewalk), openly obsessed about money. She complained about the cost of Leslie's airline tickets to Alaska, and did so to the only person she saw on a daily basis, Dorothy. Dorothy's main concern, however, was not money at all. Instead of confronting her mother, for Verna had carefully brought up her daughters to yield to parental authority, Dorothy instead vented her frustrations over her mother's frivolous concerns to her older sister Joan in letters. She retorted, "The point is that they received a $500.00 check from church and district so that so far actually they haven't gone down a penny yet." Instead of facing the pain of the potential loss of a daughter, Verna busied herself with a much lesser concern of finances to keep her mind occupied. In deep frustration, Dorothy was rightfully outraged at her mother's concern for money and seemingly not for her lost daughter. In this same letter, however, Dorothy revealed the heart of her frustration and greatest fear. She wrote, "Pa is going back to Alaska tonight if he can get a plane which I'm sure he can. I don't think he thinks they're still alive. I was convinced they were until talking to him. He didn't say as much but he gave me that impression. He's taken it pretty hard. More so than Ma." Years later Joan added, "But he healed well with his faith." While Leslie found himself home between search attempts, Dorothy attended a talk that Leslie gave at a convention dinner. During his speech, he utilized the search "as an illustration of complete frustration—being grounded, + being unable to hunt down the source of a rumor that Donna + Richard were seen + Donna was in a state of shock—and as he told it he almost broke down. His voice wouldn't come. I felt so bad for him." Dorothy witnessed her father's reaction as the complete antithesis of his wife's inability to deal directly with the pain.

While in Illinois after his first trip to Alaska, several newspapers interviewed Leslie about his trip and the difficulties of the search. Leslie reported that when Alaska was a territory, the Air Force handled searches for downed planes; but because it had only recently become a state, Alaskan authorities were not yet prepared. Up until midnight

Leslie and Verna McGladrey, passport photograph dated June 30, 1961, courtesy of author.

December 31, 1959, the Air Force handled all searches. On January 1, 1960, the state took over, according to the Waterman *Chronicle*. During Leslie's interview, he explained that although he remained in Alaska fourteen days (January 2–16), he had only flown three times due to weather conditions. "Not only is the weather bad, but the sun comes up about 9:30 and goes down before 3, so the period of operation is restricted." He reiterated that flying conditions are "always hazardous." Yet on the ground, Leslie explained, the search continued as well. "Eskimos are covering the area with dog teams on their own initiative and there is always the chance that the two would be located." Leslie had certainly held out hope. Along the perimeter of the search area, National Guard planes searched. The sea search was handled by the U.S. Coast Guard, according to an article in the *Chicago Tribune/Sun-Times*.

While in Illinois, he also had to settle personal affairs that he had neglected for many weeks while in Alaska. Hugs and kisses from his new grandson no doubt helped him find solace and contentment as he suffered through the darkest time a parent could ever face, the disappearance and potential loss of a child. But his duty as a father called him back to Alaska by the end of January for a second trip to search. After moving his wife to 309 Sherman Avenue in Evanston and conducting his TEI annual meeting, Leslie returned to Alaska. Aboard a Northwest Orient Airlines DC-7C, Leslie wrote to his wife, "Up in the Air! On the Inner Passage. I've seen 1000 miles of territory like we saw from Haines to Juneau as we flew there on our trip. The mts. are all snow covered now. . . . It's about the best flying day I've had yet. No turbulence since leaving Chicago." He wrote that in spite of all the coffee that he drank, he slept on the plane. "I seem to be more relaxed than I have been for days. I got a lot of things off my mind while home."[1] Conceivably he had resigned himself to one last search knowing that three weeks had passed since the plane disappeared and time was running out, even if she had survived.

Verna worried even more during his second trip, not so much for Donna but for Leslie,

for in the 3 days he was flying the search, he crashed once (on the airport skidded into snowbank and ruined $7,000 of [a] $15,000 plane), almost got caught over Togiak lake in fog when it unexpectedly closed in behind them + they had to spiral up from 800 to 7000 feet at 1500 ft. per minute! And set down in Togiak, a village of 200 Eskimos + 2 white teachers, + couldn't get up for 2 days because 6 in. of snow fell. Until dog sled teams pulled the hand-propelled snowplow to clear the field!

Leslie had not told his wife about this accident until he returned from Alaska, probably so as not to worry her. As frustrating as it was to not know the fate of her own daughter, she continued to be preoccupied with finances.

When he arrived in Anchorage on January 20, Leslie wrote his wife that Dillingham resident Albert Ball had taken him up for observation. They spent a couple hours searching north of Dillingham. "He and others assured me they would keep on looking," Leslie wrote to Verna. Instead of sending home comforting, hopeful, and reassuring messages as he did during his first trip, Leslie's letters now hinted that he had to survive on promises that his daughter would not be forgotten. But his frustration leaked through his prose: "Today is the nicest day I've had in Alaska. Too bad we didn't have a few like this when we had about 15 planes ready for search." His frustration mounted when he could not locate Reverend Hull or Charles Newton, forcing the frugal and distraught minister to register at a hotel. He would try later to contact the Newtons and Reverend Hull, but in the meantime, he planned to "get things under control at Chugiak." He needed to finish emptying Donna's trailer and sell her car.

The next morning, he sent off a quick postcard to his wife from Anchorage before he left for Dillingham. He had slept from 9:00 that evening until 6:00 the next morning and accomplished much the day before. He had discovered more information and planned to go to King Salmon later that day, then on to Dillingham. "Weather is warm here," Leslie wrote to Verna. As he closed his letter, Leslie reassured his wife that the search planes would be able to get up in the air and continue searching, although the days continued to be very short. Good news seemed hard to find. The positive tone in his letters, previously so full of hope in early January, failed to materialize.

From King Salmon he wrote to Verna on January 21, "Our plane left Anchorage at 8:00 + took the Cook Inlet route for 3/4 of an hour, just as the sun was coming up enough to color the southern sky. Turnagain Arm + the mtns. up Portage Glacier way + all down the line were magnificent beyond description." Truly captivated by Alaska's beauty, certainly Leslie had begun to understand why his daughter had fallen so completely for Alaska. Upon arrival in King Salmon, Leslie searched for three hours to find Lt. Earl Gay. After finally finding him, they spent two hours together. Leslie learned that Gay had carefully tracked the search areas and marked the maps with 1, 2, and 3, indicating the number of times each area had been covered. He reminded Leslie that the search would continue only in areas that had been checked only one or two times. While this news might have caused Leslie alarm, Gay indicated that he was "not in the mind to stop now or for a long time to come!" Leslie observed that "things have been slowed down. Weather has still been bad most of the time," yet he indicated that more gas and more volunteering pilots would arrive in Dillingham the following day.

Leslie had to be exhausted. Instead of staying at the air base, he procured a hotel room in town explaining that "it was too far to walk." He wrote, "You should see this hotel! I went to the entrance into a restaurant + was directed to the bar for a room. I had to climb up an open outside stairway. My desk is 3 wooden boxes with a board on top. My chair is a folding camp variety. The cot is government surplus variety. Yet I have heat, light, + water. What more could I ask out here?" Leslie went to bed early, knowing that he would fly to Dillingham the next day and needed to conserve all of his energy for the search. He spent twelve hours in bed, but slept only eight. He went to Dillingham a tired, and perhaps disheartened father. Leslie sent far fewer letters on his second trip to Alaska. He received less encouraging news this time, and instead concerned himself with rounding up assistance and taking care of Donna's affairs. He chose not to share his disappointment with his wife. After all, Charles and Mary had indicated that Richard's plane had only a week's worth of supplies on board—and it had now been more than three weeks since the plane disappeared.

When Leslie did return to Dillingham, the mood had shifted significantly, for no searches had originated from Dillingham for a week due to weather. While conditions that day were better, he reported, "no planes were up." Leslie wrote to Joan, "The search is still on. If people here won't give up, why should we." Charles Newton and Al Lee, the latter a friend of Charles who had a hunting lodge in the Matanuska area, had waited in Dillingham hoping to continue the search. According to villagers, they had become "quite discouraged at getting nothing accomplished," Leslie explained to Verna. After all, C. R. Lewis, owner of C. R. Lewis Plumbing and Heating and a friend of Charles, had also flown Charles numerous times in his own plane during the month of January.

On January 25, Leslie wrote to his wife that the previous day, a Sunday, he had preached a sermon at the Church of Christ in Dillingham for Roberta and Martha. The regular minister, Mr. Smith, and his wife were "'outside' for six months and may not ever be able to return." In the morning service, he preached on temperance, in the evening, "a regular" sermon. "They offered me a steady job!" he exclaimed. While in Dillingham, he also attended the Seventh Day Adventist church. He explained to Verna that they had a very strong church, and out of courtesy to the Wrens and the Balls, who had diligently assisted with the search, he had attended their church where Donna used to play the pump organ.

Leslie reported that on Monday, January 25, Lt. Gay, Mr. James, and another man arrived from King Salmon with more fuel, but that weather would not permit the search that day. He wrote, "If it isn't snow + fog it's wind." Mr. Wren would supervise dispensing of gasoline and supervise the search, for Mr. Gay had to return to King Salmon. Leslie then explained that he had some important duties in Chugiak and Anchorage, with frustration he added, "especially since I don't even get into the search." Some of his duties involved paying Donna's bills. He hoped to convince the bank to pay Donna's bills out of her bank account and paycheck, "as I did for the sewing machine. If they [Donna and Richard] are never found, it will make a very long drawn-out process of getting everything settled." Part frustration for feeling useless in the search, and part stress from not finding his daughter, he felt the tremendous weight on his shoulders of having to settle Donna's final affairs. This hint of despair would grow more obvious in the following days.

Dillingham residents understood his frustration and helped fill the agonizing days that Leslie spent grounded due to weather. Leslie mentioned that the Lawveres, the school principal and his schoolteacher wife, visited him and shared their Alaska pictures with him—likely the same slide show he had shown at the Willow Tree that Donna and her friends Bobbie and Marty enjoyed a year before. The Lawveres had taught at Homer, Kodiak, and several other places and therefore had very interesting photographs. Knowing of his wife's partiality for elaborate slide shows, and annoyed at the lack of flight time, Leslie must have jumped at the opportunity to see an Alaskan slide show. He planned to go talk to the Lawveres to see if they would let him speak at the High School later that day or the next. He reported to Verna that he planned to stay through Sunday, "if I can get Sunday engagements at Chugiak, Anchorage, or Elmendorf. If not, I'll start home as soon as I get Donna's affairs under proper control. Love, Leslie." He knew, finally, that Donna was lost forever.

To non–family members, Leslie and Verna tried to keep a strong front, but their fears crept through the text. Quoted in both the *Economist* and the *Chicago Tribune* in late January, Verna said that searchers no longer had much hope that the pair survived. Yet Leslie seemed to hold out more hope. He said that if they had been lucky enough to land softly, they certainly had enough food, clothing, sleeping bags, parkas, and various other survival gear. Richard could hunt moose, which locals had assured Leslie were plentiful in the area. Leslie might retain hope, but his wife did not come across in the newspapers so positive or hopeful. But who could hold out hope when tens of thousands of square miles had been searched two and three times each?

After being in Alaska more than one week during this second trip, on Thursday, January 28, Leslie wrote his wife a short note on a postcard from Anchorage, "I got a lot of things done today. Haven't sold the V.W. yet but have prospective buyers. Should move it in next two days. I'll speak in school at Chugiak tomorrow and in church on Sunday. Have reservation on 2 P.M. plane Sunday. Due to arrive in Chicago Monday morning. Will call on arrival. Love, Leslie." He avoided mention of the search, knowing that the CAP called off the search for the missing pair the day before.[2]

On the same day, Verna wrote a letter to Joan. She explained that the mail that she received helped her tremendously during those lonesome days. Every day she opened letters from someone who cared—letters from Texas, Florida, Louisiana, Missouri, Iowa, Minnesota, Ohio, Wisconsin, Illinois, Pennsylvania, North Carolina, and Alaska. They came from friends at previous churches, relatives, and friends of Donna's that the McGladreys had never met. She filled her worrisome days reading the letters, as well as visiting Dorothy, who needed assistance with her sick son Danny. He had thrown up repeatedly, and was "so 'blushed' and lifeless . . . If I weren't worried so over Donna, I could probably have taken his illness less seriously." Stress wore on Verna as well. She continued:

I already contacted Prudential (to have something to do) + have all papers ready=if necessary. If they are not found, it will be a long drawn out process.

Did I tell you? Daddy deposited her Dec. check + the bank gave him the $93.50 to complete her Singer payments! Out of her check. He hopes to pay her rent and fuel the same way plus other small bills. And he talked with the VW people + may be able to do something there. Today's letter expressed frustration. Snow, fog, high winds==no plane up for $1^1/2$ weeks. He couldn't help—just sit around Dillingham, went to—I'll send letter.

She still seemed more concerned about the financial aspects of Donna's disappearance and her husband's inability to help with the search than her daughter's disappearance. But Verna and Leslie each had to deal with the tragedy in their own manner. And both seemed to be planning for the worst.

On January 30, Leslie wrote a difficult letter to his eldest daughter. "Just a note to say the search has been suspended. Some will go back in the spring when the snow is gone, but hope of finding them alive is practically nill." It had taken him three days to tell his family the bad news. His straightforward and painfully candid letter continued, "I emptied her trailer + stored things at Newtons and Rev. Hulls. I am staying till Sunday noon to speak in the Meth[odist] church at Chugiak. I'll be home Monday. I go to see a lawyer at 10 today in regard to what I can do with the V.W." By February 1, Leslie returned to Chicago where he resumed his duties at TEI. Exactly one month before, he had taken the TEI job, and the same day was notified that his daughter disappeared in the Alaskan frontier.

Newspaper articles ceased to appear with any frequency regarding the missing couple, and Alaskans who had helped in the search had to return to their daily lives. When Leslie returned home, his heart was heavy. How could a father not remain in Alaska while his daughter might be suffering, starving, and freezing? Or at the very least, be there to collect her remains for a proper burial back in Illinois? Luckily Leslie did not have to preach sermons anymore, or be the strong man of the congregation. Instead, he could focus on the proliferation of alcohol—which he felt destroyed families, health, and even lives. Together with his faith, the solace he received from helping to save lives made him stronger over the years. He also had family to sustain him, including his two grandchildren, Karen and Danny.

As the days turned into weeks, then into months, the snow began to melt in Illinois and the crocuses and daffodils began bursting through the ground with renewed vigor, showering gardens with their brilliant colors of purple and gold, ignorant of the suffering that surrounded them. When April 19 approached, Dorothy celebrated her twenty-fifth birthday, her first birthday without her twin sister. By late April, the McGladreys had lost all hope that their daughter would return alive and began making preparations for a memorial service to be held at the Waterman Methodist Church on May 1 at 3:00 P.M. That same day, memorial services honoring Donna were held simultaneously at the Church of Christ and the Moravian churches in Dillingham, and the Methodist Church in Chugiak. Once again, cards and letters began to pour in to the McGladrey home. Verna carefully recorded each card, letter, and dollar sent as a memorial. She took great comfort sifting through the memories of a daughter lost on Alaska's frozen tundra.[3]

Back in Alaska, Charles Newton also gave up hope. According to a letter from Verna, Charles had written Verna shortly after the memorial services that he was "going to make one last good search, and then I am going to quit torturing myself." The same younger brother who moved in with Charles when he first moved up to Alaska during his high school years; the same brother who Charles hired to work for the plumbing and heating company where flying was imperative; the same brother with whom Charles entrusted partly the success of his company, as well as the well-being of the company plane; had disappeared. Charles was devastated—but at least he had a wife, Mary, and children. Royce's wife, Ruby, had lost her newborn in November shortly before Richard and Donna disappeared, so his priorities had been torn from the very first days of the search for Richard.

A month and a half after the memorial services, pilot Orin Seybert (founder and president of Peninsula Airlines) left Egegik on an emergency flight to Dillingham to transport a patient to Kanakanak Hospital. During the 1950s and 1960s, he flew regular flights in the region, and many of them involved transporting individuals to the Kanakanak Hospital, just outside of Dillingham. As he took off on June 13, Seybert recognized the urgency demanded by his ailing passenger who desperately needed medical attention and therefore rapid transport to Kanakanak. The usual flight plan took pilots north along the southeast shore of Bristol Bay north from Egegik to Naknek, cutting quickly across Kvichak Bay to Portage Creek and then following the Nushagak River to Dillingham. Instead, Orin flew north to about 58.5 degrees (about twenty statute miles south of Naknek along the coast) and cut early across the Kvichak Bay just south of Johnson Hill toward Supply Lake, then north to Black Point, then along the Nushagak to Dillingham.[4] As he caught sight of land on the southern end of Etolin Point, he noticed the sun reflecting off some metal below. He circled the marshy region, surrounded by low hills and scrub woods, to get a better look. He caught sight of it on the tundra below—a badly burned, mangled mass of a small aircraft. He reported that he could not read the registration numbers, but that the color matched the Cessna 175 that two other people had reported in the same location almost two weeks before. He reported that the fuselage was gutted, but that the wing and tail sections were still intact. Since he had no floats on his plane, he had to be satisfied to report it to the Western Alaska Airlines office after he rushed his passenger to the hospital. That same Sunday evening, Albert Ball called Charles to inform him of this newest sighting south southeast of Dillingham. Charles immediately wired Leslie to inform him. The next day, Charles and Royce left for Dillingham and flew over the site. When they saw nothing, they looked for Albert Ball for assistance.

By June 16, officials confirmed that the wreckage was indeed that of Richard and Charles Newton's Cessna 175, N-9332-Bravo. Donna and Richard's remains were found in the fuselage, badly burned by the fire that engulfed the plane immediately upon impact. The same day that officials confirmed that the downed plane was his, Charles Newton wrote the most heartfelt, difficult letter he likely ever wrote during his life.[5] He informed Leslie that a Mr. Carl Glick (a missionary) and Mr. Johnson (both of Kenai) were flying on the deck, or low, in foul weather following the coast south of Port Heiden, in order not to become lost. As they headed north, they noticed a wing at the low tide mark about thirty miles south southeast of Dillingham. They reported the sighting to the authorities, but as a very frustrated Charles put it to Leslie, "since the government powers involved prefer not to disseminate such news we heard it 2 wks. later from Albert Ball on the phone."

Charles requested that the Air Force helicopter commander take him to the site, but could not convince the commander to do so. Instead Charles had to hire a floatplane and they flew to a lake about five miles from the site and walked in. The impact of what they saw upon arrival likely sent chills through their bones. They found the Cessna about twelve miles south southeast of Black Point, just as Albert Ball had informed them a few days before. The location was not far from where Charles had nearly wrecked his plane a few years before, and just a few short miles outside of the southern border of the search area. It had crashed into the ground at "well over 160 miles per hr." and had impacted at a sixty-degree angle in a sharp right spiral; as pilots say, it was "augured in." Just as Lt. Gay had suspected, Richard had been in a fog of vertigo when he made the final distress call. "The plane exploded and burned on impact," Charles wrote. The left door had been torn off and lay more than five feet from the fuselage, the left ski gear and main gear was next to the door. "The nose gear was under the front seat and the right main gear was under the baggage compartment."

Bush pilots understand the danger of flying without instrument training and the devastating effect that can have on pilots caught in difficult situations. Fellow plumber and friend Hermann Kroener commented that as a result of his many years of flying, he would be able to fly and probably regain control of the spiraling aircraft, but Richard's inexperience made it impossible for him to recover. Hermann remembered that Richard had reported to the CAA that "he was flying straight and level, certain heading, and he was giving a speed like 160 miles an hour, which was way in excess, a plane [like Richard's Cessna 175] could never fly if it wasn't straight and level flight. So evidently, without him knowing, he had the wings level on the airplane but he didn't realize that he was heading down toward the ground at that high a speed." His wife Hilda added, "That's what they call vertigo." This is a phenomenon known only by either incredibly experienced pilots, or dead ones. Hilda and Hermann repeated a famous saying: "There are old pilots and there are bold pilots, but there are no old, bold pilots."

Dillingham pilot John Paul Bouker confirmed this theory of "vertigo." Bouker has flown for nearly twenty years in the Bristol Bay area with his own delivery service. Not being instrument rated and "hitting the wall" (complete darkness with no ground lights to give the pilot a sense of direction), he agreed that Richard probably had no clue he was headed straight toward the ground. Hermann Kroener lamented, "I knew Richard, he was a nice person, you know, couldn't think of anybody any better but somehow he just misjudged the time and the weather on that fateful trip to Dillingham. Many a pilot has made the same devastatingly incorrect decision, as well." It seems most Alaskans have lost at least one family member or friend in a plane wreck.[6]

Charles searched the wreck in vain for traces of his beloved brother and his beautiful fiancé, but all he could find of their parkas, sweaters, and three sleeping bags was a small polka dot piece of blouse and a very small piece of green shadow plaid wool shirt. Charles wrote that "The heat was so intense that 2 steel wrenches were fused together . . . death was between breaths, instantaneous and merciful. They suffered from the fire not at all." Donna's watch had stopped at 5:25 P.M., just 2 minutes after Richard's last transmission to Lt. Gay at King Salmon. Finding his brother's charred remains haunted Charles, and he recognized the area as close to the one where he had crashed several years earlier. But necessity took over and he knew he had some important, but sad duties to fulfill. He ordered two sealers to ship the remains to Anchorage.[7] The recovery of the remains would not prove simple, however, for the Federal Aviation Administration (FAA) instructed him through a second-hand source not to visit the site or remove anything until the FAA could examine the wreckage and make their determination. Once the FAA completed their investigation, Donna and Richard's remains were shipped to the Anchorage Funeral Home where Richard's awaited burial and Donna's shipment to Illinois.

Charles lamented, "Gone is the time when we must jump at a whisper and go running off on a wild good chase to follow a rumor." Charles thanked Leslie for his assistance and pined over the lost time, energy, and finances that he and the others had expended on their behalf. As he returned to Anchorage, the pilot flew a little north of the downed plane and Charles wrote that "while thinking that possibly that was the last time I would see it Chron [pilot and friend of Charles] said, 'here we are feeling sorry for them and they're up there looking down wondering when we're going to join them and really live.' So the balance of the trip wasn't half bad." He signed off by thanking Leslie for his "Christian attitude," adding that "from you I learned much." Thus would end the collection of memories shared between the two families until reconnected by this project more than forty years later.

The bodies would return to their respective homes for their final rest and the families could try to return to a semblance of normal life, no longer having to worry about the recovery of their loved ones from the Alaskan wilderness that had claimed them more than six months before. Funeral services for Richard were held at 2:00 P.M. on June 20, 1960, at the Anchorage City Cemetery. He was buried in the Veteran of Foreign Wars Tract 19, row 4, number 19. While the funeral charge was only fifty-six dollars, the total cost expended by all of the families, friends, the CAA, and CAP searching for the couple likely exceeded a million of today's dollars, none of which was recoverable. While

Donna McGladrey's tombstone on the left, Verna and Leslie's on the right
Waterman, Illinois, photograph by Dorothy Mathews, courtesy of author.

Richard laid in state waiting for his funeral and burial, Leslie had Donna's remains shipped back to Waterman in a cargo box about two feet by two feet square.

On June 20, 1960, Donna was finally brought home to rest at the North Clinton Cemetery in Waterman, Illinois, in a service conducted by Dr. Stafford. Joan remembered that her remains arrived a day later than was expected, so they had to move the funeral back a day. She smiled sadly, "She was late to her own funeral." Donna's headstone read simply, "Donna Joy McGladrey, 1935–1959."

Donna's two sisters, even forty years later, still miss her terribly. Joan pondered one summer afternoon during our interviews, "I've often wondered if it had turned out differently, what kind of family would she have had." Dorothy added, "Yeah, what her kids and grandkids would be like. They would have been wonderful musicians." Overall, they arrived at the same conclusion about their beloved sister, gone so many years, "Ah, it would've been quite different if she had stayed with us." And finally, they both agreed that Donna had learned to tolerate more and to be more patient, as her letters revealed. They truly believed Donna's spirit was at home and Donna had found happiness.

CHAPTER THIRTEEN

Epilogue
"Like a Needle in a Haystack"

Donna had found happiness in Alaska. Whether or not she would have married Richard will forever haunt both families. For the Newton family, this tragedy was the first in a series of calamities. Too much suffering had fallen in a short period of time upon this small family of pioneers. With the plane's disappearance, the family's attention turned away from helping Ruby and Royce heal after the traumatic and sudden loss of their newborn, to the search for Richard and the hope that at least this life could be saved. Royce continued to give his wife attention, but was torn by devotion to his brother Charles's search and his lost brother, Richard.

To make matters worse, Matanuska Plumbing and Heating Company was already in a financial crisis before the small Cessna disappeared. Charles and Richard's work on the Dillingham school, hired out by a general contractor, had continued for over a year, despite lack of payments by the contractor. The Newton's company had to cover the cost of purchasing and shipping items out to Dillingham without being reimbursed or paid for the supplies or their labor. In the midst of this frustrating business situation, Richard was lost in the company's plane. Instead of continuing work on contracts, Charles refocused most of his energy on looking for Richard. In January, Charles borrowed a plane that he wrecked during the search. Don Wagner, Charles's employee who respected Charles greatly, remembered that after Charles rolled the plane, "they took his student ticket away." Charles never bothered to get it back. Shortly thereafter, the general contractor on the Dillingham project went into bankruptcy. The small company took the contractor to court and while they won, they ended up having to pay lawyers and court costs. Shortly thereafter, Matanuska Plumbing and Heating Company ceased to exist.

Mary recalled many years later, "It was the best thing that ever happened to us." She explained that Charles then went to work out of the local union. He became a superintendent, for he already had tremendous experience supervising contracts. "He knew how to run a job," Mary informed me proudly.[1] As a supervisor, Charles no longer had to do any of the paperwork, which he detested. He had some very good jobs and by the 1970s, Charles, like many other construction specialists, began to work on the Alaska pipeline.[2] In fact, nearly half of the men from the Newton's small Baptist church worked on the pipeline and disappeared from their families for long stretches of the year. Women simply had to learn how to get along without their men. Mary lived without Charles for about half the time while he worked out in the "boonies." Ruby remembered Royce being gone a significant amount of time as well. In retrospect, Mary commented, "It really tickles me that some of these gals complain about their husbands being gone for the weekend or their husbands gone for the night, I said yeah, tell me about it." So the women spent their energy taking care of the children, keeping up the homes, taking care of finances and book work, as well as doing "crafty" things; partly to bide the time, but also to make their homes more "homey." Royce, Charles, and Rick (Charles's son) all worked at one time on the "slope" (the North Slope, Barrow, and Prudhoe). Life for the earlier pioneers certainly differed from the latecomers from the outside. But in the back of their minds, the Newton family would never quite forget those long six months when their lives had changed forever.

After Dorothy married M. Jack Mathews in May of 1958, they lived at 829 Foster Avenue in Evanston until September 1960 when Jack joined the military and moved his wife and son to Glasgow Air Force Base in Glasgow, Montana (now a retirement community). Dorothy left behind the grave of her sister, the grass now growing and the mound sinking lower as the months passed. She left behind her mother and father, who now lived alone in Evanston. Dorothy focused on her busy little son, Danny. Shortly, she realized she was pregnant with her second child, a tiny bundle of blue-eyed giggles born in May, 1962, whom they named

Diane. In the midst of the cold war, fearing that another Cuban Missile Crisis would emerge, Dorothy had her hands full.

The emptiness of losing a daughter and Dorothy moving so far away, compiled with adjusting to a new home and job, and Joan a half-day's drive away, forced Leslie and Verna to depend upon each other for solace. They had to be relieved to learn that their surviving twin daughter would not be so far away for long. After serving his two years in Glasgow, Jack, Dorothy, Dan, and new baby Diane moved back to Evanston so that Jack could do his residency at the Veteran's Administration Hospital. The joy of having grandchildren nearby no doubt put a softer edge on the suffering that Leslie and Verna endured. Within two years, I was born (Dorothy and Jack's third child). Before I turned six months, our growing family moved to Nebraska.

Meanwhile, back in Alaska, Donna's two Church of Christ missionary friends, Roberta and Martha, whom she had attempted to visit on that last fateful trip, continued to work for a while in Dillingham. A few years later, Roberta learned to fly, earned a commercial pilot's license, and received her instrument ratings. She eventually became a flight instructor. In 1968, the two friends boarded a twin-engine F-27 commercial airliner to visit friends in Dillingham. Just short of Lake Iliamna near Pedro Bay, an explosion blew off the tail section. When the pilots lost control of the plane, it went down and all thirty-nine people on board died—several of whom were from the Dillingham area. Everyone in Dillingham remembers that crash, so many people in town lost a loved one or friend that day. While grief overtook members of the Dillingham community, most people understood that Roberta and Martha could now be with their long-lost friend Donna once again.

Unlike the crash of that large F-27 that was found rather quickly, the search for Donna's plane had extended well into 1960. For those six months, the community held out hope, just like both families. Everyone had grown to love Donna and Richard, for they were good people who did not drink or cause trouble in town. The families back in Anchorage and Illinois held out hope as well—at first, to see their loved one again; then, hope fading until memorial services in May in Illinois and Alaska brought some closure to the overwhelming tragedy that had befallen both families.

Newspaper articles fill the final pages of Donna's album that her mother so carefully constructed. Yellowed and fragile, the articles and pages of the album tear easily, but nevertheless it has survived for years in a small mobile home in which Leslie and Verna lived, then the basement storage at Oak Crest, a Methodist retirement home in DeKalb (Illinois), Dorothy's house after Verna's passing in February 1998, and finally moved to my house where it sits in an archival box. When Verna was buried in 1998, I was defending my dissertation at the University of New Mexico. Since I reread the letters in graduate school, I had been intrigued by Donna's story, even more so after I began to research Donna's story, not realizing how much it would affect me in the end. Over forty years after Donna died, I, one of the nieces she never met, would retrace her footsteps to the Alaskan tundra. One of the first places I visited was the Anchorage Memorial Cemetery to see Richard's grave. He had no headstone. Either miscommunication from the cemetery, the intense grief of the family, or the loss of Matanuska Plumbing and Heating Company kept the family from seeing to Richard's tombstone. I learned, however, from Cemetery Director Don Wharton that the Anchorage Mayor had approved payment and installation of veteran headstones. Wharton promised me that Richard would get his veteran's marker. As of the summer of 2002, it was still not there. But Richard's headstone, at this point, was not my priority. I needed to learn as much as I could in Dillingham from her former students, if they even remembered her.

"What would I find in Dillingham?" I thought as I left behind my oversized suitcase at a bed and breakfast in Anchorage. I suppose I could have taken the big suitcase, but I did not want to overpack. I felt as if I should limit myself as Donna had. So, I packed the bare necessities for March in Alaska: wool socks, hiking boots, winter coat, mittens, hat, scarf, wind pants. I also carefully crammed into my already bulging bag a tape-recorder, microphones, batteries, and cassette tapes. I then carried onto the tiny two-prop jet my laptop, scanner, and two cameras and plenty of film. When I got onto the plane, I took out my journal and began writing. What would I find there? How much has the town changed? Would people remember Donna? What happens if the students hated her? What happens if she was a terrible teacher? Will people even talk to me? Will there be a restaurant? How will I meet people? Would Donna even approve of this project? Is this a waste of my time? Question after question I scribbled into my journal. Donna must have asked similar questions: Will the children like me? Will I do a good job? Where am I going to live? Who will be my friends? What will I do when I'm not teaching? Was moving to the Territory of Alaska the right thing to do? What happens if I want to go home tomorrow? Will people be disappointed in me? Will I do a good job? Will Daddy be proud of me? Like Donna, I would find answers to many of these questions within a few hours of arriving in Dillingham.

I arrived at Dillingham's small regional airport, consisting of a metal building with rooms that contained the ticket counters, waiting area, and telephone. In another narrow room, the boarding passengers were being herded through the security checkpoint, while their bags were being x-rayed. I arrived at the Bristol Inn, owned and operated by Choggiung, Ltd., the Alaska Native Corporation that organized after the Alaska Native Claims Settlement Act of 1971. I immediately telephoned Tim Troll, a local historian about whom I heard while at the Anchorage Museum of History and Art. He was excited to hear about my project and asked if I had met Verna Lee Heyano, who was working downstairs in the hotel. I said no, then promptly went downstairs and introduced myself. Verna Lee was a beautiful woman, with long, slightly graying hair held back by an intricately beaded barrette. She had dance fan earrings. Tim apparently told her that I was coming and she excitedly explained that she had been in Donna's sixth-grade class. We hit it off immediately, and since then I consider her one of my closest friends in Alaska. I love spending time with her, mostly because we laugh constantly.

Later that day, I met Tim Troll, who took me on a tour of Dillingham. On subsequent research trips, he encouraged me to read from Donna's letters for his radio show, "Our Story." We taped enough for three separate shows, which aired after I left that March of 2001. He explained much to me about the history of the Bristol Bay region, the canneries (the big local Peter Pan Cannery just turned one hundred years old). I had a behind-the-scenes tour of the cannery, as well as the Samuel K. Fox Museum. Most important, Tim showed great interest in my project and directed me toward numerous resources that proved invaluable to my research. And as a sidenote, he and his wife also introduced me to an Alaskan steamhouse.

We entered the plywood shack down the hill behind Tim's home and I found myself in a small narrow room with a bench built into the wall, and a window for all Alaska to see my nakedness. I undressed with Tim's wife and her friend (a local nurse), and we entered the steam bath through a narrow door. The two were "steam mates," often steaming

Author with Verna Lee Heyano at Bristol Bay Inn,
Dillingham, Alaska, March 2001.

together. The ceiling was just over six feet high, and around a large black cast iron wood stove were built-in plywood benches. The other two clamored to the highest seat, leaving me to sit next to the inferno. I had just left Nebraska's record-setting summer of temperatures over one hundred degrees, and here I sat in a room at nearly 250 degrees, sweltering, while outside snow still sat in the mountains. We bathed, took a respite in the cooling room; bathed, took a respite. Once more we entered the intense heat until I could take it no more. I could feel my lungs shriveling and my heart racing. Even the cool water in my pan provided no relief and I choked under the pressure. I wondered how sweating could possibly leave me feeling clean, but in all honesty, I have never experienced such a pure or cleansing experience in all my life.

While in Dillingham, I had the great fortune to connect with Hermann and Hilda Kroener, whom I had met on a previous visit in Chugiak. They had quickly become my other two dearest Alaska friends. On my last day in Dillingham, Hilda, Hermann, and their grandson Luke from Denver, stopped by the Bristol Inn to visit me. They had been out at their camp on the Igushik River, fishing for salmon. On a whim, around 9:00 P.M., we left Luke to play computer games (something he surely missed while he was at fish camp) while Hermann drove Hilda and me out to see Kanakanak Hospital, the hospital that called Orin Seybert on that fateful mission that flew him over Richard's plane, since I had never seen it. We drove past Gustie Wahl's homesite, across the road from Squaw Creek and Gustie's boat yard, and past the original townsite of Dillingham, or Olsonville, where Hilda grew up. We drove down the road where Hermann and Hilda haul their skiff in and out of the Nushagak and drove along the beach, noticing the tide coming in by the buoys marking the set nets along the beach. We then drove up to the hospital and Hermann enthusiastically pointed out a smaller white building with green trim that he had worked on so many years before. "They say it's the only building that never had problems with plumbing," Hermann proudly commented. "It's because we used silver solder, which is more expensive." Then we drove out beyond the hospital to the huge VOR beacons, which pilots use to guide them safely home. When we turned around at the end of the road, I took a photograph of the huge cross put up by Gustie Wahl around 1999 across the river at Nushagak where the first Russian Orthodox church used to sit as early as 1812. This immense cross had been built by Wahl and, in around 1999, the community helped him transport it on pontoons and drag it over with fishing boats—finally hauling it up and securing it with guy wires. Following this photo op, we began to head back to Dillingham when Hilda mentioned that sometimes the salmonberries are ready this time of year.

I had no idea what a salmonberry was, and Hilda offered to stop and see if we could find some. Out on the west side of the bay behind the hospital, the tundra flattened out above the river. Even though it was 9:30 at night, we could see for miles in the misty, overcast evening. We stepped out of the truck and crossed the road. I followed Hilda dutifully onto the Arctic tundra. She began shouting, "I found blueberries! BLUEBERRIES!" Out there on the tundra, without large trees or any other windbreak for miles, it was windy and cool, but I did not feel it. I had on my wool socks and Merrell hiking boots and trudged out farther onto the soft, squishy tundra. I slogged over to Hilda, who was cradling a blueberry bush delicately in her left hand. She pulled a berry and handed it to me, and I obliged her with a grin. "They're ripe!" she said with a big smile as she excitedly trudged off in search of the luminescent salmonberries.

We walked, hunched over, picking and popping. Every minute or two, Hilda would holler at Hermann, "Hermann, here's a bunch of blueberries! Ripe blueberries!" We wandered farther and farther away from the truck, following the trail of blueberries. We found a few cranberries, mossberries, and then Hilda hollered, "Sandra, come over here! Salmonberries! Ripe Salmonberries!" She said, "There's something in them that stops cancer," and with a smile popped the big berry into her mouth. We were out there, in the middle of what seemed like nowhere, for over a half hour collecting and eating berries of all kinds.

It was an amazing experience. After having read *Two Old Women* by Velma Wallis, I had begun to understand the role that every piece of sustenance, every morsel from the natural environment, played in the lives of traditional Alaska Natives. I marveled at the energy and time it must have taken to collect enough for an entire family for the severe winter months since the berries were half the size of a dime. I thought about the long tradition, and how Hilda and Hermann both took such great pride in her heritage and the lessons it had taught her—and now she shared with me. I felt incredibly honored.

I did learn not to eat the crowberries, though. Hilda could not remember why, but she knew we were not supposed to eat them. She found edible and nonedible mushrooms, then trounced off toward the lonely tree to find more salmonberries with their almost luminescent glow. It was getting darker, however. Even my 800 film would not allow me to take photographs anymore. My hiking boots were getting wet, and since I had only shorts on, I suppose I should have been cold. The exhilaration of hunting for berries with people who knew Donna and her more-often-than-not boyfriend Richard Newton, the beauty of the tundra and its fascinating colors and plants (including the Arctic cotton), kept me from noticing the conditions that cooled by the moment. But it was starting to get dark and Hilda began to worry about Luke a bit, so we made our way back to the truck. Hermann turned on the heat in his truck as we turned back toward Dillingham, but Hilda and I quickly became hot. I was exhilarated and nearly speechless. I would never forget that night, with the grey skies and wind, light mist and swampy tundra, and being in the company of such good friends collecting berries as Alaska Natives had done there for hundreds of years. To me, at that moment, time did not exist. It was as if I had entered into the mystery of becoming one with the ages, connecting with the past in a way that only being in nature allows. The spirituality of the place touched me as well, knowing that I walked upon the very ground that Donna spied from several hundred feet in the air, describing its enduring beauty.

When Charles Newton wrote that fateful letter in June 1960, the end of the search for Richard and Donna had finally come. Finding the plane and bringing home Donna's remains signaled the end to a long period of great suffering, wondering, worrying, and sorrow. But for me, who learned of Donna's story many years later, closure did not come. For some reason, I felt compelled to find the wreckage. In four separate trips over a two-year period, I had retraced every one of Donna's Alaskan footsteps, at least that I could determine or pursue. I needed to witness the final image of Donna's footprint in Alaska, where Donna's soul, released from her body, soared. So I began to research the location of the accident, as well as the circumstances that surrounded it, by talking with bush pilots with many years of experience. One of those pilots was Hermann Kroener. As always, Hermann was gracious and offered useful information and maps.

When I first approached Hermann about the location of the wreckage, he seemed quite interested that John Paul Bouker, owner of Bay Air in Dillingham, told me that it was Peninsula Air President Orin Seybert that had originally found Donna's plane. Hermann remembered that the plane was below a little village called Portage Creek. I told Hermann that in order to give me a sense of what it was like to fly on a bush plane, my good friend Tim Troll had convinced John Paul to take me on one of his runs to the village of Portage Creek to drop off the school counselor. In his years as a pilot, John Paul had seen a plane wreckage farther west. Hermann was determined, "They [Donna and Richard] were still a little bit off course, but not that much." I needed to trust Hermann; he has flown the region for more than forty years, going back and forth to his wife's fish camp on the Igushik from Anchorage. Moreover, he had been at the crash site. Hermann remembered, even though so many years had passed, that he and Charles rented a floatplane and landed at a nearby lake [likely Supply Lake], then hiked about five miles to the crash site. He brought out an FAA map and carefully plotted the location according to Charles's letter, twelve miles south southeast of Black Point (just a bit north and west of Portage Creek, and according to Hermann Kroener, the promontory is also known as Black Slough). For nearly an hour, he wrestled with his map, his measuring tools, and his memory, while Hilda and I talked. In the end, however, he had pinpointed where he thought the plane might be—from his memory of having seen it both by plane and on foot on the swampy tundra, so many years ago. He then gave the map to me.

During my July 2001 research trip, I contacted Orin Seybert, who surprisingly remembered seeing the wreckage. It continues to amaze me how these tragedies leave an indelible mark in so many people's memories—even those who seem to have no direct connection to those who perished. I sat down and I listened to Orin's story about how he spotted the plane. Yes, he was coming up from Egegik, but not on a direct course. He had flown along the coast and headed north to Dillingham at Johnson Hill. About three to five miles inland, he saw the plane. This trajectory would have put the sighting about twelve miles south southeast of Black Point, which is where Charles reported the accident's location originally in his letter to Donna's father in 1960. Orin carefully marked the location of the wreckage on another map. Now I had two maps that clearly illustrated the location of the crash site in a location southeast of Black Point.

In March 2002, the weather did not cooperate, Bristol Bay had seen a LOT of snow that year. Even if the weather was good, I would not be able to see the wreckage through the snow. So, I planned perhaps my final research trip in the summer of 2002, late July. I felt guilty, thinking I would not have enough to do on this final journey—but just like my fears about the first trip, I found more than I expected. Once again, I arrived in Dillingham, eager to talk with Donna's former students, colleagues, and friends. When I ran into Tim Troll, he asked me if I would like to find the crash site. I jumped at the chance. He set it up for the very next day with John Paul Bouker.

We had originally planned to leave at 1:00 on Friday afternoon, but the overcast skies and rain delayed our trip for an hour. I sat in the hotel room, busily typing, rewriting, and reworking the manuscript as I awaited the phone call from Tim. When he called, he said, "It looks like the weather is good, are you ready?" So I headed downstairs and met Tim, who drove me out to the airport where we met the owner/operator of Bristol Bay Air. I had been introduced to John Paul Bouker before. He was Tim's steam-mate, had short red hair, and chewed nicotine gum with determination to quit smoking so he could be around longer for his family. After he filled up the right wing with fuel, he invited us in. Before I knew it, Tim had crawled in the back seat, whereupon I committed two major aviation blunders. I used the struts to balance my foot as I tried to climb into his single engine, small plane; and then I lightly grabbed the door for balance. Gently, but determined and concerned, he prevailed upon me: "Please don't stand on the struts"; then, "Please don't grab my door." Rather embarrassed at being such a *Cheechako*, or greenhorn, I said perhaps too defensively, "Ya gotta tell me these things, I'm not used to flying." He was kind and gentle, and quickly gave instructions to me about buckling up and handing my camera bag to Tim to get it out of the way. My gracious host was nothing but pure business, concerned with our safety and the maintenance of his plane. Who could blame him?

John Paul then taxied the aircraft, in what seemed like no time at all, to the taxiway leading to the runway. He passed a plane, which looked like it was ready to hit the runway and take off, quickly looked up the runway, and then before I knew it, turned west onto the runway. Within seconds we were in the air heading south. He flew Tim Troll and me on a straight line from Dillingham to Egegik, crossing the muddy Nushagak, and south past the old community with the huge cross. We flew across tundra and scrub forest where winding trails of caribou and moose connected forest with tundra meadow and ponds. Small lakes dotted the paths between small hills, or hummocks, and forest groves. As we flew farther south, I wondered what my reaction would be if we found the plane. Then John Paul pointed out Etolin Point, and I hastily snapped a picture—I didn't know what else to do.

We came closer to the open waters, separating us from Egegik and the Aleutian Chain, my first glance at Bristol Bay that shared boundaries with the Bering Sea. This is the closest I had ever been to Russia, the chain, and all of the King Crab fishers who put their lives in harm's way daily—the most dangerous job in the world.[3] I refocused as we grew closer. Then John Paul said what I had anticipated and feared most: "The plane is in this area here." We began our search, circling and crossing Larson Creek at many trajectories, all somewhat in line with the Egegik heading from Dillingham. As the sun popped from behind the low-flying clouds, I saw its reflection on the glimmering ponds a few hundred feet below us. On one of our first passes toward Etolin Point, both John Paul and I shot upright in our seats as a plane-shaped figure came into view dead ahead of us. I snapped two photographs as my heart raced. I began to feel the anticipation, fear, excitement, anxiety, at the very prospect of seeing the plane. As we came closer, we both recognized it as yet another pond that simply reflected the sun. He explained that it had been twelve years since he saw the wreckage—one day that he boldly flew a direct line from Egegik to Dillingham, a very dangerous proposition indeed. Back then, he saw the wreckage, circled above it a few times, then stopped by Dick Armstrong's place to report what he had found. Dick had explained that it was the plane of the school-teacher, lost so many years before. As we kept circling, I began to real-ize how Leslie McGladrey must have felt—hoping to catch a glimmer of metal in the snow covered hummocks of Alaska in January 1960. I often wondered, "How in the hell does anyone find anything out here?" Just then, John Paul again said, "It's right here in this area, on the side and top of a hill," in full view. I had never attempted to look for a plane before and had no idea what I was looking for. I saw some-thing white and my heartbeat started racing again—only to see the white object fly away with its mate. Swans dotted the glorious tundra. I saw something else! Wait, just another puddle on the swampy tundra. Oh, is that the plane? My heart raced again—nope, just a small flock of white birds or some white rocks. Each time after my heart senselessly raced, my heart would slow and my stomach would churn ever so slightly. Was I excited or nervous? What would I do if we found the

The hummocks and ponds of Bristol Bay region without much snow
illustrate how difficult a search might have been in January after
a snow. Searching for Donna's plane on Etolin Point in July 2002,
with John Paul Bouker and Tim Troll. Photograph by author.

plane? Would I cry? Would I react by just taking pictures? And how many would be enough?

But we did not see the plane, and I became frustrated, thinking we were searching the wrong area. After all, Hermann Kroener told me that it was twelve miles south southeast of Black Point—I was sure we were too far west. Orin Seybert told me that when he saw the plane, he was not in a direct line from Egegik, but had flown up the coast to a place somewhere short of Johnson Hill, before he took a direct heading to Dillingham. John Paul recognized the type of hill upon which the plane sat, but we could not find the wreckage. Nevertheless he had seen it and knew it was there.

Leslie wrote about similar feelings of frustration to those that I had. His were obviously much stronger, compounded by having the search his sole purpose for coming to Alaska, of having to wait for days for the weather to clear, and of hoping to find his daughter alive. In fact, after he left Alaska the first time to move his household to Sherman Avenue, he gave a public speech at the TEI convention dinner, which drew upon his recent anguish. He must have spoken of peering through a plane window into the snowy tundra, hoping to catch a glimpse of a cream and silver plane, with its small splash of red on the wing and body. Having searched on a relatively sunny day in the summer and not finding the plane, I can only imagine how frustrating that search must have been in the dead of winter with drifting snow. We even had a relative location and knew upon which side of a small hill the plane lay. He had no knowledge of the plane's location, only that he must find his daughter somewhere out on the frozen and desolate tundra.

As we continued to circle, I began to feel guilty about taking up John Paul's time, making his other passengers that he kicked off the plane wait while we flew around in circles—seemingly in aimless designs, in a sense mimicking the caribou and moose tracks below. But those caribou and moose tracks had a purpose, for the trails had been there for generations, leading their travelers to water, food, and shelter. We, on the other hand, were following a path in circles and lines, not knowing where we would turn or what we might find when we finally arrived there. I told John Paul that I really appreciated his helping me search, but that I knew that he had other things to do. John Paul said we had flown over the top of the plane, he was certain, "but you really have to know what you're looking for." He told me about a B-29 that crashed near Portage Creek. He flies out there all the time, but he has only seen it twice. He told me of another plane, halfway between Etolin Point and Nushagak that he had only seen a couple times as well. "The sun has to catch it just right," he explained.

As we turned north toward Dillingham, I looked over my shoulder to the east longingly, wanting to grab the controls and head us back again. But instead, I watched out the window as we flew away from Donna's beckoning spirit. On the way back to Dillingham, I saw no moose, no caribou, no beaver, but saw signs of them everywhere. I saw huge beaver dams dotting the edges of the lakes. Soon we flew just barely east of Nushagak and again saw Gustie Wahl's immense cross. When we landed, ever so softly—for John Paul is an excellent bush pilot—the engine slowed and stopped with a slight lurch. I unbuckled my seatbelt as Tim said quietly, "Like a needle in a haystack." That phrase has haunted me ever since.

We had departed Dillingham around 2:05 P.M., but did not return until about 3:30 P.M. The next passengers had given up waiting at the airport, apparently, for they were nowhere to be found. Tim told John Paul to "write it [the bill] up and send it to him," and when I offered, Tim would not hear of me paying for it. I begged him to let me cover it—after all, it took fuel, time, and energy, for we had been flying for almost an hour and a half. Tim said, "Let's just wait to see what he writes up." I left it at that, for Alaskans are truly the most generous people you will ever meet.

Admittedly, I was overwhelmed by my experience. I tried to tell Tim about how Leslie's heart must have raced when he thought he saw the plane, and the sinking pit in his stomach when he realized it was nothing. He asked me if that's how I felt, and I quickly answered yes. Out of excitement, I said. We both knew it was far more than just that. He then told me that he, too, had seen the B-29 by Portage Creek, but it was not one big piece of plane. It consisted of pieces of metal strewn across an area that, if the sun didn't catch it just right, you would not be able to see. That was his gentle way of letting me know that I might find even less of this forty-year-old wreck. As it turned out, we found nothing but the beauty of nature in lakes, streams, ponds and puddles, tundra trails, caribou, moose, gulls, and swans that drew Donna to love Alaska. But the trip was worth it. I witnessed the topography in which Donna's spirit found its home. She marveled at the rivers, the color of the berries and turning leaves, the gracefulness of the swans, and the pristine beauty of the wilderness. Although Donna's family had to wait for months before her body returned for burial, it struck me that her spirit immediately was embraced by the beauty that she loved.

I could not remain in Dillingham forever. The night before I left, perhaps for the last time as a researcher studying Donna's life, I walked over to the Dillingham Hotel managed by Pete Olson, one of Donna's students. I needed to return an informational sheet about Dillingham that he lent me the day before, during my interview with him. As I stepped up to the desk, three Native men in their twenties or thirties turned to see who had come up the stairs. As they turned to Pete, one of them said, "Oh, isn't she pretty! Look at those dimples!" That was the first time that I can remember being complimented so enthusiastically on my dimples. It seemed fitting that the compliment came in the Dillingham Hotel. Although it is a different building now, the name and the spirit of that particular place evoked a strong feeling of connection to Donna, and where she had lived so many years before. Pete apologized for them, saying, "It looks like they're out early tonight." I laughed and responded, "Hey, I'll take a compliment from anyone!" I returned his documents and hopped down the stairs, guessing how many times Donna had heard the very same thing.

The next day, I headed to the airport to return to Anchorage. Saddened, I wondered if this would be my last trip to Donna's home. My friend Tim was waiting for the same plane, heading south to Oregon to join his family on vacation. On a wall map that hung in the waiting room at the airport terminal, I showed him where I thought the plane lay, and he reminded me that John Paul was simply trying to show me the location of the plane that he had seen. Then he told me that he had gone to find the gravesite of another teacher in a remote Alaskan bush community. He searched and searched, but could not find it. He felt ripped off, as if someone had let him down. Why hadn't someone kept it up for him, he playfully asked. But then again, he was the first person in probably ten years that attempted to find her grave. He told me that he wondered, as we flew with John Paul, "Were we meant to find the plane?" I admitted that I had thought the same.

Perhaps I was not meant to see the plane. Perhaps this was a lesson that I needed to learn: I cannot always find everything, I was not meant to uncover every story, and I was not meant to understand why they made the choice to fly that day. Perhaps I was just meant to chase Donna's shadow and tell the story she left to me, as ambiguous in death as were her affections for Richard in life.[4]

Appendix A

THE OLD MAID'S SONG: LESLIE D. MCGLADREY'S VERSION

I'll sing you a song of a burglar bold
Who went to rob a house.
He opened the window and then crept in
As quiet as a mouse.
He looked for a place to hide himself
'Til the folks were all asleep.
And then said he, "By Jiminy!
I think I'll take a peep!"
So under the bed the burglar crept,
He crept close to the wall.
He didn't know it was an old maid's room
Or he wouldn't have made the call.
He thought of all the money he'd get
As under the bed he lay.
But at 9 o'clock he saw a sight
That made his hair turn gray.
At 9 o'clock an old maid came in:
"Oh, I'm so tired," she said;
She thought that all was well that night,
And forgot to look under the bed!
She took out her teeth, and her big glass eye,

And the hair from off of her head.
That burglar, he had 90 fits
As he looked from under the bed.
From under the bed the burglar crept,
He was a total wreck.
The old maid wasn't asleep at all;
She grabbed him by the neck.
She didn't scream, nor yell, nor cry;
She was as cool as a clam;
Said she, "The Saints be praised!
At last I've got a man!"
From under her pillow, a pistol she drew;
She aimed it right at his head;
"Young man! If you don't marry me
I'll shoot off the top of your head!"
She held him closely by the neck;
He had no chance to scoot.
He looked at the teeth, and the big glass eye,
And said, "Madam, for Pete's Sake, SHOOT!"

[Leslie used to sing this song to his daughters and grandchildren while they were growing up.]

Appendix B

Vocal: "Prayer for the Innocent," by George McCay (February 8, 1955)

Organ: Chorale-Prelude "Beloved Jesu," by Johannes Brahms (February 7, 1956)

Vocal (Soprano): "Psyche," by Emile Paladilhe, accompanied by Mrs. Gerson at the Piano (April 17, 1956)

Vocal: "Gesang Weyla's," by Hugo Wolf (November 13, 1956)

Vocal: "Fussreise," by Hugo Wolf and "Velvet Shoes," by Randall Thompson, accompanied by Phyllis Wong at piano (November 18, 1956)

Organ: Chorale-Prelude "O Sacred Head, Now Wounded," by Johann Kuhnau; Fugue on the Kyrie by Francois Couperin le Grand; and Chorale-Prelude "As Jesus Stood Beside the Cross," by Samuel Scheidt (November 20, 1956)

Vocal Quartet: "Emitte Spiritum Tuum," by Schuetky-Singenberger, with Phyllis Wong, Barbara Moore, and Nanci Weeks (November 27, 1956)

Organ: Canon in B Major, Op. 56, No. 3, by Robert Schumann (February 12, 1957)

Vocal: "Silent Noon," by Vaughn Williams (March 5, 1957)

Lenten Vespers: Miserere (Psalm LI) IV. Deliver Me, with Phyllis Wong (April 14, 1957)

Organ: All Saints' Day Meditation: "Gaudeamus," by Everett Titcomb (June 1, 1957)

Vocal (Mezzo-Soprano): "Voi Che sapete," *Marriage of Figaro*, by Mozart, with Jessamine Ewert ('59) on piano (June 1, 1957)

Source: Photo album constructed by Verna McGladrey for Donna McGladrey, courtesy of author.

Appendix C

Letter from Leslie D. McGladrey to Donna Joy McGladrey

Tuesday evening

Dear Donna,

Mother just told me of her recent telephone conversation with you. I am glad that you got the contract and hope you sign it and go back for another year.

This whole situation gives me an opportunity to say a few things that may be helpful to you. After a person graduates from a college he soon finds himself enrolled in a post graduate course in the "University of Hard Knocks." I know for I have been in that school for a long time!

Another observation I might make is that there is a marked difference between theory and practice. It all seemed so easy and thrilling during student days. Now it turns out to be hard, hard work day after day. Some of the theories did not work. You are on your own and have to work out your own salvation.

You are in a period when you have not gained full confidence in yourself and your abilities. You have made some mistakes. We all do. It isn't very important what happens to you. The important thing is how you take what happens. You are in a time of testing. This is a rather critical time. If you run away from it all, you will have permanent difficulty in gaining self-confidence. If you face it squarely with the determination to win, you will win. Mistakes and failures are the stepping stones to success. Actually you haven't failed at all. You have met some difficult situations and you haven't pleased everybody. That's all it amounts to. Let it go at that.

This enclosed booklet came in the mail today and I am enclosing it with the suggestion that the camp from June 29th to July 4th might be just the thing for you. I had theory of preaching in my theological training. I went out to preach and found myself making more mistakes than you ever thought of making. I went back and took more training and it meant far more when I had had some experience. Something of this nature, or a summer school session might be worth all the sacrifice it would take.

Don't worry about it all. I worried myself into ulcers at your age and it didn't do me a bit of good. Do your best and let it go at that. Mother and I are betting on you. We know you have got what it takes.

Love,
Daddy

Appendix D

Letters from Bobbie and Marty (Roberta Tew, and Martha Jay)

[During the summer of 1959, Donna received messages from her friends, Roberta and Martha, the missionaries at the Church of Christ in Dillingham. The handwritten personal messages to Donna added to their form letters follow.]

> Dillingham, Alaska
> June 16, 1959
> [From Bobbie]

Hi!

Just a note along with this so you'll think you got a letter! The weather here is beautiful now—at least yesterday and today. I'm surely hoping it will continue.

Wish you had been here yesterday. We had a nice boat ride and a picnic. It was surely loads of fun! We are hoping to go by boat to Naknek tomorrow with Lyle Smith, but aren't sure yet. It would sure be a nice excursion.

Guess Rich has told you about Herman. We've had such a blessing in fellowship with him. He's sure a swell person. Of course Richard is sort of 'droopy' now 'cause he misses you so. We do too—a little! (Really lots!) Wish you were coming here this fall.

We have surely been praying the Lord will use you greatly to win souls for Him. It often takes much time and prayer, but Praise His Name, our God is <u>all</u> powerful.

Must close now. Be good & write again <u>real</u> soon. We love you, miss you, & pray always His richest blessings shall be yours.

Love in Christ,

II

P.S. here are some 'mouse catchers.' When the mice catch a glimpse of these they'll fall over in a dead faint!

Dillingham, Alaska

July 30, 1959

[From Bobbie]

Dear Donna,

Just a few extra lines. We enjoy your letters so much, and are surely getting anxious to see you.

My, it <u>surely</u> would be lots of fun to fly over and drive around with you. We would enjoy so much an opportunity to visit with you as well as see some more of Alaska. We'll check and let you know for sure, meanwhile write and let us know for sure when you would want to do it.

Well, must close and get all these newsletters sent. 'Bye now. Write <u>real</u> soon and have a nice trip. May His richest blessings be yours.

Love,

Bobbie

[Another handwritten note, from Marty]

'Tis I again! Must do my little part or I won't hear from you.

The last few days have been beauties, so warm and sunny. Such a switch from the usual cloudy and windy days.

There was a surprise baby shower for Tressie last Tues. and believe me she was surprised. She received many pretty things. She is hoping to see you before she goes outside.

Hurry and come back to Alaska. We want to see you again soon. With love and best wishes.

Marty

Appendix E

Letter from Merlin to Verna, Dorothy, and Danny, January 9, 1960, Larson Air Force Base, Washington

[excerpt]

There's something you can do here, too. Some letters of appreciation and encouragement to some of the following people would keep the pot boiling:

1. Lt. Col. Carleton, Commander
   King Salmon Air Force Station
   King Salmon, Alaska

He houses, sympathizes, flies searches when the authorities aren't looking, provides transportation and meals for Leslie and the Newtons. He is cooperative <u>far far</u> beyond the call of duty. Poor guy's lonely: wife, sons 16 and 13 in Florida. He has remote Alaska tour (one of several isolated tours). A note of appreciation would help.

2. Myron Moran, Dillingham—The main spring of the Dillingham search, a community leader, knew both Donna and Rick.

3. Airman White, King Salmon HDS Motor Pool—diamond in the rough, drives jeep, tries to go as observer on searches. Had deep interest and guts to call all men in his barracks together and say, "We're all just goin' a say a prayer tonight for dem two kids out there in the tundra." . . .

4. Lt. Earl Gay, C.A.P.

King Salmon, Alaska

Search commander who works long hours, applies vast knowledge as professional weather forecaster and radio operator and pilot to search.

5. Mr. Emmert &/or Rev. Wayne Hull, Chugiak.

They took initiative to prove Donna was on aircraft and to call you. Mr. Emmert put V-W in police custody, sent Mr. McKinley teacher—pilot to join search. Wayne Hull is CAP Chaplain on duty at Dillingham as chaplain and observer.

6. Chaplain (Col.) E. I. Corriker [Carriker]

Alaska Air Command, Elmendorf A.F. Base

Anchorage, Alaska

He stretched regulations to put Leslie on military air travel status in Alaska, thus allowing him to eat in government mess hal[l]s, etc. Ch. Carriker tied in all possible civilian and military help, contacted newspapers, the Hulls, the Newtons, et al. Took hours from a busy schedule to set us up with parkas, boots—all sour dough equipment (over his own signature). Ch. Carriker volunteered to fill Wayne Hull's pulpit to release him for CAP duty. Ch. Carriker is very worried about his wife. She goes to hospital for very serious "exploratory" next week—5 children.

7. Chaplain (Lt. Col.) John Smeltzer

Staff Chaplain, 10th Air Division

Elmendorf A.F. Base, Alaska

John got first coordinated effort started in 10th Air Div. Hq. air search section. He was my original caller from Alaska a half hour after you called me the first time. John took Leslie to dinner from chapel service just after he landed on Sunday 3 January. He brought Leslie and Ch. Carriker to meet my plane, took us to his home for supper, thence to the search Hq. to get our first briefing. He and his wife were extremely cordial and helpful.

8. Lt. Betty Wolverton

ISO CAP Squadron

Elmendorf A.F.B., Alaska

Betty is the Information Services officer. The more scoop, baby pics or any human interest you can pumpto her, the more she'll keep the search in the paper. She's eager newspaper type, but very kind and deeply interested in rescue project.

Appendix F

Donna Joy McGladrey was born April 19, 1935, in Mora, Minnesota. She attended grammar school in Plainfield, Mendota, and Chicago, Illinois. She graduated from Parker High School, Chicago in 1953, was a 1957 graduate of the School of Music of MacMurray College, Jacksonville, Illinois and had started work toward her Master's degree in music at Northern Illinois University, De Kalb, Illinois. She taught music in the public schools of Northbrook, Illinois, Dillingham and Chugiak, Alaska. She was a member of the Methodist Church, active in church life wherever she went and served as organist and choir director in the Methodist Church while in Chugiak.

On December 30, 1959 Donna and her fiancé, Richard Newton, were lost on a flight from Anchorage to Dillingham. To date, no trace of the young couple has been found. She leaves to mourn her loss, her parents, Rev. and Mrs. L. D. McGladrey of 309 Sherman Avenue, Evanston, Illinois, a twin sister, Mrs. Dorothy Mathews of 829 Foster Avenue, Evanston, Illinois, an older sister, Mrs. Joan Engelsen of 1706–23rd Avenue, N.E., Minneapolis, Minnesota, a grandfather, W. J. McGladrey of 5224–45th Avenue So., Minneapolis, Minnesota, a niece, Karen Engelsen, and a nephew, Daniel Mathews.

Appendix G

June 16, 1960

Mr. McGladrey

Dear Friend

This is the hardest letter I hope I ever have to write. About one month ago a pilot, Mr. Carl Glick of Kenai, a missionary was flying "on the deck" in foul weather following the coast south of port Hieden and being followed closely by Mr. Johnson of Kenai. Because they had to follow the coast or become lost they both sighted a wing at the low tide mark. Since the Bureaucratic powers involved prefer not to disseminate such news we heard it 2 wks. later from Albert Ball via phone. Knowing that the next series of low tides in that area would be mon and tue just passed we arranged to check out another rumor or sighting or whatever you can call it on Sunday Eve (13th). We received another call from A Ball advising us that he had seen 32 Bravo at a new sighting S.SE. of Dillingham.

Monday after wiring you we took off to Dillingham and upon arrival took A. Ball out to show us the site as we didn't see it going in.

The craft was in its proper position in relation to the Ground but badly damaged and burned. After asking the A.F. Helicopter commander to take me in with him and being refused on the ground of too much load. (He had 6 or 7 men in a 16 man craft) I chartered a Float Plane and flew to a lake about 5 miles from the site and walked in.

Mr. Guy [Gay] had informed Mr. Richardson (sat) at Rescue Control that he definitely was not sending a copter in.

At any rate upon arrival at the scene we found that the plane which was located about 12 miles S.SE. of Black point had gone in at about a 60 degree angle in a sharp right spiral at well over 160 miles per hr. If you remember, Gay had put Rich into the overcast on instruments at 5:19 and Donna's watch stopped at 5:25 just 2 minutes after the last transmission

The plane exploded and burned on impact. The left door was torn off and lay about 5 or 6' out and a little behind its opening. The left ski and main gear was lying about 5' behind it. The nose gear was under the Front seat and the right main gear was under the baggage compartment. They were known to be wearing 2 knit sweaters. Each had a parka, and 3 sleeping bags were in the plane, however, the only cloth found was a small polka dot piece of blouse and a very small piece of green shadow plaid wool shirt. The Heat was so intense that 2 steel wrenches were fused together. The entire Fusilage except the epedaige or tail Feathers was melted down to a few small blobs of metal. Death was between breaths, instantaneous and merciful. They suffered from the Fire not at all.

The right wing was completely burned. The only salvageable part was the left elevator which wasn't worth getting out.

On the next day after this which was wed, we were instructed second hand not to visit the site or move away parts until such time as the FAA could make an examination. Had I not already been there I would most certainly have gone in then. Never in my life have I seen such non-co-operation and downright hinderance by our supposed public servants. I'll walk alone from now on and just hope they give me a wide berth.

Knowing that there was some difficulty in the shipment of human remains I had ordered 2 sealers from Anchorage via n.c.h. [n.c.l.?] previous to the time when I spoke to Chaplain Carriker and ask him to explain the Facts to you thinking that I could ship direct to you but as it turns out Donna is now in the Anchorage Funeral Chapel awaiting your instructions.[*]

Without your help much of the search would have been impossible even tho the time energy and money were lost.

Gone is the time when we must jump at a whisper and go running off on a wild goose chase to follow a rumor.

We owe another debt of gratitude to Western Alaska personell and E. C. Chron.[†]

The packages which you requested were consolidated and I am sending you the slips which I should have done sooner. I certainly hope you receive them in good shape.[‡]

On the last trip out back to Anch while passing a little north of the downed craft and while thinking that possibly that was the last time I would see it Chron said "Here we are Feeling sorry for them and they're up there looking down wondering when we're going to join them and realy live.["] So the balance of the trip wasn't half bad.

Please advise me if there is any further thing which I can do. I'd be only too glad to do it.

Your Friend

Chas. A.

Thank you for your Christian attitude
From you I learned much

Chas. A,

[On Verna's copy of Charles's transcribed letter, Verna inserted the following information: "This last statement is the one that means much to us. Knowing Charles as an ardent and active So. Baptist, belonging to a group that is intolerant of the established churches, a man who felt the Methodists had lost their fervor, we are particularly impressed by this comment. How true the Christian friendships and faith jumps artificial human barriers!"]

---

[*]On a transcribed copy of this letter that Verna likely typed out for family and friends, she inserted various commentaries. At this point, she writes, "As it turned out, she was supposed to have been in Dillingham awaiting our orders; and considerable delay was caused by their flying her out to A. without permission. We sent the telegram to D. and undertaker answered, and then we telegraphed A.—V.M."

[†]At this point, Verna inserted "Baptist minister pilot near Chugiak."

[‡]At this point, Verna inserted "we did."

Appendix H

December 27, 1960

Dear Joan,

What can I say? How can I ever thank you? I received the sweater yesterday and it is beautiful and fits perfectly. It gives me happiness in remembering Donna but also sorrow. I couldn't help shedding a few tears.

I knew she had started sweaters for Roberta and me, but I thought they were in the plane with her. Roberta and I mentioned several times how wonderful it would have been if the sweaters had not been destroyed—that we would have been happy with them even unfinished. Needless to say, I am overjoyed having received the sweater and can't begin to tell you Joan how I appreciate your finishing it and sending it to me.

Donna spoke of her family often. From the things she said I know she loved you very dearly. She was an exceptionally wonderful gal loved by everyone, including me.

Thank you again, and I pray God will bless you abundantly.

I'm planning, the Lord willing, to return to Dillingham in Feb. The sweater will not only be a comfort to wear, but I shall be very proud to wear it.

[Martha Jay]

Jan. 6, 1961

Dear Joan

I have "put off" writing this letter, because I just didn't know how to express my sincere appreciation for your finishing the sweater Donna was making. I know it must have taken much time and effort when you were very busy with your family. Thank you so very much.

It means so much to know that Donna spent time on part of the sweater and of course it is a treasure to me. She showed us one of the sweaters after she had just begun it, when we were with her in Anchorage in Sept. of '59. Anyhow, we just took it for granted that both of the sweaters were with her in the plane, and had burned. It is such a blessing to have something she made.

Martha and I are both making preparation to return to Dillingham sometime in March or April. We will spend the next two weeks on tour of some churches, presenting to them a resumé of the mission work in Dillingham.

Of course we will miss Donna when we return, as she was a precious blessing in Dillingham. However, we are thankful for the realization that her life was in the hand of God, and praise Him for our privilege of fellowship with her.

Thank you again, Joan, and May our Lord bless you richly for sharing with me in such a sweet way.

Sincerely,
Roberta Tew

Notes

INTRODUCTION

1. Frederick Jackson Turner first presented his ideas about the closing of the frontier in "The Significance of the Frontier in American History," which he first delivered to a gathering of historians in 1893 in Chicago. This significant work has become a foundation for contemporary study of the history of the American West.

2. See Appendix A for text of song.

3. Professor Jameson co-authored with Susan Armitage the standard graduate school text for Western Women's history courses, *The Women's West* (Norman: University of Oklahoma, 1987), and *Writing the Range: Race, Class, and Culture in the Women's West* (Norman: University of Oklahoma, 1997). She is also author of *All That Glitters: Class, Conflict, and Community in Cripple Creek* (Urbana: University of Illinois Press, 1998).

4. Please see the bibliographic essay for Chapter 8 for full reference for *Tisha* and a list of other sources for women in Alaska.

CHAPTER ONE

1. The parsonage is now a public building housing city offices.

2. It was not uncommon for families to close off rooms in a house to conserve energy, even going so far as to bring mattresses in and sleep on the floor.

3. Incidentally, the girls' uncle Merlin obviously enjoyed music, as did his brother Leslie. While in England, Merlin joined a quartet and broadcast on the Columbia Broadcasting System. Both brothers were blessed with beautiful singing voices, and Merlin continued to encourage his nieces from afar.

4. Named for famous nineteenth-century industrialist George M. Pullman, the town was known as a model industrial town. He owned the town, but his anti-labor tactics, along with the depression of the late nineteenth century, led to labor strikes. Pullman became the focus of the labor movement and when the military arrived to quell strikers, six people were killed. Pullman refused arbitration and, with his health failing, died three years later in 1897 of a heart attack.

5. Regarding Merlin's military service and promotion, at the end of 1943 Merlin wrote, "I do practically identical work as a Capt. as I did when I was a Lt." By June 1944, he made Chaplain Major (according to him, the youngest one in the "ETO—by some years"). In March 1945, he was awarded the Bronze Star.

6. Kendall College in Evanston was later called Evanston Collegiate Institute, a two-year institution.

CHAPTER TWO

1. Information from this chapter came from interviews with Dorothy Mathews and Joan Eik in the summers of 2000 and 2001, and via e-mail correspondence to clarify sections. Oral interviews taped, transcribed, courtesy of author.

2. Not until the 1970s, with the Environmental Protection Act and the Clean Rivers Act, did this change—that is, until George W. Bush revised it in 2003.

3. Gunneling involved standing on the gunnels (outside rail) of the canoe just in front of the back seat and bouncing up and down gently, which in turn caused the canoe to move forward through the water.

CHAPTER THREE

1. They were named the "Whiz Kids" for their participation in a radio quiz show called "Whiz Kids." Not all the children at the University of Illinois Laboratory School had participated in the show. Donna and Dorothy's parents did not have a lot of money, yet they hoped to give their daughters an educational opportunity—perhaps beyond their means.

2. See Appendix B for list of performances.

3. Dorothy later reflected that this certainly made sense and helps explain Donna's insecurity as she left home for college and during her first teaching jobs.

4. After a year in Alaska, Donna told Joan that "the ones [children] in Alaska were more interested in what she was trying to do and the spoiled ones [Northbrook] weren't." She immediately recognized the differences between the children as related to their social class and whether or not they were "spoiled."

5. See Appendix C for complete text of letter from Leslie to Donna.

CHAPTER FOUR

1. Muriel Speers for the Department of the Interior, Alaska Indian Service, "Post War Planning Survey," File 431, Dillingham, Box 39, Record Group 75, Juneau Area Office, General Subject, Correspondence 1933–63, National Archives, Pacific Alaska Region, Anchorage. The report was filed for "Station: Dillingham Bristol Bay" with a date of "Feb."

2. A potlatch is an elaborate ceremony wherein a community member gives away his or her possessions to other community members as a way to gain status within the tribe. Memorial potlatches among the Tlingit served several purposes, one of which was to signal the end of mourning and another to transfer possessions and names to the deceased's successor. Wendell H. Oswalt and Sharlotte Neely, *This Land Was Theirs: A Study of North American Indians*, 5th edition (Toronto: Mayfield Publishing Company, 1996), 260–61.

3. Some villagers dumped their chemical buckets in pits behind homes, having few options in a community without a sewer system.

4. Incidentally, the term "fisher" is the term of choice in the region, as non-gender specific.

5. The fishers in the region still refer to PAF as "Pay After Fishing," since only after the fishing season ended would the totals be tallied and checks distributed to the fishers.

6. Today the old school houses government offices, as well as the *Bristol Bay Times*, the local newspaper.

7. Unfortunately, census reporters stopped utilizing the regional designation of "Bristol Bay" as a category after 1950, so tracking population becomes a bit more difficult.

8. Joan recalled that "the lack of tact and the overuse of negative descriptions was typical of the way Donna spoke. I would describe it as a safe way to vent, safely and without cuss words; but [it] also shows naivete and a bit of arrogance."

9. The Opland Hotel was built by Alfred J. Opland in 1946–47.

10. Donna's sister Joan recalled years later that Leslie McGladrey's mother had been involved in the Women's Christian Temperance Union (WCTU). In turn, Leslie carried on her interest in avoiding alcohol and took this interest into rehabilitation work. He did major work on alcohol problems, later becoming head of Temperance Education, Incorporated. He even conducted radio shows in Chicago regarding temperance. His attitude permeated the McGladrey household, "Mother being more voracious than Dad," Joan recalled; they "couldn't even use wine vinegar." These attitudes left an impression on their daughters.

11. Aleknagik sits on the southeastern tip of Lake Aleknagik. The northwest end of this lake today extends into Wood-Tikchik State Park, a collection of nearly a dozen large lakes, most of which are interconnected by rivers and host some of the best trout fishing in the world.

12. Donna wrote more than eighty letters home to family and friends. Special thanks to Whitney Rine of Lincoln for counting the number of letters Donna penned. All letters from Donna to her family are located in the family's private collection, courtesy of author.

CHAPTER FIVE

1. During my first research trip to Dillingham, it became apparent that, comparatively, prices have not changed that much over the past forty years. In July 2002, Dillingham had no fresh strawberries. My next choice, bananas, rang in at a hefty $1.69 per pound (compared to $.29 per pound in Lincoln, Nebraska).

2. "Incidentally, we put out the fire with no damage," JoAnn Armstrong later told me. Although I could not track down Ann Carr, I am still curious about her side of the roommate story. Perhaps someone who reads this will remember some old letters stashed away that their Grandmother Carr wrote them from Dillingham between 1958–59.

3. Tressie Vander Hoek, interview by author, March 2002, Anchorage, Alaska, taped and transcribed. All subsequent quotes from Tressie Vander Hoek emanate from interviews taped in March 2002.

4. Unfortunately though, at times the sewage in the leach pond would percolate up as the spring thaw arrived, usually in May or June.

CHAPTER SIX

1. Hilda Kroener, interview by author, March 2002, Chugiak, Alaska, taped and transcribed. All quotes from Hilda Kroener emanate from interviews taped in March 2002.

2. Juanita Pelagio, interview by author via telephone, March 2002, Anchorage, Alaska.

3. Hilda Kroener continued with music after Donna had left Dillingham: "I think after Donna left we didn't have a music teacher and guess who they chose to lead the class in music? . . . Me." Hilda lamented, "And I think if I wouldn't have gotten married, I still should've pursued it, but I love music. I should've become a music teacher, but I'm not sorry I got married, you know." She said it with a wink and a smile, for her husband Hermann was sitting across the table from her, measuring and studying aeronautical charts of southwest Alaska for a later part of our interview.

4. The lack of attendance could also have been related to other socioeconomic factors including what Donna perceived as the high rate of alcoholism and joblessness in the community.

5. Verna Lee Heyano, interview by author, March and July 2001 and 2002, Dillingham, Alaska. Interviews from March 2001 and 2002 were taped and partially transcribed. All subsequent references from Heyano come from these interviews and follow-up telephone and e-mail conversations in the subsequent years.
6. Just recently, the school board in Dillingham has made a conscious effort to include more culturally oriented curriculum based on traditional cultures in the region.

CHAPTER SEVEN

1. Meeting his future wife, Hilda, would not be that easy for Hermann, for Hilda's father raised his children with strong discipline. Mr. Olson insisted that his children disappear into another room when neighbors came to visit. Even Charles Newton asked one time why he never met Hilda when he worked at their house. Some Dillingham residents even used to joke, "Whose daughter is that?" when Hilda occasionally did appear. After Hermann finally met her in 1960 they began to date, and the story she told illustrates her father's wonderful sense of humor. Her father was so indebted to Hermann for finishing the plumbing job that Richard and Charles had begun, that he promised Hermann anything he wanted when the job was over. Mr. Olson had no idea that Hermann and Hilda would begin to date, and that later Hermann would ask Mr. Olson for his daughter. Hilda's father told Hermann years later, "Hermann, I don't trust plumbers anymore. The first one that came along took my daughter. The next one that comes along might take my wife!"
2. The WSCS was an organization, now called the United Methodist Women, which is still dedicated to service and mission.
3. In the 1950s, the Lily Pond had enough water to serve as a landing strip, but since the canneries began pumping water from it for their processing, it no longer had sufficient water surface upon which pilots could land in the summer or iced over in winter.
4. On March 25, David Carlson reported that "The temp has risen to +20 but the wind remains from the north. It is nice to feel the more modest climate and seems about time too." The next day he reported that the temperature was above freezing all day. By March 29 (Easter Sunday), he reported that the weather was "nice at 5:30 this morning when the Moravian Sunrise service was held at the cemetery." Two days later he reported: "Mild weather again. The water is beginning to flow down the road now."
5. Bobbie and Marty had set up a tent Summer Bible School at the salmon tent camps, located where the public boat harbor now sits just west of the Peter Pan Cannery boat yard. The Summer Bible School was for everyone, but mostly only tent community members attended. Unfortunately, the tent community had neither sewer nor garbage service, nor running water; hence, the area had

a serious problem with all kinds of daily waste. "The stench was terrible," Mary Newton recalled in interviews many years later.

6. This thoughtful note appeared in Verna's transcription of Donna's letters, the original, however has since disappeared.

7. Neither Mary nor Ruby Newton, Richard's sisters-in-law, remembers hearing about Richard building a house for Donna and himself.

CHAPTER EIGHT

1. Enrollment records came from two major sources: Alden M. Rollins, *Census Alaska: Numbers of Inhabitants, 1792–1970* (Anchorage: University of Alaska Library, 1978); and, "Look North to Dillingham," Alaska: Standard Industrial Survey, Department of Economic Development, Industrial Development Division (Pouch EE, Juneau, Alaska, 99801).

2. Verna kept the letters written to Donna by Bobbie and Marty over the summer of 1959 (See Appendix D), but interestingly, there is no record of her corresponding with Richard.

3. Mary and Ruby Newton believed that before school started, she "must've been living in Richard's trailer. He must've been gone or something, it sounded, I thought it [Donna's letters] said something about it. Maybe I misunderstood." For quite a while, Richard lived with his mother, although he did have a trailer by Mountain View, the Matanuska Plumbing and Heating Company shop.

4. Margaret Swanson, Chugiak, interview by author, July 2002, taped, not transcribed. Subsequent references to Margaret Swanson emanate from this interview unless otherwise noted.

5. Marjorie Cochrane, *Between Two Rivers: The Growth of Chugiak—Eagle River*, with A Fiftieth Anniversary Update "The Eagles Return to Yukla Valley" by Lee Jordan (Anchorage: AT Publishing, 1997), 74. Much of the historical information in this segment about Chugiak, where otherwise not noted, comes from this book.

6. Ibid., 110.

7. Tressie Vander Hoek, however, felt an undercurrent of something being wrong—as if the people there did not like Donna. Donna was not being honest with Tressie about Richard. She apparently did not feel as able to tell her about the problems that seemed to creep back into her relationship with Richard.

CHAPTER NINE

1. Paul also owned the quonset huts next to the school.

2. Mrs. Newton filed papers for the homestead on June 14, 1956, remaining the required number of months out of every year for the next five years to prove up

on the claim. On June 5, 1961, she acquired the title, but instead of continuing to homestead, she moved to Oregon where she lived out the remainder of her life with her Oregon-based children.

3. From the very first year, Chugiak Elementary School had to utilize quonset huts because they did not have enough space in the new school building.

CHAPTER TEN

1. Charts depicting sunrise and sunset compiled by the Astronomical Applications Department, US Naval Observatory, Washington, DC, for the region indicate the following times for sunrise and sunset in Anchorage, 10:15 A.M. and 3:49 P.M., and Dillingham, 10:29 A.M. and 4:44 P.M.

2. Kvichak is pronounced "queé jack."

3. The "heading" is the compass direction in which the airplane's longitudinal axis points. Therefore, when the pilot is changing his heading, he is turning laterally (as opposed to altitude).

4. Verna McGladrey, "The Alaskan Wilds; or, Was it God's Will," edited collection of Donna's letters, unpublished manuscript, courtesy of author.

CHAPTER ELEVEN

1. The sun rose on January 4, 1960, at 10:12 A.M., and set at 3:57 P.M., leaving less than six hours of daylight. "Rise and Set for the Sun for 1960, Anchorage, Alaska, Astronomical Applications Department, United States Naval Observatory, Washington, D.C." http://aa.usno.navy.mil/cgi-bin/aa_rstable2.pl (accessed on December 17, 2003).

2. Merlin launched a campaign to keep their memory alive and keep up interest in the search by providing information and photographs to Lt. Betty Wolverton and area newspapers. Merlin McGladrey to Verna McGladrey, January 1960, from Dillingham, King Salmon, and Anchorage, courtesy of Joan Eik and author. See Appendix E for Merlin's letter to Verna.

3. When Leslie returned later that year, Les Fetrow took Leslie fishing. "He wanted to try fishing in Alaska and I took him to a lake up in the valley that I knew had fish in it, and I think he did catch a fish up there, didn't he? He may have been the only one that caught one that day. . . . I was up in a tree. I had my line tangled in a tree, and I looked down at him and he says, 'what are you doing up there?' He was in the stern of the boat, he had a fish on." He laughed heartily as he finished his story, "oh, I had fun with her father." Les Fetrow, interview by author, July 2001, Chugiak. Interview taped but not transcribed.

4. "Search Continues for Missing Plane," *Bristol Bay News*, 21st Edition, January 15, 1960.

CHAPTER TWELVE

1. On the back of the postcard, he wrote across a reproduced image of the DC-7C, "Got here OK. Just called coordination center. Search still on. Go to King Salmon tomorrow morning. Am going to bank. VW, Singer, etc this PM, Love, Me." Leslie had filled his plate with necessary tasks, taking care of selling the VW Beetle and shipping the Singer Sewing machine back home. Leslie McGladrey to Verna McGladrey, postcard n.d. [likely either January 19 or 20, 1960], Anchorage, Alaska, courtesy of Joan Eik and author.

2. "Newton Hunt Is Suspended," *Anchorage Daily Times*, January 27, 1960.

3. See Appendix F for Obituary Notice.

4. Orin Seybert, now president of Peninsula Air (PenAir) explained that bush pilots rarely fly that much over open water because they are always aware that they might have engine failure. As he put it, "if you have failure over water, you drown." At least over land you have a fighting chance. Orin Seybert, interview by author, July 2001, Anchorage. Interview taped but not transcribed.

5. See Appendix G for the full text of this letter.

6. See Sheila Nickerson, *Disappearance, A Map: A Meditation on Death and Loss in the High Latitudes* (New York: Doubleday and Company, 1996). Nickerson writes about the loss of individuals in Alaska throughout history and its effect on those left behind.

7. A sealer was an airtight container for their remains.

CHAPTER THIRTEEN

1. Mary Newton, Palmer, Alaska, interview with Mary and Ruby Newton by author, June 2002, interview taped but not transcribed, courtesy of author. All subsequent quotes from Mary or Ruby Newton emanate from this interview.

2. The Trans-Alaska Pipeline System was built to transport the more than nine billion barrel oil field at Prudhoe Bay in 1968. This pipeline was an engineering marvel, spanning more than eight hundred miles across Alaska from the North Slope to the Prince William Sound. Claus-M. Naske and Herman E. Slotnick, *Alaska: A History of the 49th State*, 2nd edition (Norman: University of Oklahoma Press, 1987), 241, 251–55.

3. Because the Bering Sea is rather shallow, storms whip the water into a fury, causing large fishing vessels to sink and their fishers to perish in the cold and angry waters.

4. I must thank Christine Starr, a novelist, for the beautiful final few words of this story. She quickly found in those few words what I have labored for years to portray.

Bibliographic Essay

INTRODUCTION

Information regarding the frontier thesis can be found in Frederick Jackson Turner's "Significance of Frontier in American History," in *The Frontier in American History* (New York: Dover Publications, 1996). Information about other teachers in Alaska prior to Donna are listed under Chapter 8, but the Robert Specht's *Tisha: The Story of a Young Teacher in the Alaskan Wilderness* (New York: St. Martin's Press, 1976) is most commonly remembered and was the first that informed my understanding of a teacher's experience in the Alaskan Bush.

Interviews with numerous individuals in Alaska, as well as follow-up telephone, letter, or electronic mail conversations provided the foothold needed to clarify certain details as I began thinking about this introduction. Those people included Verna Lee Heyano, Hilda and Hermann Kroener, Tressie Vander Hoek, Ruby and Mary Newton, Tim Troll, and finally Mary Anne Mateson (from Oregon).

Mostly, the family of Donna McGladrey informed this chapter, through official, taped, and transcribed interviews, as well as innumerable personal, telephone, and electronic mail conversations. Joan Eik and Dorothy Mathews also reviewed countless versions of this manuscript to correct any misstatements that may have inadvertently crept into the text.

CHAPTER ONE

Information about Donna's childhood and her family, from this and all subsequent chapters come from extensive (recorded and transcribed, as well as unrecorded) interviews, telephone calls, and e-mails with Joan Eik and Dorothy

Mathews beginning in June 1999 and continuing until the manuscript was submitted. Verna and Leslie McGladrey's honeymoon photograph album and Donna and Dorothy McGladrey's childhood albums informed the first three chapters of this book, as well as segments about Dillingham and the aftermath in chapters 11 and 12.

Letters from Merlin W. McGladrey while stationed in Great Britain also referred to the girls' activities during the war. For example, in letters to their Uncle Merlin, the girls must have mentioned strawberries, for he wrote to his nieces that the "strawberries sound marvelous. My last fresh strawberries were in 1942." Merlin W. McGladrey to Leslie McGladrey and Family, June 25, 1944, Joan Eik's private collection, courtesy of Joan Eik and author. He wrote many letters to his family during his years of service, which have been preserved, transcribed, and distributed to family members.

All of these letters, documents, and albums are in the family's private collection.

CHAPTER TWO
Besides the interviews and family's collection of documents, photographs, and memorabilia, numerous sources influenced this chapter. Regarding Camp Nawakwa, in 1987, Dorothy Mathews wrote a personal memoir, prepared for a Nawakwa Memory book, which she entitled "Nawakwa." During an interview, she remembered this short memoir and gave me a copy. Regarding summer camp in northern Wisconsin, "YMCA Family Camp Nawakwa," www.nawakwa.com (accessed January 14, 2002), proved quite useful. Incidentally, Camp Nawakwa continues to be operated by the Metropolitan Chicago area YMCA, although they now have another office in Lac du Flambeau, Wisconsin. Most of the families that return to Nawakwa, however, continue to hail from the Chicago region (or have roots in the area). Also, for a history of Pullman, see Almont Lindsey, *The Pullman Strike: The Story of a Unique Experiment and of a Great Labor Upheaval* (Chicago: University of Chicago Press, 1994).

Environmental factors had a great impact on Donna's decision-making process, especially as she grew older. John Opie's *Nature's Nation: An Environmental History of the United States* (New York: Harcourt Brace College Publishers, Inc., 1998) certainly informed this chapter, particularly to substantiate Donna's descriptions of Chicago during the 1940s and 1950s. Also, information about the role of pesticides in the environment can be found in the path-breaking work by Rachel Carson, *Silent Spring*, with an introduction by Vice President Al Gore (New York: Houghton Mifflin Company, 1993).

CHAPTER THREE
Most of the information about Donna's high school and college experiences, including activities and friendships, come from her childhood album,

so carefully constructed by her mother. Items referenced include: "Carnival Spirit Rules Tonight at Parker High: Proceeds from Program Will Buy TV Set," Neighborhood Section, *Chicago Daily Tribune,* April 24, 1952, part 5, page 1; Letter of Recommendation for Donna Joy McGladrey from Henry Jarvis, Senior Division Teacher, Parker High School, Chairman of Campus Life, to The Colonial Dames Scholarship Committee, March 17, 1953; the program for the MacMurray College Choir and the Wabash College Glee Club (actually performed on March 4, 1955, but the broadcast was delayed), "Wabash College Program," program, March 4, 1955; "Class Day Recognizes '57 Seniors," newspaper clipping (unknown source); United Press International, "Father Has High Hopes: Rev. McGladrey Thinks Daughter Will Be Found Alive," *Chicago Star-Tribune,* February 6, 1960; and telegrams sent by the Commissioner of Education, Don M. DaFoe to Donna, family's private collection.

For information about Potlatches, see Wendell H. Oswalt and Sharlotte Neely, *This Land Was Theirs: A Study of North American Indians,* 5th edition (Toronto: Mayfield Publishing Company, 1996); and Sergei Kan, *Symbolic Immortality: The Tlingit Potlatch of the Nineteenth Century* (Washington, DC: Smithsonian Institution Press, 1989).

Information about the music program at MacMurray College comes from "Music Program Overview," Department of Music Education, MacMurray College, www.mac.edu/academ/music.htm (accessed January 12, 2002).

Numerous letters written by Donna before 1958, found by Joan Eik over the course of this research, provided valuable clues as to Donna's development into an adult, including her lack of self-confidence, sense of insecurity, unattainable high standards, and frustration at Dorothy's impending marriage to Jack.

During the editing process, Dorothy and Joan wrote comments on sticky notes and placed them in the manuscript. For example, Dorothy postulated that the fact that Donna was the favorite may have set up unrealistic expectations for her outside of the family. She never received "from the outside world the recognition that she had from home." Note to author on manuscript by Dorothy Mathews, October 2002.

Incidentally, the last names of Dorothy and Donna's roommates were excluded because more than forty years later, Dorothy cannot recall Barb and Lynn's last names.

Finally, interviews with Mary and Ruby Newton (Richard Newton's sisters-in-law) during research trips to Alaska informed me regarding the 1950s in Dillingham. Mary and Ruby Newton, Palmer, Alaska, interview by author, March 2001. Interviews taped and transcribed, courtesy of author.

CHAPTER FOUR

Information about Donna's life are taken from her letters to parents and sisters Joan and Dorothy as found in the family's private collection. Most of the letters emanated from the first semester she lived in Dillingham. Author has compiled and nearly completed editing the entire collection of letters from Donna to her parents, Joan, and Dorothy, as well as letters Donna wrote to her best friend June Swatosh (from Illinois). Included in that compilation are also letters written by Roberta Tew and Martha Jay (her Church of Christ missionary friends), Leslie McGladrey and Merlin McGladrey, and Charles Newton. Over four hundred pages of transcribed letters resulted.

The Dillingham Public Health Center, established in 1948, was located in the basement of the school until 1958 when the current health center opened. Kanakanak Hospital, a native hospital, only treated Alaska Natives, unless in the case of an emergency. Before and during WWII, the hospital had one physician to oversee a hospital filled with tuberculosis patients. The 1919 influenza epidemic hit the region hard, as did scarlet fever in the 1930s. Information regarding the public health center came in part from Herbert E. Knapp, Secretary, Parent-Teacher's Association, to C. Earl Albrecht, M.D., Commissioner of Health, Juneau, February 2, 1954 (as found in Julie Rolf, compiler, *History of Dillingham Public Health Center*, Dillingham, Alaska). This is a collection of historical documents pertaining to the health center on file in a notebook at the health center in Dillingham.

The Moravian Church was originally constructed in September 1954. The building still sits at what would have been just beyond the east end of the runway on the east end of Dillingham. It serves as a small shed today and has recently been painted blue. The Russian Orthodox Church, originally constructed in 1916 in Aleknagik, when Aleknagik's population shifted to Dillingham in 1948, moved the church building to Wood River Road, where it still sits today. Built in 1939, the Church of Christ sat on the west corner lot of Main and Second Avenue West. It sat across from the Dillingham school where Donna taught, but has since burned down. The Church of Christ held their Sunday services at the local Chinese restaurant down by the City Harbor and Docks when the author visited in 2001–2. Information regarding the community buildings can be found in Dillingham Historic Preservation Commission, *Inventory of Historic Buildings in Dillingham*, Phase 2 (Dillingham: City of Dillingham, 1993), Mimeograph. Special thanks to Tim Troll for allowing me to borrow and copy this document. Interestingly, before electricity came to Dillingham, most homes utilized windmills to generate electrical power throughout the community.

Information about the school and local community "happenings" came from the school newspaper entitled *The Blizzard*, 1948–61 (the run lasted longer, but only these years were utilized in this research), microfilm, Alaska Newspaper Collection, Alaska Room, Loussac Library, Anchorage.

Information about Donna's teaching career in Dillingham does not exist with the Dillingham School District, the Bureau of Indian Affairs, or the State Department of Education. The original telegrams and teaching contracts, however, remain preserved in Donna's childhood memory album. The family has no record of Donna's original letter of inquiry to DaFoe, but the telegram she received from Mr. DaFoe indicates she did send a letter. Other information from her teaching career in official documentation include Territory of Alaska, Department of Education, Standard Contract Form for Teachers and Administrators (Territorial Schools), also located in Donna Joy McGladrey's album.

Regarding distance of Dillingham from Anchorage, the mileage varies, depending on whether one looks at the flight path or a straight line (as the crow flies). The number I chose to utilize here is according to the Bristol Bay Native Association, "Dillingham," http://www.bbna.com/dlg.html (accessed January 24, 2002).

Statistical information about population and characteristics of population come from two major sources: Alden M. Rollins, *Census Alaska: Numbers of Inhabitants, 1792–1970* (Anchorage: University of Alaska Library, 1978); and, "Look North to Dillingham," Alaska: Standard Industrial Survey, Department of Economic Development, Industrial Development Division (Pouch EE, Juneau, Alaska, 99801), 1969. Community economic figures come from *Dillingham Community Profile*, Sheets 1–2 and poster (Dillingham: City of Dillingham, n.d.). Information regarding housing styles from Steve J. Langdon, *The Native People of Alaska* (Anchorage: Greatland Graphics, 1993); The Alaska Native Heritage Center in Anchorage, Alaska; and Muriel Speers for the Department of the Interior, Alaska Indian Service, "Post War Planning Survey," File 431, Dillingham, Box 39, Record Group 75, Juneau Area Office, General Subject, Correspondence 1933–63, National Archives, Pacific Alaska Region, Anchorage. The report was filed for "Station: Dillingham Bristol Bay" with a date of "Feb."

The story about berry picking was adapted from June Cherry, *Ak'a Tamaami*, Vol. 1, No. 1 (Togiak: Togiak High School, Spring 1980).

Dorothy (Erickson) Anderson began teaching English at the Dillingham School in the fall of 1959, the year that Donna left. She remembered that by the time she got to the school, there were lots of band instruments, "some of which are still around at the school." Dorothy Anderson, interview by telephone by author, July 25, 2001, Dillingham, Alaska. Dillingham hired a combination music and physical education teacher, Mrs. Smith, for the year 1959–60, who left in the middle of the year. Dorothy taught music starting midyear. Although not trained in band, she did continue the singing programs. Emily Olson, also a student of Donna's, remembered that Mrs. Smith had a serious disagreement with the principal and left. The students staged a protest and marched back and forth in front of the school to demand that the principal keep Mrs. Smith, not let her go. Emily Olson, interview by author, March 2001, Dillingham, taped and transcribed, courtesy of author. During that time, Leslie D. McGladrey witnessed the strike and mentioned it in a letter home. Interviews formed the basis for this story, as well as the majority of personal recollections that inform this chapter: Emily Roberts, Verna Lee Heyano, JoAnn Armstrong, Lyle Smith, Dorothy Anderson, and Tim Troll (all from Dillingham); Hilda and Hermann Kroener (Chugiak); Tressie Vander Hoek and Sue Hahn (both from Anchorage); Joan Eik (Minnesota); and Dorothy Mathews (Nebraska).

Information about weather and daily activities around town came from the David Carlson Diaries, which can be found in several volumes at the Samuel K. Fox Museum and the Dillingham Public Library, Dillingham, Alaska. The diaries are currently being transcribed by a local resident. In particular, the following dates provided the basis for some text (all from 1958): September 14, 17–18, and 30; October 10, 15, and 17; and December 2. David Carlson was the school agent for Dillingham, but also played a key role as a community builder. He sat on various committees including the Chamber of Commerce, Public Health Committee (for which he served as president), Parent-Teacher Association, and owned a local cold storage facility and store. He lived in an eight-by-eleven-foot log and wood frame home, begun in 1935 and finished by 1939, just east up main street from the school. During his fifty plus years in Dillingham, he kept a daily journal in which he recorded town development, business, weather, crime, and much more. He and his wife Mary (who, like Donna, played the piano and organ) added a 19 x 35 feet one-and-a-half-story addition onto the house finished in 1939, and later a two-story wing and a one-story kitchen in 1958.

Information about the Lowe's theater from Dillingham High School History Class of 1972–73, John Parker, Compiler, *The Last of Yesterday* (Dillingham High School: Dillingham, Alaska, 1974), 37–39; and, Interview and Public Health Committee Minutes, December 19, 1960, Dillingham Public Health Center, notebook compiled by Julie Rolf.

Many thanks to Heather Hadley, archival assistant, for forwarding the following records from the Department of Education and Early Development, Division of Libraries, Archives and Museums, Alaska State Archives, Juneau: Donna Joy McGladrey, Teacher's Experience Record, September 12, 1958, Department of Education, Territory of Alaska (indicating her Alaska Teacher's Certificate Number: H 8729-5-63); Alaska Educational Directories, School Year 1958–59 (issued by the Alaska Department of Education, Don M. DaFoe, Commissioner of Education) and School Year 1959–60 (Issued by the Alaska Department of Education, Theo J. Norby, Commissioner of Education).

CHAPTER FIVE
For the sake of brevity, sources listed in Chapter 4 continued to inform Chapter 5.

CHAPTER SIX
Donna's letters provided the foundation for this chapter, all of which she sent from Dillingham.

Interviews with George Krause and Wayne Schroeder provided valuable information as well. Mr. Krause corroborated the story about the airplane wreck, as written by David Carlson in his diary on January 26, 1958. Hilda Kroener, Verna Lee Heyano, and Emily Roberts filled in the blanks about the students and some parents' perception about PTA meetings. Verna Lee Heyano was a sixth grader in 1957–58, and Hilda Kroener, an eighth grader. David Carlson's diary also described Donna's concert at Lowe's, as well as other news from around town. David Carlson Diary, February 11, 1959; David Carlson Diary, April 3, 1959, Dillingham Public Library, Dillingham.

Information about graduating seniors came from *Choggiung* (Dillingham: Dillingham Public School Yearbook, 1962), author's private collection.

CHAPTER SEVEN

Once again, Donna's letters provided much valuable information for this chapter. All of her letters emanated from Dillingham.

Interviews with those who knew Richard Newton or Donna, provided a wonderful balance to Donna's letters: Hilda Kroener, Dorothy (Erickson) Anderson, Mary Newton, interview by author (telephone), Palmer, Alaska, July 7, 2001, Palmer, Alaska/Lincoln, Nebraska; Marie Andrews, interview by telephone, Anchorage, Alaska, July 24, 2001; Tim Troll, interview by author, Dillingham, March and July 2001, March and July 2002; and, JoAnn Armstrong, interview by author, July 2001, Dillingham, Alaska. Finally, the story about Bobbie and Marty having a Bible Camp at the Fish Camp came from Mary Newton. Mary Newton, interview by author, July 2001, Palmer, Alaska. Interview taped and transcribed, courtesy of author.

Regarding Donna's difficulties finding a permanent residence, Marie Andrews did recall that Donna lived in the upstairs manager's apartment of the Opland Hotel that they had subsequently purchased. Marie Andrews, interview by telephone by author, July 2001, Anchorage, Alaska. Not taped, notes taken, courtesy of author.

The Dillingham Historic Preservation Commission, *Inventory of Historic Buildings*, Phase 2; Muriel Speers report; and, Alden M. Rollins, *Census Alaska: Numbers of Inhabitants, 1792–1970* (Anchorage: University of Alaska Library, 1978), n.p.; provided historical data essential to understanding the communities, the buildings, and sanitation issues.

Even though Donna reported to her family that children there knew nothing of "real" music, in her appreciation of good music, she had company among adults of Dillingham. David Carlson had a collection of classical music, and others in town played piano and organ, and sang. Mary Carlson often played the organ at the Moravian Church; Donna filled in when she was unable to play. David Carlson's diaries, once again, provided many observations, as well as informed the above. David Carlson Diary, March 17, 1959; March 25–31, 1959.

Books written by or about school teachers in Alaska include such classics as Robert Specht's *Tisha: The Story of a Young Teacher in the Alaska Wilderness* (New York: St. Martin's Press, 1976); Hannah Breece, *A Schoolteacher in Old Alaska: The Story of Hannah Breece*, ed. and introduction by Jane Jacobs (New York: Random House, 1996); Hap Gilliland, *Wolf River: The Saga of a Teacher's Adventures in Alaska* (Billings, MT: Council for Indian Education, 2001); Abbie Morgan Madenwald, *Arctic Schoolteacher: Kulukak, Alaska, 1931–1933* (Norman: University of Oklahoma Press, 1992); Alice M. Brooks and Willietta E. Kuppler, *The Clenched Fist* (Philadelphia: Dorrance, 1948); and Edna Borigo, *Sourdough Schoolma'am* (Chicago: Adams Press, 1969). More recent books include Wilford Corbin, *A World Apart: My Life Among the Eskimos of Alaska* (Homer, Alaska: Wizard Works, 2000); and Katherine McNamara, *Narrow Road to the Deep North: A Journey into the Interior of Alaska* (San Francisco: Mercury House, 2001). Other sources for teaching in Alaska included Helen L. Simpson, *Alaska Teaching* (Spenard, Alaska, 1956); and William Deane Overstreet, "A Survey and Analysis of the Reasons Teachers Gave for Leaving Their Positions in Alaska in 1960" (master's thesis, University of Washington, 1960).

Census data comes from Alden Rollins, *Census Alaska: Numbers of Inhabitants, 1792–1970* (Anchorage: University of Alaska Library, 1978).

Once again, Donna's letters proved invaluable.

Rudimentary information about the Yellowstone earthquake can be found at "Quake Lake: 1959 Hedgen Lake Earthquake, Largest in Montana," www.westyellowstonenet.com/attractions/quake_lake.htm (accessed August 16, 2002). This article was abridged from (Revised) by Carl W. Stover and Jerry L. Coffman, "Seismicity of the United States, 1568–1989," U.S. Geological Survey Professional Paper 1527 (Washington, DC: United States Government Printing Office, 1993).

Much of the information from this chapter regarding Richard, if not from Donna's letters, comes from interviews with Mary and Ruby Newton (wives of Charles and Royce respectively), and MaryAnne Mateson, Richard's younger sister. Mary and Ruby Newton, interview by author, Palmer, Alaska, March 2001. Interview taped and transcribed, courtesy of author.

Current and former residents of Chugiak provided invaluable information about the community: Margaret Swanson, interview by author, Chugiak, Alaska, March 2001; Shirley Maulden, interview by author, Chugiak, Alaska, March 17, 2001. Incidentally, Shirley Mauldin is a great supporter of the Chugiak Methodist Church and my host for the day who drove me around to the homes of Les and Dorothy Fetrow, Natalie Brooks, Zona Dahlmann, and Margaret Swanson. That day, Shirley mentioned her first washing machine, all electric in 1949. Once she dry-cleaned in her washer by pouring gasoline in the washer and putting the clothes in. (To which Margaret replied, "Oh, that wasn't very smart.") At the time Shirley lived in Napa, California, and it took quite a while of hanging the clothes outside to get the smell out." Shirley kindly gave me a copy of Marjorie Cochrane, *Between Two Rivers: The Growth of Chugiak–Eagle River*, with A Fiftieth Anniversary Update "The Eagles Return to Yukla Valley" by Lee Jordan (Anchorage: AT Publishing, Inc., 1997), from which I included many background details of Chugiak. Another monograph that informed this chapter is Claus-M. Naske and Herman E. Slotnick, *Alaska: A History of the 49th State*, 2nd edition (Norman: University of Oklahoma Press, 1987).

Finally, interviews with Joan Eik and Tressie Vander Hoek answered many questions about the summer and fall of 1959 that Donna did not address in her letters home.

CHAPTER NINE

Appropriately, Donna's letters from Chugiak formed a basis for this chapter.

Interviews with Donna's colleagues, friends, and Richard's family, assisted tremendously with this chapter: Zona Dahlmann, Chugiak, Alaska, March 17, 2001; Margaret Swanson, Chugiak, Alaska, July 2001.

Finally, some of the interviewees had interesting recollections about Chugiak. One teacher remembered that the Eklutna children were not really encouraged to go to school, thinking that sometimes their community discouraged them from attending school. Shirley and Zona both recalled that in the earliest days, only about fifteen people used to attend the early Methodist Church, and likely half of them were Fetrows.

Nearly the entire section of this chapter based on her experience at Susitna Homestead is taken from Donna's lengthy letter to her parents on October 13, 1959, written while living in Chugiak, Alaska; courtesy of author. Some peripheral information, however, came from informants Hilda and Hermann Kroener as well. Astronomical observations come from "Willow, Alaska, Rise and Set for the Sun for 1959, Alaska Standard Time, Astronomical Applications Department, U. S. Naval Observatory, Washington, DC 20392-5420," http://aa.usno.navy.mil/cgi-bin/aa_rstablew.pl (accessed December 17, 2003).

CHAPTER TEN

Key astrological observations come from "Anchorage and Dillingham, Alaska, Rise and Set for the Sun for 1959, Alaska Standard Time, Astronomical Applications Department, U. S. Naval Observatory, Washington, D.C., 20392-5420," http://aa.usno.navy.mil/cgi-bin/aa_rstablew.pl (accessed December 17, 2003).

Key interviews gave important perspectives on the disappearance: John Paul Bouker, interview by author, Dillingham, Alaska, July 2001. John Paul Bouker, professional pilot and owner of a cargo service based out of Dillingham, interview by author while on a short flight from Dillingham to Portage Creek, March 2001 and a longer one in July 2002. Zona Dahlmann also provided key information during our interview in Chugiak in March 2001.

I simply could not have written this chapter without the assistance of Hermann and Hilda Kroener and their son Marvin. Hermann carefully studied my description of the flight path, as well as my conjecture about possible trajectories, and added his input. Hermann later pored over the chapter making key corrections based on his forty-plus years flying that very route as a bush pilot. With that tremendously intuitive and insightful information, I was able to understand those final hours far better. Hermann and Hilda Kroener and Marvin Kroener, Chugiak, Alaska, March 2001 and 2002.

Information about Earl Gay came from Marie Andrews, who informed me that he later worked for the FAA. He was killed in a motorcycle accident in California during the 1960s. Marie Andrews, interview by author (telephone), Anchorage, Alaska. July 24, 2001.

The transcription of the last transmission by Richard to Lt. Earl Gay comes from Donna Joy McGladrey's photograph album. Other items collected and preserved in the photograph album by Verna McGladrey that informed this chapter include: "Weather has Ended Search: Wait Lengthening Daylight Hours to Hunt for Donna McGladrey," [February 1960, unknown newspaper]; "Search Continues for Missing Plane," *Bristol Bay News*, 21st Edition, January 15, 1960, Naknek, Alaska, 1; "New Clues Reported in Search for Newton," *Anchorage Daily Times*, January 9, 1960; and, "Hint Teacher Was Aboard Missing Plane," *Anchorage Daily News*, January 5, 1960.

Communication between the McGladrey family members (including various letters as well as the tape and transcript of the Christmas tape the family made for Donna) informed this chapter as well. In one letter, Merlin tried to reassure his brother Leslie: "a week's food for two . . . heater with 5 gallons white gas. . . . They were dressed in arctic clothing." Merlin McGladrey to Leslie McGladrey, Larson Air Force Base, Washington, January 11, 1960.

The recollection of Reverend Wayne Hull's telephone call to Leslie was typed by Verna McGladrey, "Was it God's Will?" unpublished manuscript, author's private collection, 67. Since she was not on the telephone, of course, this is likely a paraphrased recollection of what Leslie told Verna.

CHAPTER ELEVEN
Astronomical information comes from "Rise and Set for the Sun for 1960, Anchorage Alaska," Astronomical Applications Department, United States Naval Observatory, Washington, D.C., http://aa.usno.navy.mil/cgi-bin/aa_rstablew.pl (accessed December 17, 2003).

Letters between the McGladrey family members informed this chapter.

A wonderful source on the "disappeared" is Sheila Nickerson, *Disappearance, A Map: A Meditation on Death & Loss in the High Altitudes* (New York: Doubleday, 1996). The Alaska poet laureate from 1977 to 1981 and writer in residence at the Alaska State Library, Nickerson wrote in part about those losing loved ones in plane wrecks. She noted that while the newspapers seem to carry the story for a few days, unless the case is unusual, reports begin to dwindle until they disappear entirely after a few weeks. Newspaper articles found in Donna's photograph album provided reference as well: "Search for 2 Spurred," and "Hunt Still Continues for Pair," *Anchorage Daily Times*, January 13, 1960; and, "Weather Has Slowed Hunt: Civil Air Patrol Will Continue Its Hunt for Donna McGladrey," January 15, 1960, *Chronicle*, Waterman, Illinois; "Search Continues for Missing Plane," *Bristol Bay News*, 21st Edition, January 15, 1960, Naknek, Alaska, 1, on microfilm in Alaska Room, Loussac Library, Anchorage, Alaska; and, *Mukluk Tell-Ya-Gram, An Alaskan Methodist Newsletter* from Rev. H. Wayne Hull, Chugiak, Alaska, January 15, 1960, author's private collection.

Once again, interviews with friends and colleagues were invaluable: Margaret Swanson, Chugiak, Alaska, March 17, 2001; Zona Dahlmann, Chugiak, Alaska, March 17, 2001; and, Les and Dorothy Fetrow, Chugiak, Alaska, March 17, 2001.

CHAPTER TWELVE
Family letters and newspaper articles found in Donna's photograph album primarily informed this chapter.

Newspaper articles found pasted at the back of Donna's childhood album, just beyond the image of Donna and Richard on their way to Susitna Homestead, included such headlines as "Still Search Missing Girl: Rev. McGladrey Tells of Wide Hunt Against Odds," January 16, 1960, *Chronicle*, Waterman, Illinois; "Father Has High Hopes: Rev. McGladrey Thinks Daughter Will Be Found Alive," February 6, 1960, United Press International, *Chicago Tribune/Sun-Times*; "Push Search For Girl Lost On Plane Trip," *Economist Newspapers*, Wednesday, January 27, 1960; "Father Has High Hopes: Rev. McGladrey Thinks Daughter Will Be Found Alive," February 6, 1960, United Press International, *Chicago Star Tribune*; "Newton Hunt Is Suspended," January 27, 1960, *Anchorage Daily Times*; "Searches for Plane," March 1960, *Together*; "Memorial Service Planned for Donna McGladrey May 1," April 28, 1960, *Kanabec County Times*, Mora, Minnesota; *The Blizzard*, April 29, 1960, Dillingham, Alaska; courtesy of author.

Finally, this chapter could not have been written without the assistance in interviews of Orin Seybert, Anchorage, Alaska, July 21, 2001, interview taped but not transcribed; Joan Eik and Dorothy Mathews, Blaine, Minnesota, June 24, 2000, interview taped and transcribed; John Paul Bouker, over Etolin Point, Alaska, July 2002; and Hilda and Hermann Kroener, Chugiak, Alaska, March 2002.

CHAPTER THIRTEEN

The epilogue is based on my own experience in Alaska, as well as interviews with Don Wagner, Anchorage, July 24, 2001; Mary Newton and Ruby Newton, Palmer, Alaska, March 2001; Hermann and Hilda Kroener, Chugiak, Alaska, March of 2001 and 2002; Jack Mathews, Lincoln, Nebraska, October 2003; Tim Troll, Dillingham, Alaska, July 26, 2002.

Hermann in particular remembered that the fuselage of the F-27 still sits where it fell to the ground. Jack Mathews, an airplane enthusiast, recalled that the F-27 ceased to be available in the U.S. due to major mechanic failures like this one, but he thought that the company that produced the aircraft continued to make the F-27 available in Latin American markets. Jack Mathews, interview by author, Lincoln, Nebraska, July 2003.

Index